TRACTORS
OF THE WORLD

TRACTORS
OF THE WORLD
OVER 220 OF THE WORLD'S GREATEST TRACTORS

MICHAEL WILLIAMS

p

To Jayne

This is a Parragon Publishing Book
First published in 2005

Parragon Publishing
Queen Street House
4 Queen Street
Bath BA1 1HE, UK

Copyright © Parragon 2005

ISBN 1-40545-326-5

Editorial and design by
Amber Books Ltd
Bradley's Close
74–77 White Lion Street
London N1 9PF
www.amberbooks.co.uk

Project Editor: Michael Spilling
Design: Zoe Mellors
Picture Research: Natasha Jones

Printed in China

PICTURE CREDITS

All pictures courtesy of Michael Williams except the following:
Peter Adams: 30, 71t, 74, 122, 124, 131, 255m, 275, 286 (both);
Amber Books Ltd: 3, 8, 9, 10t, 36 (both), 38t, 39, 56t, 57, 67, 83l, 92 (main), 93, 96 (both), 99t, 106t, 115, 127 (both), 133, 134t, 136t, 163 (main), 180 (both), 188 (main), 199 (both), 211 (main);
Cheffins: 219;
Corbis: endpapers
Elkhorn Valley Museum: 52;
Andrew Morland: 26, 31 (both), 32, 33 (both), 44t, 48, 49, 50, 53, 64 (both), 68 (both), 69, 70, 79, 80, 81, 83 (main), 84 (both), 87, 97, 99 (main), 106 (main), 112, 113;
David Williams: 7, 13, 22 (both), 25, 28b, 29, 34 (both), 35, 45 (both), 46 (both), 47, 51t, 60 (both), 61, 65 (both), 73 (both), 94 (both), 95, 104, 108t, 110 (both), 111, 118, 123, 125, 128, 134(main), 136 (main), 137, 139l, 141, 143, 145, 147, 148, 150, 151, 161, 162, 163t, 164 (both), 165, 166 (both), 169 (both), 171 (main), 174, 175 (both), 176 (both), 183 (both), 184 (both), 185, 186, 187 (main), 190, 192-3, 193, 195t, 196 (both), 204 (both), 205 (both), 208t, 211t, 212 (both), 213, 217r, 223 (both), 227t, 228, 234 (both), 235, 239 (both), 251 (both), 256, 263.

CONTENTS

Tractor Power

The development of farm tractors has had an enormous impact on farming efficiency, and the result in countries with a mechanized farming industry has been that a small number of people working on farms can now produce enough food for the remainder of the population.

Above: *Giant tractors such as this Steiger Panther provide big-acreage farms with massive power for pulling high-output implements.*

Left: *This John Deere 435 is an example of the tractor industry's switch from spark-ignition engines to diesel engines during the 1950s and 1960s.*

The change has been dramatic. Before the first tractors appeared, when food production relied on animal power plus a relatively small contribution from steam engines, farming employed well over 50 percent of the working population in North America and much of Europe. Since then productivity has increased so much that just two or three percent of the population provides enough food for themselves and for the nonfarming 97 percent or so.

Productivity

Obviously tractor power is not the only reason for this increased output. We have more productive strains of crops and livestock, more effective veterinary products and pesticides, and we use more fertilizer, but mechanization and the use of tractor power have made a massive contribution to farming productivity.

Another indication of the impact of tractor power on food production is the changing population of draft animals recorded in official statistics. Census figures for the number of horses on American farms reached a peak in 1919 at just over 20 million, and there were also more than five million mules. Since then the number of working animals has fallen steadily, while tractor numbers have continued to increase. There has been a similar pattern in Britain, where the four principal heavy horse breeds have virtually disappeared from farms as working animals, although they are still maintained by enthusiasts. Britain's oldest heavy horse breed is the Suffolk Punch, and 80 years ago it provided the power for much of the work from plowing to harvest on many of the arable farms in the eastern counties of Britain. Today the Suffolk Punch is officially on the rare breeds register, and the population is actually smaller than that of the giant panda.

Apart from powering threshing drums in North America, steam engines never made a massive contribution to farm mechanization. They were too big and expensive to replace animal power on the small- and medium-acreage farms, and the American and European manufacturers of portables, traction engines, and cable-plowing engines soon felt the impact of competition from tractor power. It was an easy win for the tractor companies, and the response of some of the big steam engine manufacturers is included in this book. Some such as J. I. Case moved into the tractor market at just the right time to catch the wartime boom in tractor sales, while the initial reaction of the British company Richard Garrett was to remain loyal to steam, redesigning the traction engine as a steam-powered tractor.

Design Development

When the first tractors appeared more than 110 years ago they were designed mainly for powering threshing machines. The design improvements that have been introduced since then to produce the highly productive and versatile modern tractors that have replaced both animal power and steam engines on farms are outlined in this book.

Some of the progress has been made in big strides, and this category includes Henry Ford's cheap and cheerful mass-produced Fordson, the first diesel-powered Benz tractor, International Harvester's Farmall rowcrop tractor, the first rubber tires demonstrated on the Allis-Chalmers Model U, rubber tracks introduced on the Caterpillar Challenger, the Deutz Intrac and Mercedes-Benz MB-trac systems tractors, four-wheel drive, and last but certainly not least, the Ferguson System.

But design improvements have also come in more modest steps such as increasingly user-friendly gearboxes, improved access for engine maintenance, increased maneuverability, and better instrumentation. However, there have also been plenty of ideas that simply failed to attract enough customers, and these include various three-, six-, and eight-wheel drive tractors and the County Sea Horse amphibious tractor that was driven across the English Channel.

Several tractors from the 1950s onward were equipped with hydrostatic transmissions, and this is again a development that has so far failed to achieve the level of popularity that some people expected. Hydrostatic drives have some important advantages, including infinitely variable speed adjustment without using the clutch pedal or altering the engine rpm, and with no gears to crash a hydrostatic tractor could be ideal for inexperienced drivers. However, the main disadvantage of a hydro drive is that the power losses are significantly

Below: *Rumeley OilPull tractors established a reputation as rugged heavyweights. An attempt to develop a new lightweight model range in the 1920s was less successful.*

Above: *Canadian-based Goold, Shapley, and Muir was one of a large number of tractor companies that failed to survive the intensely competitive era of the early 1920s.*

greater than for most mechanical transmissions. There are plenty of situations where the benefits should easily outweigh this one disadvantage. However, in spite of this, the disappointing sales figures forced International Harvester to abandon its ambitious Hydro tractor range.

Another recent development that already appears to be well established is the transportation tractor, designed to offer a faster travel speed for trailer work or travel between farms. It is an idea that started with the Mercedes -Benz Unimog truck/tractor in Germany— although this is probably more truck than tractor, and was developed in a much more agricultural version as the Trantor in Britain. The Fastrac from JCB provides even more of a dual-purpose tractor, designed for slow-speed jobs such as plowing as well as a speed of 31mph (50km/h) on the road.

Tractor power was provided initially by gas-burning spark-ignition engines, with diesels becoming increasingly dominant starting in the 1950s. Diesel power is now firmly the standard for farm tractors, and experiments with alternative power units such as high-tech steam engines, fuel cells, and gas turbines have so far made no impact on the popularity of diesel.

Safety

Although there has been a steady stream of mechanical developments affecting the performance of tractors in the field and on the road, the tractor industry's efforts to improve the comfort and safety of drivers have, until recently, been much less impressive. For the first 30 years of development the drivers of most tractors worked within easy reach of exposed gear wheels, chain drives, and other moving parts, a situation that would horrify a modern safety inspector.

It took even longer for safety cabs to be fitted to protect the driver from death or injury if the vehicle overturned. Even modern tractors can overturn when working on steep land or working too close to a drainage ditch, and the problem was aggravated on some of the earlier tractors by a high center of gravity. A particular problem on the Fordson Model F tractor was a habit of rearing over backward owing to a design fault in the position of the drawbar hitch, and in his book *Henry Ford and Grass Roots America*, Reynold M. Wick quotes contemporary newspaper reports suggesting that, by 1922, 136 drivers had been killed in accidents involving Model F tractors on American farms.

When, eventually, the tractor manufacturers started fitting safety cabs it was not because the accident statistics showed clearly that some form of protection was needed in order to save lives, but because they were forced to fit them by government legislation. Some of the blame for this situation must rest with the customers who bought the tractors: if they had demanded proper safety cabs the tractor industry would have been quick to respond.

Comfort

Driver comfort has also been a low priority. It took about 60 years for the majority of drivers to be offered more than a basic metal seat on a springy steel mount, and on some of the earliest tractors there was not even a driver's seat. Cabs for weather protection also remained a rarity until the 1950s, and it took a further 30 years before proper cab and axle suspension systems arrived to help absorb some of the bounce and vibration when a tractor was working over rough ground.

Exactly why tractor drivers had to wait so long to enjoy a more comfortable working environment when even the earliest vans and trucks were equipped with cabs and sprung axles is a mystery. One explanation may be that customers were reluctant to pay extra for a tractor with higher standards of driver comfort, but, ironically, there is now plenty of evidence to show that it increases output because drivers tend to select a higher gear or choose a faster engine speed if their tractor is more comfortable.

Considering how long it took to achieve any significant progress in providing tractor drivers with a better working environment, the situation has certainly changed quite dramatically during the past 25 years or so, with driver comfort moving rapidly up the list of design priorities. Tractor salespeople confirm that customers are demanding much higher levels of comfort, and a spacious, well-equipped cab with a deluxe seat is one of the key factors in the competition for sales.

Above: *This cutaway picture shows the transmission that delivers the engine power on the big Steiger STX440 tractor from Case I.H.*

Below: *County's FC series tractors with a load platform behind the front-mounted cab were one of the innovative designs of the 1960s.*

Robot Tractors

Now that the leading tractor manufacturers are offering really high standards of driver comfort, the next stage could be to eliminate the driver and use robot tractors for many of the more repetitive jobs on farms. This is not a new idea, and as long ago as 1958 a team of engineers at Reading University, in England, demonstrated a tractor with a tracking system that could automatically follow signals from a cable buried beneath the ground. This system was considered to be so successful that an improved version was developed commercially, and at least two installations were sold to large-scale fruit growers, who used the buried cables in their orchards to guide a driverless tractor for routine grass mowing under the trees.

There were, inevitably, problems with the buried cable guidance system, and with various radio-controlled remote-guidance systems that were demonstrated by several companies, including Ferguson in the United States and Ford in Britain. The latest systems may prove to be more acceptable, using advanced electronics, computerized control systems, and signals from the Global Positioning System (GPS) network of satellites to pinpoint the position of the tractor with an accuracy of less than three feet.

Much of the technology needed to produce driverless tractors is already standard equipment on many tractors, and this includes the interlinked electronic control systems that manage the engine, transmission, and rear linkage of many of the medium- and high-horsepower models. This means that instead of needing a driver to coordinate the optimum settings for the main working components, the job can be handled by a computer and the results are likely to be more precise than even a skilled driver can manage. Add a GPS-linked control for the steering and a fail-safe mechanism to stop the tractor if there is something in the way, and the driver's job could be under threat.

Various electronically controlled robot tractors have been demonstrated, but at this stage they are not being used to replace the driver. Instead they are making the driver's job easier and more productive by removing some of the routine aspects of tractor operation. How long this will continue is not clear, and it will no doubt depend on the quality of work and the reliability of the driverless tractors.

What is certain is that the next 10 or 20 years of tractor development should be at least as interesting as the past few decades have been.

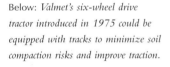

Below: *Valmet's six-wheel drive tractor introduced in 1975 could be equipped with tracks to minimize soil compaction risks and improve traction.*

chapter 1

The First Tractors

The first tractors were developed in the United States in the 1880s, when the farming industry was expanding rapidly with millions of acres of good farming land in the American midwest being cultivated for the first time. Most of the machinery was powered by horses and mules, but steam power was making an increasing contribution, and the first tractors were designed to replace steam engines for powering threshing machines.

Above: *Tractors such as this rare British-built Crossley were designed for versatility and were capable of operating general field machinery as well as powering a belt to drive stationary equipment.*

Left: *Three-wheel designs attracted many manufacturers during the early years of tractor development, including Case with their distinctive 10-20 model, and the idea was later adopted for rowcrop tractors.*

The first American tractors were big and heavy, and designed mainly to replace steam engines for powering stationary agricultural equipment. The British approach was different, and the designers produced smaller, lighter tractors that would replace horses for pulling equipment such as cultivators and hay machinery in small fields; the little Ivel tractor was the classic example.

Steam power had most of the advantages at first. By the 1890s, when the first tractors were working, steam-engine technology was backed by more than 100 years of development and the engines were extremely reliable. The new gasoline-powered tractors were just the opposite. The engines were crude, inefficient, and temperamental, and reliability was a serious problem for another twenty years or more.

Poor reliability was one of the reasons why farmers on both sides of the Atlantic were so cautious about switching from animals and steam power to using tractors. However, the impact of World War I (1914–18) brought about significant changes in farming practices in North America and Europe. Large numbers of men and horses left the farms for the battlefields of Europe, and many farmers found themselves having to use tractor power for the first time in order to maintain food-production levels. Postwar manpower shortages ensured the tractor was here to stay.

FROELICH

⚒ 1892 Froelich, Iowa

FROELICH

Tractor history dates back to about 1889, when an American named John Charter used a gasoline engine mounted on the chassis and transmission of a steam-traction engine to power a threshing machine.

More experimental tractors appeared in 1892 and, like the Charter, they were used for threshing work. One of them was built by John Froelich of Froelich, Iowa, a village named after his father. John Froelich was a contractor who operated steam-powered threshing equipment in the Dakotas, and he decided to build a gasoline-powered traction engine to replace one of his steam engines.

Early Design
The chassis was built by a local blacksmith and was mounted on a set of traction-engine wheels. Froelich bought a Van Duzen engine, which was typical of the efficiency standards available from gasoline engines in the early 1890s. With just one enormous cylinder providing 2,155 cubic inches (35.5 liters) capacity it produced only 20hp (14.8kw).

Above: *This replica version of the original Froelich tractor was built by Deere and Co. to feature in a movie about the company's history.*

It was probably the first tractor with a reverse gear, which must have simplified the driver's job when maneuvering into position for threshing work, but there were few other concessions to driver comfort or safety. The driver stood right at the front of the tractor, and the only seat was the top of the fuel tank. The driving position was within easy reach of the engine's huge spoked flywheels, and the transmission gears were also exposed and easily accessible. There was, however, a large container for drinking water in case the driver was thirsty.

Waterloo Gasoline Traction Engine Co.

The tractor- or gasoline-powered traction engine worked well, and its success encouraged John Froelich and a group of businessmen to start a company to build more machines based on the same design. The company, based in Waterloo, Iowa, was called the Waterloo Gasoline Traction Engine Co., but the first two tractors built in 1893 failed to satisfy their customers and were returned to the factory.

Following this setback the company was reorganized in 1895. It stopped building tractors and concentrated on engine production instead, the name was changed to the Waterloo Gasoline Engine Co., and John Froelich left in 1895. But this was not the end of the story. Later, when it returned to tractor production, Waterloo was so successful that Deere & Co. bought the company in order to enter the tractor market—making the 1892 Froelich the earliest ancestor of all John Deere tractors.

Specifications

Manufacturer:	John Froelich
Location:	Froelich, Iowa
Model:	N/A
Type:	Self-propelled threshing engine
Power unit:	Single-cylinder engine
Power output:	20hp (14.8kw)
Transmission:	Exposed gears
Weight:	N/A
Production started:	1892

Left: *Operator safety was a long way down the list of priorities when the Froelich tractor was built with its completely exposed flywheels and gearing.*

CASE

🔧 1892   Racine, Wisconsin

CASE EXPERIMENTAL TRACTOR

By the early 1890s the J. I. Case Threshing Machine Co. was one of America's leading manufacturers of agricultural steam engines, and it was well on the way to becoming the biggest in the world.

Specifications

Manufacturer: J. I. Case Threshing Machine Co.

Location: Racine, Wisconsin

Model: Experimental

Type: Self-propelled threshing engine

Power unit: Patterson single-cylinder engine

Power output: 20hp (14.8kw)

Transmission: N/A

Weight: N/A

Production started: 1892

Most of the big steam-engine makers did not respond to the challenge from the new internal combustion engines until it was too late. The Case approach was different, and the company built an experimental tractor in 1892 and compared it with a steam traction engine.

"Balanced" Engine

Some gasoline engines used by the tractor pioneers had a single horizontal cylinder, which produced a rocking motion as the big piston traveled back and forth. Case chose the William Patterson "balanced" engine with two opposed pistons in a single cylinder, and this worked more smoothly. The engine was mounted on the chassis and wheels of a Case traction engine, with a canopy that appears to protect the engine but not the driver.

Primitive ignition and fuel systems used on the early gasoline engines caused reliability problems, and the Patterson engine was no exception. Steam engines, with many more years of development behind them, were more reliable, and Case stopped work on the Patterson-powered tractor to concentrate on its successful steam engines instead.

Above: *The roof over this prototype Case tractor in this 1890s photograph seems to provide some protection for the engine, but leaves the driver exposed to the rain.*

HART-PARR

✖ 1903   Charles City, Iowa

HART-PARR 18-30

The partnership between Charles Hart and Charles Parr began at the University of Wisconsin, where they studied engineering and shared an interest in engine design. After graduating in 1896 they formed a company to build engines based on ideas they developed as students, and these included using oil instead of water in the cooling system, presumably to avoid frost damage.

Right: This 1903 Hart-Parr 18-30 was one of the heavyweights from the early years of American tractor design, and it is now in the Smithsonian Institution.

Specifications

Manufacturer: Hart-Parr Co.

Location: Charles City, Iowa

Model: 18-30

Type: Self-propelled threshing engine

Power unit: Oil-cooled twin-cylinder engine

Power output: 30hp (22.2kw)

Transmission: Single-speed gearbox

Weight: 15,680lb (7,119kg)

Production started: 1903

Tractor production began when the Hart-Parr company moved to bigger premises in Charles City, Iowa, and Tractor No. 1 was completed in 1902. The third model was the 18-30, built in 1903 and powered by a two-cylinder kerosene- or paraffin-burning engine with oil cooling.

Cooling Tower

A distinctive feature of the 18-30 and many other Hart-Parr models built during the next 15 years was the big rectangular tower at the front of the tractor. This was part of the cooling system, taking exhaust fumes from the tractor's engine and using them to induce an upward blast of air inside the tower to cool oil circulating from the engine.

As the model number suggests, the two 10-in (3.9-cm) bore and 13-in (5.1cm) stroke cylinders produced 30hp (22.2kw) on the belt pulley, with 18hp available at the drawbar. The 18-30 weighed 6.9 tons (7 tonnes), a lightweight compared with the 27-ton (27.4-tonne) Hart-Parr 60-100 built in 1911.

IVEL

1902 Biggleswade, Bedfordshire, England

IVEL

Dan Albone was the son of a market gardener and, like Harry Ferguson and Henry Ford, his main interest was engineering and he left home to start a small workshop where he made bicycles and axles for railroad trucks and cars.

Albone's business was based in Biggleswade, Bedfordshire, in England, which is where he began experimenting with tractors, and in 1902 he completed his first prototype model. It was a three-wheeler with a two-cylinder engine mounted on a steel frame. A large tank for cooling water was mounted at the rear of the tractor, with the weight over the driving wheels to improve traction.

Various makes of engine were used, and the 8hp (6.03kw) of early versions eventually reached 24hp (17.7kw) in 1913. While American manufacturers were building heavyweight tractors to power threshing machines and plow the prairies, Albone realized that a small, light tractor could replace horses for jobs such as pulling a mower or a binder, and his tractor weighed only 26cwt (1,300kg).

Above: *Several different engines were used to power the Ivel tractor, and different power outputs were quoted ranging from 8hp (6.03kw) to 24hp (17.7kw).*

Tractor power remained a novelty in Britain, and sales were disappointing, but the Ivel acquired an impressive list of export successes to 18 countries by 1906. A specially modified Ivel was built for a fruit grower in Tasmania—probably the first orchard tractor—and Albone designed a narrow version for a French vineyard. Ivels also won gold and silver medals at shows throughout the world, with the total reaching 24 by 1906.

Tractor Variants

Albone showed considerable imagination developing alternative uses for his tractors. One Ivel was equipped as a fire truck, complete with water pump and crew, and gave a fire-fighting demonstration.

Another tractor, with armor cladding and wide-opening rear doors, was demonstrated as a battlefield ambulance. Army chiefs were shown how the belt pulley could power water purification and ice-making equipment at a first-aid station, and the tractor could transport medical supplies over rough ground.

The tractor could also be used to help bring in the wounded, using the big rear doors to shelter stretcher bearers. Apart from firing bullets to test the armor, the military men showed little interest in an idea that, 10 years later, might have saved thousands of lives on European battlefields.

With further development the Ivel could have become an international success story, but Albone died in 1906 aged 46. The Ivel, once described as "undoubtedly the great attraction" at the Paris agricultural show and "the most successful agricultural motor yet placed on the market" by a newspaper in Argentina, faded into obscurity.

Specifications

Manufacturer: Ivel Agricultural Motors

Location: Biggleswade, Bedfordshire, England

Model: 1904 version

Type: General purpose

Power unit: Two-cylinder, horizontally-opposed engine

Power output: 18hp (13.32kw)

Transmission: Single-speed gearbox standard, two-speed optional

Weight: 3,360lb (1,525kg)

Production started: 1902

Left: *In spite of winning an impressive array of gold and silver medals and attracting customers in 18 countries, the Ivel attracted only disappointing demand in the UK.*

RANSOMES

⚒ **1903 Ipswich, Suffolk, England**

RANSOMES

The Ransomes family began making farm equipment in Ipswich, Suffolk in 1789, and during the second half of the nineteenth century they were one of the leading manufacturers of agricultural steam engines.

Below: *Some pioneer tractor-makers did not bother to fit brakes, but the first Ransomes tractor featured four-wheel braking with foot and hand controls.*

In 1903 Ransomes Sims & Jefferies, as the company was then called, demonstrated its first tractor. The power unit chosen for the model was a 20-hp (14.8-kw) four-cylinder gasoline engine made by Sims, a leading manufacturer of car engines.

The tractor was also equipped with what appears to have been an unusual gearbox, with three speeds forward and three in reverse. The transmission also operated the belt pulley, providing the choice of 220, 450, or 1,000rpm settings at the rated engine speed.

The braking arrangements were also unusual. A foot pedal disengaged the clutch and at the same time applied a transmission brake on the drive to the wheels, and a hand lever applied the brakes to all four wheels.

Brakes

This was probably the first example of four-wheel braking at a time when many tractor manufacturers considered that brakes were unnecessary. Work rate with a three-furrow plow was said to be 0.5 acres (0.2 hecatres) per hour using 1.5 gallons (4.5 liters) of gasoline.

The tractor was demonstrated and taken to shows in 1903 and 1904, but no sales are recorded and the project was abandoned.

Specifications

Manufacturer: Ransomes Sims & Jefferies	
Location: Ipswich, Suffolk, England	
Model: 20hp	
Type: General purpose	
Power unit: Sims four-cylinder engine	
Power output: 20hp (14.8kw)	
Transmission: Gearbox with three speeds forward and in reverse	
Weight: 4,704lb (2,136kg)	
Production started: 1903	

FORD
✗ 1906/7   Detroit, Michigan

FORD EXPERIMENTAL TRACTOR

Below: Henry Ford's first experimental tractor was assembled from Ford car components to reduce development and production costs.

Although Henry Ford's childhood on the family farm in Michigan left him with little enthusiasm for working with horses, it did produce a life-long interest in developing tractor power to improve farming efficiency.

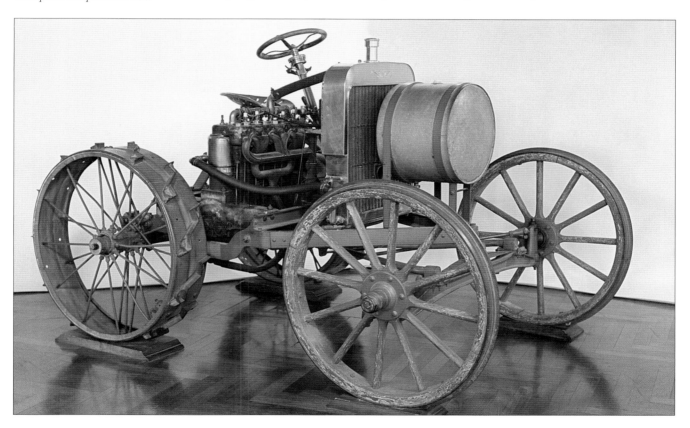

Specifications

Manufacturer: Ford Motor Co.

Location: Detroit, Michigan

Model: Experimental

Type: General purpose

Power Unit: Ford four-cylinder engine

Power output: 24hp (17.7kw)

Transmission: N/A

Weight: 1,500lb (681kg)

Production started: 1906/7

Ford is principally remembered for his immense contribution to the car industry, but he also revolutionized tractor design and production, using his enormous financial resources and mass-production expertise to make affordable tractor power available to many farmers for the first time.

Ford's Tractor

Ford tractor development began in 1906 or 1907 with an experimental model built by Joseph Galamb, one of Henry Ford's most trusted engineers. He used mainly existing components, and these included the 24-hp (17.7-kw) engine and gearbox from a Ford Model B car and the steering gear and front axle from a Model K car. The front wheels may also have come from a Model K, but the rear wheels were probably from a binder.

The tractor's front axle had a leaf-spring suspension, but it was included because it was part of the Model K design and there is no evidence that Ford and his engineers were particularly concerned about driver comfort. Tractor drivers had to wait another 90 years before axle suspension systems were widely available.

MARSHALL

✖ 1908 Gainsborough, Lincolnshire, England

MARSHALL 60HP

After a long and distinguished history as steam-engine manufacturers, the Marshall company of Gainsborough, Lincolnshire, in England, made its first move into the tractor market in 1907, when it announced its 30-hp model, powered by a paraffin-fueled engine.

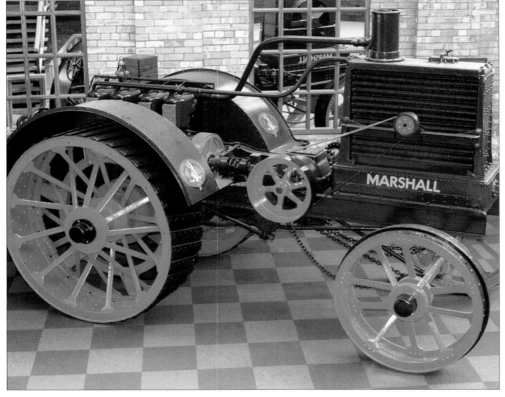

Above: *This Marshall tractor was originally exported to Australia, but it recently made the return journey to Britain, where it has now been fully restored.*

Specifications

Manufacturer: Marshall Sons & Co.
Location: Gainsborough, Lincolnshire, England
Model: 60hp
Type: General purpose
Power unit: Marshall two-cylinder engine
Power output: 60hp (44.4kw)
Transmission: Three-speed gearbox
Weight: 22,000lb (9,988kg)
Production started: 1908

The new model, weighing about 4.9 tons (5 tonnes), was big by British standards and was designed mainly for export. Marshall targeted countries with big farms such as Canada and Australia, where its steam engines were already well established and had built up a name for long-term reliability.

An additional model followed in 1908, powered by a rear-mounted, four-cylinder engine consisting of a pair of its two-cylinder 30-hp (22.2-kw) engines mounted side by side to give a 60hp (44.4kw) output. The cylinder bore and stroke were both 7in (17.8cm) and the rated engine speed was 800rpm.

Mixed Fortunes

The Canadian market was dominated by American-built steam engines and tractors. Marshall competed strongly, entering its 30- and 60-hp tractors plus a steam-traction engine in the Agricultural Motor Competition held in Winnipeg, Manitoba, in 1909.

The results were disappointing, as the 30-hp tractor came third in a class of three and the steam engine was withdrawn. The new 60-hp tractor came second in a class of five, however, and in the same year it also achieved valuable publicity by winning the Gold Medal award at the prestigious Brandon Fair, in Manitoba.

Above, left: *Marshall was one of several British steam-engine manufacturers that built big, heavyweight tractors for export to far corners of the British Empire.*

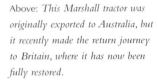

SAUNDERSON

⚒ **1910 approx   Elstow, Bedford, England**

SAUNDERSON UNIVERSAL MODEL G

Below: There was enough space in front of the radiator on the Saunderson Universal tractor for a wooden box to carry tools, spare spark plugs, and other essentials.

Britain's urgent need for tractor power to increase food production during World War I affected even the Royal Family. There was plenty of scope to plow more land on the royal estate at Sandringham in Norfolk, and when King George V decided to buy a tractor he chose a Saunderson Model G.

Specifications

Manufacturer:	Saunderson
Location:	Elstow, Bedford, England
Model:	Universal G
Type:	General purpose
Power unit:	Two-cylinder engine
Power output:	20hp (14.8kw)
Transmission:	Three-speed gearbox
Weight:	N/A
Production started:	1910 approx

The order was placed in 1916 and it took two days to drive the tractor the 80 miles (129km) from the factory to the Royal estate. The company gained valuable publicity from the order and from the subsequent reports about the tractor's progress on the Royal estate, and there was more publicity from the Saunderson family farm, probably the first in the country to be farmed entirely with tractor power. Other successes with the Model G included an agreement for a French company to build the tractor under license.

Saundersons

H. P. Saunderson, a baker's son, started building tractors in 1900. The Model G was available from about 1910, powered by a Saunderson–designed two-cylinder vertical engine that was described as 20hp (14.8kw) and later as 25hp (18.5kw).

After the war Saunderson faced financial problems and in 1924 the Manchester-based Crossley engineering company bought the Saunderson company and attempted to market the tractors for road haulage, but production ended within about two years.

CASE
⚒ **1912   Racine, Wisconsin**

CASE 20-40

While the J. I. Case Threshing Machine Co. was developing the world's best-selling range of agricultural steam engines, it continued to watch the progress of tractor power, and by 1911 the company decided to build a range of tractors to sell alongside its traction engines.

With the benefit of hindsight, both the decision and its timing were correct. Demand for tractor power was growing strongly in North America, and the dramatic expansion during World War I was only a few years away. The other factor that probably played a part in the decision was the steady improvement in engine reliability in the almost

20 years since Case engineers had built their first experimental tractor in 1892.

The first production model was the Case 30-60 of 1911, and this was followed by the 20-40 tractor early in 1912. Both models were ruggedly built, and both shared some components with Case traction engines. The 20-40 was easily the most popular of the two

Above, top: The twin-cylinder Case engine was started manually with a ratchet-and-pawl mechanism, using an extension lever to fit into the socket. Above, left: The Case 20-40 was one of the most popular of the big North American tractors during the 1914–18 war.

models, and it was also one of the most popular of the American heavyweight-style tractors, with production continuing until 1920.

Case Engines

Case bought in the engines for the first few 20-40 tractors, but within just a few months their own engine was available, and this was the power unit used for the remainder of the production run. Both engines were a two-cylinder design with the cylinders horizontally opposed to improve the balance and reduce vibration, and both were started manually using a length of wood that slotted into a ratchet-and-pawl mechanism to turn the engine over.

A two-speed gearbox provided travel speeds of 2 and 3mph (3.2 and 4.8km/h) at the engine's 475rpm rated speed. The cooling system was based on the rectangular tower over the front axle, using exhaust fumes from the engine to increase air movement for heat removal. A water pump and fan were added later to make the engine cooling more efficient.

Confirmation of the good design of the 20-40 came at the Winnipeg trials in Manitoba with a gold medal award in 1913. In 1920 the 20-40 was one of the first tractors to take part in the new Nebraska tests, where its main claim to fame was achieving one of the lowest scores in the wheelslip test—probably because at a total weight of 13,780lb (6,256kg) it was among the heaviest tractors tested.

Specifications

Manufacturer: J. I. Case Threshing Machine Co.

Location: Racine, Wisconsin

Model: 20-40

Type: General purpose

Power unit: Case two-cylinder horizontally opposed engine

Power output: 40hp (29.6kw)

Transmission: Two-speed gearbox

Weight: 13,780lb (6,256kg)

Production started: 1912

Left: *The heavy-duty steel-girder framework with a slow-speed horizontal engine were classic design features when the big Case was introduced in 1912.*

HART-PARR

1912 **Charles City, Iowa**

HART-PARR 40

By 1912 Hart-Parr had lost its leading position in the North American sales charts to International Harvester, but it was still one of the major manufacturers with a wide range of models.

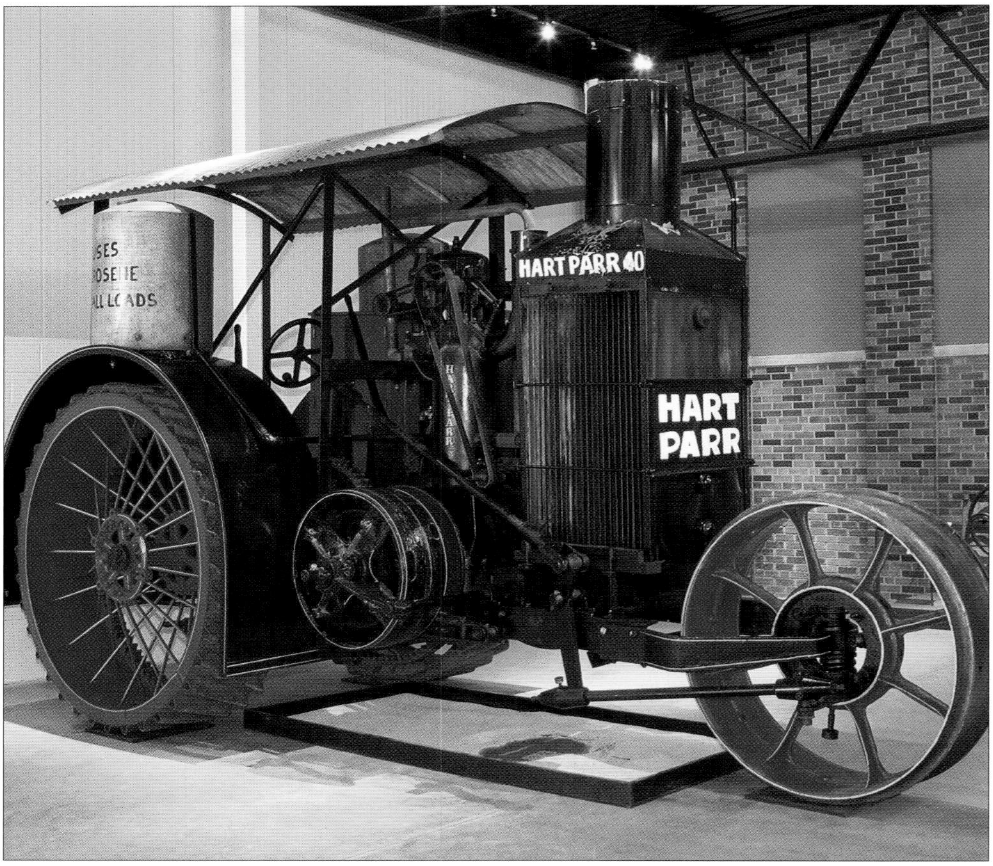

Specifications

Manufacturer: Hart-Parr Co.
Location: Charles City, Iowa
Model: 40
Type: General purpose
Power unit: Two-cylinder oil-cooled engine
Power output: 40hp (29.6kw)
Transmission: Two-speed gearbox
Weight: N/A
Production started: 1912

Above: *Hart-Parr built a series of heavyweight models with a distinctive cooling tower at the front, but the unusual feature of the model 40 was the tricycle-style wheel layout.*

The Hart-Parr reputation was based on building big tractors, and its new 40 model with a 20-40 power rating was in the heavyweight tradition. It featured Hart-Parr's usual oil-cooled engine design with a big rectangular cooling tower at the front of the tractor, and the canopy with a corrugated metal roof over the engine and driver's platform was also a typical Hart-Parr feature.

Tricycle Layout

The tricycle-style wheel layout with a single front wheel was different. Most previous Hart-Parr tractors were based on a conventional four-wheel design, and the first exception to this was the 15-30 three-wheeler introduced in 1909. A three-wheel layout can be useful in some situations, and particularly for rowcrop work, but the advantages of a single front wheel on a heavy tractor such as the new 40-60 model appear to be outweighed by the disadvantages.

Hart-Parr retained its usual two-cylinder kerosene-burning engine design for the 40, with power delivered through a two-speed gearbox with the usual bull wheel and pinion final drive. Maximum travel speed was 4.0mph (6.4km/h).

MUNKTELLS
1913 Eskilstuna, Sweden

MUNKTELLS

Below: Tractor production in Sweden made an impressive start with this Munktells model powered by a 874-cubic-inch (14.4-liter) engine, an early ancestor of the Volvo car.

Tractor production in Sweden started in 1913 when the first Munktells model arrived. The company, based in Eskilstuna, had been building steam engines since 1853, and its first tractor was designed to provide sufficient power to replace steam engines for jobs such as threshing on large farms.

Specifications

Manufacturer: Munktells

Location: Eskilstuna, Sweden

Model: 30hp

Type: Self-propelled threshing engine

Power unit: Two-cylinder semi-diesel engine

Power output: 40hp (29.6kw) (maximum)

Transmission: Three-speed gearbox

Weight: 17,936lb (8,136kg)

Production started: 1913

Gross weight of the tractor with full fuel and cooling water tanks was 8 tons (8.1 tonnes), and this was carried on driving wheels measuring almost 6ft 6in (1.9m) in diameter. The engine was a semidiesel capable of burning a wide range of fuels, and the two cylinders provided a massive 874 cubic inches (14.4 liters) of capacity.

First Swedish Tractor

Rated power output was 30hp (22.2kw), but the manufacturers also claimed a 40-hp (29.6-kw) maximum output from the same engine. The maximum forward speed was a leisurely 2.75mph (4.4km/h) with the three-speed transmission in top gear.

Munktells built about 30 of the tractors between 1913 and 1915. Most were sold to big farms and estates in Sweden, but there were also exports as far afield as Russia and Argentina. Munktells later merged with the Volvo car and truck company, and tractors built after 1950 were sold under the Volvo BM name. Volvo's tractor operation was later combined with the Valmet company in Finland, where tractor production was concentrated. The Volvo brand name was later dropped in favor of Valmet, now known as Valtra.

WALSH AND CLARK
⚒ 1913 Leeds, Yorkshire, England

WALSH AND CLARK VICTORIA

Cable plowing with steam was developed in Britain and soon spread to other European countries. The engine remains at the edge of the field where it powers a winding drum that pulls the implement back and forth across the field on the end of a wire cable. The main advantage is that the weight of the steam engine does not damage the soil.

It was inevitable that sooner or later someone would substitute a tractor for the usual steam-powered cable-plowing equipment. The first company to do this was Walsh and Clark of Guiseley, Leeds, which built the first of their Victoria series engines in 1913, winning a silver medal for it at the 1915 Royal Show. An improved version followed in 1918.

Appearance

Victoria engines are deceptive because they were designed to look like a traditional steam

Above: Looking like a steam-traction engine, this is the Victoria plowing engine, with a cable drum slung under the massive boiler-shaped fuel tank.

engine complete with "boiler" and chimney. The boiler walls were made of 0.25-in (6-mm) thick steel plate and formed the fuel tank, holding enough paraffin for four days' work, and they also provided the tractor's main frame. The chimney took the exhaust fumes from the engine, helping to induce an air flow through the radiator at the same time.

The winding drum or windlass was suspended beneath the "boiler," just as it is on a steam plowing engine, and the power unit that drives the windlass was mounted on top of the boiler. Walsh and Clark chose a petrol/paraffin engine with two horizontal cylinders. Cylinder bore and stroke measurements were 7.0in and 8.0in (17.8cm and 20.3cm), and the operating speed was 600rpm.

Cable Plowing

Cable plowing usually involves a pair of engines working on opposite sides of the field, using their winding drums to pull a plow or cultivator backward and forward between them. One engine is equipped with a windlass for right-hand working and the other is a left-hand version. The 1918 Victoria engines could sustain a 3,500-lb (1,587-kg) pull on the cable, and a pair of engines with a 10-furrow two-way plow could cover up to 10 acres (4 hectares) per day, the makers claimed, although some fields were unsuitable for cable plowing because of an irregular shape or because they were not sufficiently level.

Most cable sets were operated by contractors, and some switched from steam to the Victoria engines to avoid problems of supplying coal and water to the field. The Victorias could also work in areas where the water quality was unsuitable for steam engines.

Production of the Victoria engines ended in the early 1920s as more efficient tractor power made cable work obsolete.

Specifications

Manufacturer: Walsh and Clark
Location: Leeds, Yorkshire, England
Model: Victoria (early version)
Type: Cable-plowing tractor
Power unit: Twin-cylinder horizontal engine
Power output: 22hp (16.3kw)
Transmission: Three-speed gearbox
Weight 12,294lb (5,588kg)
Production started: 1913

Below: The twin-cylinder horizontal engine that powered the winding drum on the Victoria plow engine was mounted on top of the fuel tank.

INTERNATIONAL HARVESTER
1913 Chicago, Illinois

INTERNATIONAL HARVESTER MOGUL 12-25

The International Harvester Company achieved unrivaled success during their early years in the tractor market. Tractor production began in 1905 and by 1910 I.H. had become the world's biggest manufacturer, claiming a one-third share of the United States market.

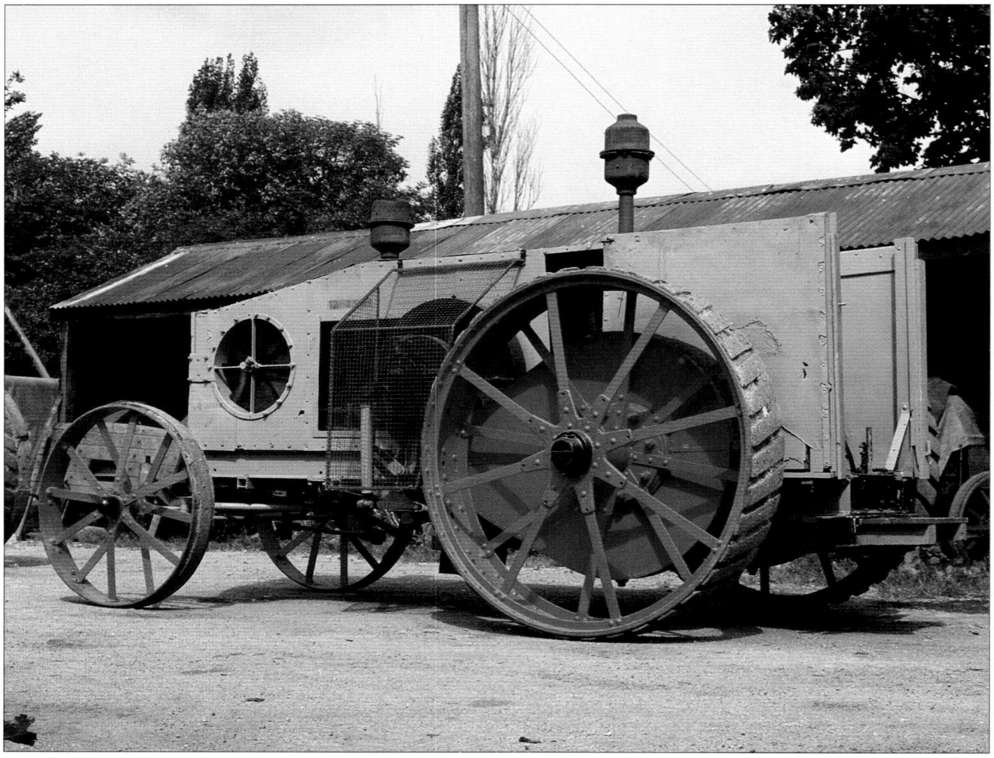

Specifications

Manufacturer: International Harvester Co.	
Location: Chicago, Illinois	
Model: Mogul 12-25	
Type: General purpose	
Power unit: I.H. two-cylinder horizontally opposed engine	
Power output: 25hp (18.5kw)	
Transmission: Two-speed gearbox	
Weight: 9,856lb (4,475kg)	
Production started: 1913	

Above: *International Harvester enclosed the chain-and-sprocket drive on its Mogul 12-25 tractor to protect it from possible damage caused by dust, mud, and stones.*

The success was based on big tractors, but a policy change brought a number of smaller models including the 12-25 in 1913. "Small" is, of course, a relative term, and the 12-25 in working trim weighed almost 4.5 tons (4.6 tonnes); the I.H. publicity described it as a "light" tractor in the United Kingdom, but medium weight in the United States.

Advanced Design

Some of the design features were a significant advance compared with earlier I.H. models, and this includes the chain-and-sprocket final drive which was fully enclosed to provide protection from dirt and stones. The 12-25 was also the first tractor from I.H. with a radiator and powered fan instead of a hopper-style cooling tower, and the automotive-type steering was an improvement over the previous chain-type steering systems.

The 12-25 was powered by a two-cylinder engine with the cylinders horizontally opposed. A high-tension magneto provided the spark, and lubrication was based on an automatic force-feed oiler. A two-speed gearbox provided a 4mph (6.4km/h) top speed.

AVERY

1913 Peoria, Illinois

AVERY 40-80

The market for heavyweight tractors in the United States and Canada grew rapidly during the five years from about 1910 as more land was plowed for wheat, and in 1913 Avery designed the 40-80 model to compete in this sector.

Above: *Avery tractors were popular at the heavyweight end of the market, and at 10 tons (10.1 tonnes) the 40-80 model was one of the classic heavyweights.*

Right: *Avery's power unit for the 40-80 was a four-cylinder engine with the cylinders horizontally opposed, a popular arrangement that reduced the vibration.*

Specifications

Manufacturer: Avery Co.

Location: Peoria, Illinois

Model: 40-80

Type: General purpose

Power unit: Four-cylinder horizontally opposed engine

Power output: 80hp (59kw)

Transmission: Two-speed sliding-frame gearbox

Weight: 10 tons (10.1 tonnes)

Production started: 1913

It weighed about 10 tons (10.1 tonnes) and, like most of its rivals, the 40-80 was ruggedly built, but it also had plenty of conventional design features. The power unit was a horizontally opposed four-cylinder, a popular design at that time as the cylinder movements helped to reduce vibration.

The 500rpm engine speed was typical of heavyweight tractors, and the cooling tower with exhaust-induced air movement was also conventional.

Many of the 40-80's rivals also shared the same chain-type steering mechanism, a feature borrowed from steam-traction engine design, and the bull gear and pinion final drive also came from the age of steam.

Gear Shift Mechanism

The Avery's gear shift mechanism was more unusual, consisting of a sliding frame that allowed the driver to change the drive-shaft pinions manually when selecting one of the two forward speeds. It could be awkward to operate, it eliminated any hope of a slick gear shift, and it would certainly not meet modern safety standards.

HART-PARR
✗ 1915 Charles City, Iowa

HART-PARR LITTLE DEVIL

Even companies such as Hart-Parr, which had helped to pioneer the development of heavyweight tractors, were interested in smaller, lighter models starting in about 1913.

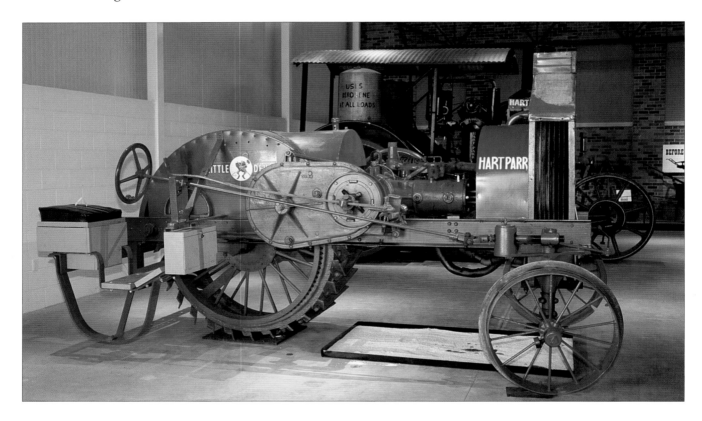

Hart-Parr's first down-market tractor was announced in 1914 and was called the Little Devil. It was a three-wheeler, with two wheels for steering while one extra-wide wheel centrally positioned at the rear provided traction. The driving position on the right-hand side of the rear wheel offered reasonable visibility forward and to the right, but the view to the left of the tractor was badly obstructed.

Design Features
The Little Devil's good design points included a fully enclosed engine and chain-and-sprocket final drive. The engine was a two-cylinder,

two-stroke developing 22hp (16.3kw) at the 600rpm rated engine speed, and the specification also included a gearbox with two forward speeds, but no reverse.

To make the Little Devil travel backward, according to C. H. Wendel's *Encyclopedia of American Farm Tractors*, the driver slowed the engine to idling speed, cut the ignition until the engine almost stopped, then suddenly adjusted the timing lever to make the engine misfire. With a bit of luck, the misfire would persuade the engine to run backward in order to reverse the tractor while one of the forward gears was engaged.

Above: *The Little Devil was Hart-Parr's first attempt to respond to the demand for lighter tractors.*

Specifications

Manufacturer: Hart-Parr Co.	
Location: Charles City, Iowa	
Model: Little Devil	
Type: General purpose	
Power unit: Two-cylinder two-stroke engine	
Power output: 22hp (16.3kw)	
Transmission: Two-speed gearbox	
Weight: N/A	
Production started: 1915	

SAWYER-MASSEY

1913 **Hamilton, Ontario, Canada**

SAWYER-MASSEY 20-40

Massey-Harris grew rapidly to become one of the leading farm-machinery companies, but it continued to specialize in machinery, ignoring steam power and delaying its entry into the tractor market.

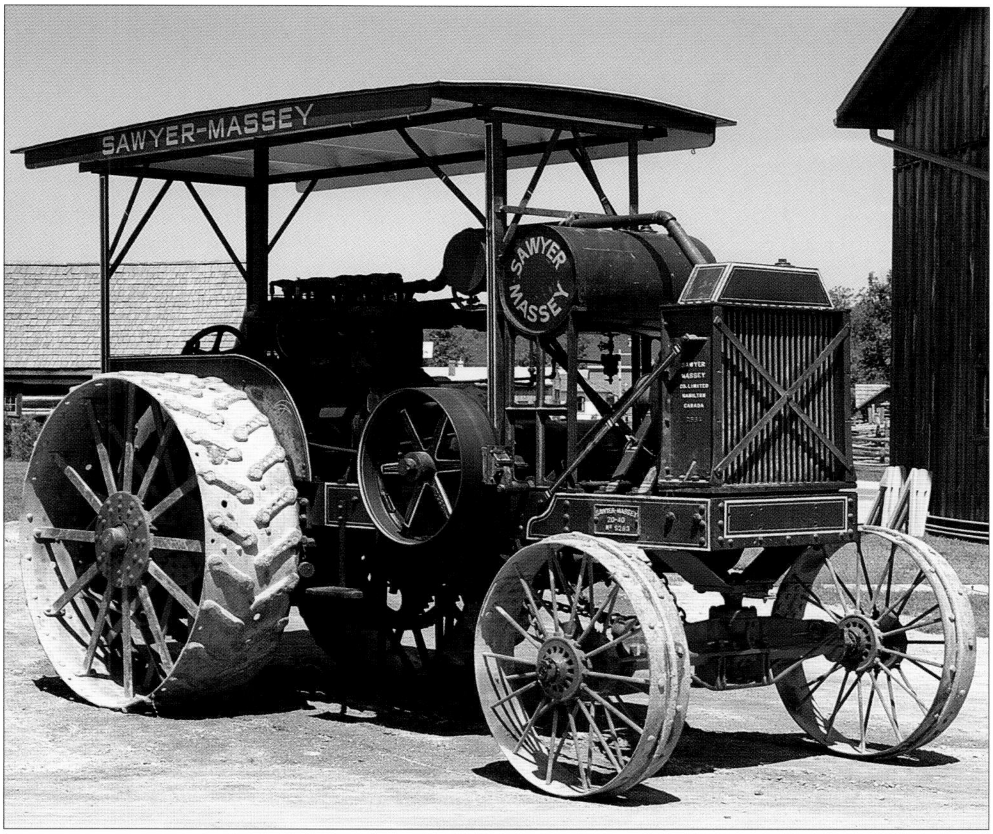

Right: *When the Canadian-based Sawyer-Massey company diversified into the tractor market, the Massey family had already sold its controlling interest in the company.*

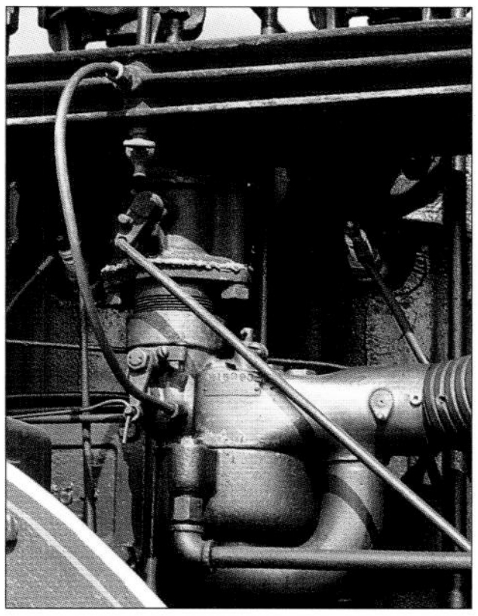

Above: *Sawyer-Massey chose a four-cylinder engine for its 20-40 tractor, placing the weight near the rear of the chassis for increased wheel grip.*

Specifications

Manufacturer:	Sawyer-Massey Co.
Location:	Hamilton, Ontario, Canada
Model:	20-40
Type:	General purpose
Power unit:	Four-cylinder engine
Power output:	40hp (29.6kw)
Transmission:	N/A
Weight:	N/A
Production started:	1913

The Massey family had a different policy. They were the biggest shareholders when the Massey and Harris companies merged in 1891, and in the following year they bought a 40 percent share in the L. D. Sawyer Co. of Hamilton, Ontario, a leading steam-engine manufacturer. Following the Massey investment, the company name changed to Sawyer-Massey and production expanded.

Sawyer-Massey

Tractor production followed in 1910, but at that stage the Massey family sold its interest in the company. Sawyer-Massey went on to develop a range of tractors, starting with a 22-45 model, which competed in the 1911 Winnipeg Agricultural Motor Competition. All models were powered by Sawyer-Massey four-cylinder engines with individual vertical cylinders.

The engine was over the rear axle, where the weight improved traction, leaving the cooling system and some empty space in front of the engine. The layout, shown by the 20-40 model, allowed Sawyer-Massey to claim that 75 percent of the weight was over the rear wheels.

The Sawyer-Massey 20-40 was one of the top-selling models, remaining in production until the early 1920s.

MOLINE
⚒ **1914 Moline, Illinois**

MOLINE UNIVERSAL MOTOR PLOW

The motor plow was very definitely designed to replace horses or mules for pulling cultivators and other machinery, and between about 1915 and 1920 they sold in large numbers in North America and, to a lesser extent, in several European countries.

Although they were slow, often under-powered and acquired a reputation for being awkward to use and unstable, motor plows were a relatively low-cost alternative to a conventional tractor, and they offered many thousands of small-acreage farmers their first realistic opportunity to make the switch from animal power to power farming. Motor plows were built by some of the big tractor companies in the USA, but they were also manufactured by many of the small businesses that mushroomed into the tractor market during the World War I sales boom.

The most successful and probably the best designed of the American motor plows was the Moline Universal. The first version was built in 1914 by the Universal Tractor Manufacturing Co. of Columbus, Ohio, but in the following

Above: Motor plows enjoyed a surge of popularity during World War I, and the Moline Universal was the leading model.

year the design was bought by the Moline Plow Co. of Moline, Illinois, and Moline introduced a number of improvements.

The power unit for the original Universal was a two-cylinder engine built by the Reliable company, and this version remained in production after the Moline takeover. Moline also introduced an additional version called the Model D, which was powered by a four-cylinder engine. Model D production started with a bought-in engine, but in 1917 this was replaced by an engine designed and built by the Moline company.

Advanced Features

The cylinder dimensions of the Moline engine were 3.5-in (8.9-cm) bore and a 5.0-in (12.7-cm) stroke, and the designers also added advanced features from the car industry, including an electric governor. In 1918 the Universal was the first tractor equipped with an electric starter, and a headlight was also included in the equipment list. Other design improvements introduced on the Model D included a heavy concrete disk attached to each driving wheel to provide extra weight for improved stability.

Demand for motor plows faded rapidly after about 1919, and production of the Moline Universal version ended in the early 1920s. In 1929 the Moline Plow Co., then known as the Moline Implement Co., was one of three companies involved in the merger to form the Minneapolis-Moline Power Implement Co.

Specifications

Manufacturer: Moline Plow Co.	**Power output:** 18hp (13.32kw)
Location: Moline, Illinois	**Transmission:** N/A
Model: D	**Weight:** 3,590lb (1,630kg)
Type: Motor plow	**Production started:** 1914
Power unit: Moline four-cylinder engine	

Left: *The Moline Universal was available with a choice of engines, and in 1918 it became the first tractor to be equipped with an electric starter motor.*

INTERNATIONAL HARVESTER

1914 Chicago, Illinois

I.H. MOGUL 8-16

Like most of its competitors in North America, International Harvester concentrated on building heavyweight models during its early years in the tractor market, but in 1914 the company announced a new model aimed at the smaller end of the market.

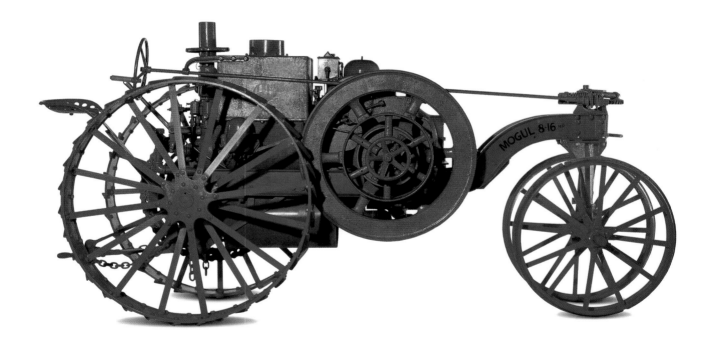

The 1914 introduction was the Mogul 8-16 model from the I.H. factory in Chicago, and it was followed in 1915 by another relative lightweight in the Titan series from the Milwaukee, Wisconsin, factory. The two newcomers were an important development for I.H. because they successfully brought the company's tractors to a much wider sector of the farming industry.

The Mogul series tractor with its 8-16 power rating—8hp (6.03kw) at the drawbar and 16hp

(11.8kw) at the belt pulley—was the smallest model in the I.H. range, but it was engineered well and had a reputation for long-term reliability.

No-frills Design

Some of its success was due to a basically simple, no-frills design with little to go wrong. The engine was a big single-cylinder with an 8-in (20.3-cm) bore and 12-in (30.5-cm) stroke, and it produced its rated power at a leisurely 400rpm. Even by 1914 standards the hopper-

Above: International Harvester's Mogul 8-16 was one of the best small tractors of its day, in spite of some old-fashioned features such as a hopper-cooling system.

cooling system, using a big rectangular tank placed over the rear axle, was low tech and, if there were problems, it was easy to repair.

The final drive was a massive roller chain and sprockets delivering power from the two-speed planetary gearbox and providing a leisurely top speed of 2mph (3.2km/h). The steering was also fairly basic, with a long straight rod linking the steering wheel to a worm gear above the front wheels.

Weight Distribution

In spite of its small size and modest power, the 8-16 weighed 5,020lb (2,279kg), a result of the sturdy design. Most of the engine and cooling-hopper weight was concentrated over the rear axle, and the weight distribution was one reason why the smallest of the Mogul series acquired a reputation as a good plowing tractor. Some were exported to Britain to help with the wartime plowing campaign, and they performed well under British conditions.

Production ended in 1917, but by then the 8-16 had been joined by a more powerful model known as the Mogul 10-20. The 8-16 and the 10-20 were basically similar, apart from the addition of fenders, or mudguards, over the 10-20's rear wheels, and the 10-20 engine had a slightly bigger bore measurement to provide the extra power.

Specifications

Manufacturer: International Harvester Co.

Location: Chicago, Illinois

Model: Mogul 8-16

Type: General purpose

Power unit: Two-cylinder engine

Power output: 16hp (11.8kw)

Transmission: Two-speed gearbox

Weight: 5,020lb (2,279kg)

Production started: 1914

Below: *Some Mogul 8-16s were exported to help with the wartime plowing campaign in Britain, where its reliability and rugged build made it a popular choice.*

INTERNATIONAL HARVESTER
⚒ **1915 Milwaukee, Wisconsin**

I.H. TITAN 10-20

For much of the first 50 years of tractor history International Harvester was the most successful manufacturer worldwide, and the Titan 10-20 model was among the most important and successful tractors the company built.

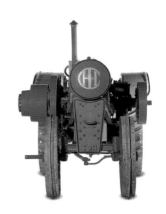

Production started in 1915 and, when the last of the 10-20s rolled off the production line at the I.H. factory in Milwaukee, Wisconsin, the build total was approaching 80,000.

Reliability
Although they looked quite different, the Titan and Mogul models shared a number of important features. Both were ruggedly built and, at a time when some manufacturers were experimenting with new ideas, the engineers at International Harvester chose a more traditional approach based on a steel-girder frame and a heavy, slow-revving two-cylinder engine. The result, by 1915 standards, was a reputation for reliability that helped International Harvester

Above: The Titan 10-20 was another of the lightweights that helped to make International Harvester the leading tractor company before the arrival of the Fordson.

to take the lead in the small to medium sector of the market.

The cylinders of the 10-20 engine were horizontal with the crankshaft at the front and the cylinder head just in front of the driver. Cylinder bore was 6.5in (16.5cm) with 8-in (20.3-cm) stroke, and the 20-hp (14.8-kw) rated output was produced at 500rpm. The fuel was kerosene, but an injection device added water to control the temperature and prevent pre-ignition. The ignition system was based on a high-tension magneto with an impulse starter.

Cooling System

The big 39-gallon (117-liter) capacity cylindrical tank located over the front axle was the cooling system, which matched the general simplicity of the 10-20, relying on heat difference and a steam impulse to circulate the water to and from the engine and avoiding the need for pumps and cooling fans. It was a system that was already becoming dated when it appeared on the Titan, but it worked well and contributed to the 10-20's reliability.

A two-speed gearbox provided a top gear speed of 2.8mph (4.5km/h) forward and in reverse, with the final drive through two exposed chain-and-sprocket drives. The weight of the 10-20 was 5,225lb (2,372kg), making it the lightest model in the Titan series, and the overall height was only 67in (170cm) compared with from 110in (279cm) and higher for other Titan models.

Few design changes were made during the production life of the 10-20, but the obvious change was a switch to bigger rear fenders, or mudguards, introduced in 1919.

Specifications

Manufacturer: International Harvester Co.
Location: Milwaukee, Wisconsin,
Model: Titan 10-20
Type: General purpose
Power unit: Two-cylinder horizontal engine
Power output: 20hp (14.8kw)

Transmission: Two-speed gearbox
Weight: 5,225lb (2,372kg)
Production started: 1915

Below: *Engine cooling for the Titan 10-20 was based on a water supply in the big cylindrical tank over the front wheels; circulation was based on temperature differences.*

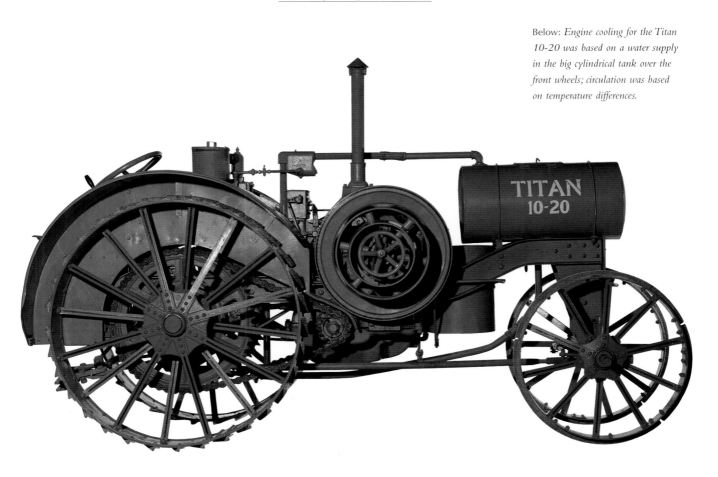

CASE
✖ 1915 Racine, Wisconsin

CASE 10-20

Tractors with a three-wheel layout enjoyed considerable popularity on American farms during World War I, and this is when the first Case three-wheeler appeared.

It was the 10-20 model announced in 1915, and an unusual feature of the design was the fact that all the wheels were different sizes. The steering wheel was the smallest, the left-hand rear wheel was normal width, but the right-hand rear wheel, the one that normally transmitted all the pulling power, was much wider.

It is not entirely clear what the benefits of the unequal wheel sizes were supposed to be, but some of the disadvantages are fairly obvious. The position of the small front wheel, which was on the right-hand side in line with the biggest rear wheel, was not visible from the driver's seat, making it impossible for the driver to see which way the wheel was pointing before engaging the clutch. This is why there was a small red arrow above the wheel to show the direction it was facing.

Above: As the driver did not have a clear view of the Case 10-20 tractor's front wheel, an arrow mounted above the wheel showed the driver which direction it faced.

The extra-wide rear wheel presumably helped reduce soil compaction when traveling over cultivated ground, but it must also have created problems when plowing because it is much wider than the furrow bottom.

Although the left-hand rear wheel does not normally transmit any engine power, it could be locked on the axle to give two-wheel drive. Presumably this would put a considerable stress on the transmission when turning corners with both wheels under full power.

Engine

Case chose a four-cylinder vertical engine for the 10-20, making it the first production Case tractor to break away from the company's long-established two-cylinder layout. Cylinder bore and stroke were 4.25in (10.8cm) and 6.0in (15.2cm), respectively, and the rated engine speed was 900rpm. The engine was mounted transversely across the main frame, and this was presumably considered to be a success on the 10-20 because the same arrangement was to appear on all the new models introduced by Case over the next 12 years. The 10-20 weighed 5,080lb (2,306kg) in total, and the transmission provided one forward gear with a travel speed of 2.0mph (3.2km/h).

The 10-20 remained in the Case range until 1920, and in that year it was tested at Nebraska and produced a maximum output of almost 23hp (17.02kw) with the engine speed raised to 980rpm.

Specifications

Manufacturer: J. I. Case Threshing Machine Co.
Location: Racine, Wisconsin
Model: 10-20
Type: General purpose
Power unit: Four-cylinder vertical engine
Power output: 23hp (17.02kw) (maximum)

Transmission: Single-speed gearbox
Weight: 5,080lb (2,306kg)
Production started: 1915

Below: *A close-up of the main driving wheel at the rear of the 10-20 shows the exposed gear wheels that provide the final drive.*

chapter 2

The Impact of the Fordson

The most important development in tractor history during the last years of World War I was the launch of the Model F Fordson. It is almost certainly the most successful tractor ever built, bringing the benefits of affordable mechanization to many thousands of smaller farms for the first time, and it also had a huge impact on the tractor industry, putting many rival manufacturers out of business and influencing tractor design and development throughout the 1920s.

Above: *Brakes were still a long way down the priority list for most tractor design teams, but Lanz engineers provided this wooden block brake on their first Bulldog tractor.*

Left: *The end of the war in 1918 brought important newcomers into the European tractor market, including Renault, with its tank-based tracklayer.*

Henry Ford's Model F was not the only important development at that time. Case also produced a family of cross-mount models based on a transversely mounted engine layout, and these are certainly among the classic designs from the early 1920s, and engineers at International Harvester produced a series of highly successful tractor designs including the 8-16 Junior, plus the 10-20 and 15-30 models.

The I.H. team even found time to experiment with steam-powered tractors, and in Britain the Garrett company produced its Suffolk Punch steam tractor. But this was the final phase of agricultural steam power, leaving the internal combustion engine as the sole power source for mechanized farming.

Most of the tractor engines from this period used spark ignition with gasoline- and paraffin-type fuels, but the first of the Lanz Bulldog tractors arrived in 1921 with its semidiesel engine. The Lanz Bulldogs remained Germany's most important tractor series during the next 30 years, and they were, in later years, a significant factor in the successful adoption of the semidiesel engine in a number of European countries.

ALLIS-CHALMERS

1915 **Milwaukee, Wisconsin**

ALLIS-CHALMERS 6-12

Although the fashion for motor plows in the United States did not last long, sales were sufficient to attract dozens of small companies, plus a few big names such as Allis-Chalmers.

Above: *The Allis-Chalmers 6-12 was a typical American motor plow, with the engine power delivered through the big driving wheels at the front.*

Specifications

Manufacturer: Allis-Chalmers Co.
Location: Milwaukee, Wisconsin,
Model: 6-12
Type: Motor plow
Power unit: Le Roi four-cylinder engine
Power output: 12hp (9kw)
Transmission: Single-speed
Weight: 2,500lb (1,135kg)
Production started: 1915

Above, left: *Allis-Chalmers ventured into the motor-plow market with the 6-12 model, but sales were disappointing, and as a result the company had to slash the price to clear its unsold machines.*

The Allis-Chalmers 6-12 General Purpose model was available from 1915 with the typical motor-plow layout placing the weight of the engine over the driving wheels at the front. Generous underside clearance allowed mid-mounted implements to be used, with the driver at the rear using extended controls to operate the engine and steering.

A four-cylinder Le Roi engine developed its 12-hp (9-kw) rated output at 1,000rpm, and in the 1920 Nebraska test session it achieved some of the best fuel economy figures of any tractor tested that year. In spite of the impressive fuel economy, demand for the 6-12 was disappointing, and price was probably a factor. Allis-Chalmers listed the 6-12 at $850 in 1919 when the Model F Fordson price was $750. The Fordson was obviously a "proper" tractor with more power and more work potential than the motor plow—and it was the Fordson that attracted the customers.

End of the Line

Allis-Chalmers stopped building the 6-12 in 1922 when only 500 had been sold. At that stage, according to one report, there were still about 200 unsold 6-12s sitting in the factory; these were eventually disposed of at discount prices in 1923. The Allis-Chalmers name was well respected and the 6-12 was probably well designed, but motor plows were simply going out of fashion as ordinary tractors took over.

INTERSTATE

c. 1916 Waterloo, Iowa

INTERSTATE PLOW MAN 15-30

The huge surge in the demand for tractor power in the United States and Canada during the 1914–18 war attracted a flood of new companies into the market, and many of them disappeared again within just a few years.

Right: *In spite of a Buda engine and a rugged design, the Interstate Plow Man and the smaller Plow Boy model made a quick exit from the tractor market.*

Above: *Tough competition and Henry Ford's price-cutting policy for his Model F Fordson made life difficult for some of the smaller manufacturers such as Interstate.*

Specifications

Manufacturer:	Interstate Tractor Co.
Location:	Waterloo, Iowa
Model:	Plow Man 15-30
Type:	General purpose
Power unit:	Buda four-cylinder engine
Power output:	30hp (22.2kw)
Transmission:	N/A
Weight:	N/A
Production started:	c. 1916

The failure rate among the new arrivals was high, and failure was the fate that faced the Interstate Tractor Co. based in Waterloo, Iowa, where it was presumably a near neighbor of the Waterloo Boy company. Many of the failures—perhaps the majority—were due to poorly designed products that failed to attract customers, but this may not have caused the downfall of the Interstate company.

Sturdy Design

Its biggest model, the Plow Man 15-30, seems to have been at least as well designed as some of its more popular rivals; it was so sturdily built that at least one of the few survivors runs almost as well now as it did when it was new more than 80 years ago, and it is powered by a Buda engine of a type that was used by plenty of other manufacturers during World War I and had built up a reputation for reliability.

Interstate was established in 1915, according to C. H. Wendel's *Encyclopedia of American Farm Tractors*, and the two principal models were the 10-20 Plow Boy and the Plow Man. In spite of the Plow Man's virtues there is some evidence that the company was facing financial difficulties from an early stage, and it appears to have ceased trading in about 1919.

CLAYTON

For a brief period during and immediately after World War I British farmers showed increased interest in crawler tractors, and it has been suggested that this was to some extent encouraged by the enormous publicity that followed the success of Britain's tracklaying tanks as they coped with difficult battlefield conditions.

Several UK-based companies moved into the crawler-tractor market to compete with Caterpillar, Cletrac, and other imports from North America. The most successful was the Clayton, which was made by the Lincoln-based Clayton and Shuttleworth company. The Clayton tractor was available from about 1916, and the first two years of production were boosted by the UK government, which placed substantial orders for the tractors for use in the wartime plowing-up campaign.

War Service

The Clayton in the photograph above, dating from 1918, has a War Department emblem stamped on the brass serial-number plate,

Above: *This is one of a batch of Clayton tracklayers that were ordered by the British government for use in the wartime plowing campaign.*

indicating that it was probably one of the original government tractors.

The Clayton was basically a simple design, with the fuel tank distinctively mounted above the engine compartment. It featured a steering wheel instead of the more usual steering levers, and the steering mechanism operated through two fully exposed cone clutches—one on each side—that controlled the drive to the tracks. When sharp turns were needed the driver could use foot-operated brakes to lock one of the tracks, forcing the tractor to swivel around in little more than its own length.

Engine

Most of the Clayton tractors were equipped with a four-cylinder Dorman engine adapted to run on paraffin, but Aster engines were also available. The output from the Dorman power unit was described as 35hp (26kw), but toward the end of the production run this increased to 40hp (29.8kw). A two-speed gearbox provided a top speed of 4mph (6.6km/h), with 3mph (4.8km/h) available in reverse.

Clayton continued to build the crawler tractor until the mid-1920s when production was temporarily suspended. It was reintroduced again in 1928, but this was also a short-lived arrangement because Clayton and Shuttleworth was taken over in 1930 by Marshall of Gainsborough.

All the tractor development activity carried out at Marshall in the early 1930s was concentrated on its single-cylinder diesel, and production of the Clayton crawler tractor ended in about 1931.

Development

It seems, with the benefit of hindsight, that Marshall should have made the decision to put some resources into improving the Clayton tractor. When the Marshall company took over, the Clayton was a well-established design with a good reputation, even if it did need updating. A combination of the single-cylinder Marshall engines plus the Clayton would have provided an impressive tractor range for Marshall to sell in the 1930s.

Specifications

Manufacturer: Clayton and Shuttleworth

Location: Lincoln, Lincolnshire, UK

Model: Clayton

Type: Tracklayer

Power unit: Dorman four-cylinder engine

Power output: 35hp (26kw)

Transmission: Two-speed gearbox

Weight: not known

Production started: c. 1916

Left: Driver comfort and safety were a low priority when the Clayton tractor was designed, with the steel trackplates and the belt pulley just a few inches from the driver's feet.

EMERSON-BRANTINGHAM 12-20

Emerson-Brantingham had ambitions to become one of the leading tractor companies when it embarked on a takeover spree in 1912. The list of companies it bought included the Gas Traction Co., which built the Big 4 range of heavyweight tractors, and the Rockford engine company, plus the company behind the Reeves steam engines and big tractors.

Specifications

Manufacturer:	Emerson-Brantingham Implement Co.
Location:	Rockford, Illinois
Model:	12-20
Type:	General purpose
Power unit:	Four-cylinder engine
Power output:	20hp (14.8kw)
Transmission:	Two-speed gearbox
Weight:	4,400lb (1,816kg)
Production started:	1916

The company's biggest success came not from the acquisitions, but from an in-house design by Emerson-Brantingham engineers. It was developed from the 12-20 Model L, a three-wheeler with a single drive wheel at the rear. The Model L joined the E-B range in 1916, but in 1917 it disappeared again, to be replaced by the 12-20 Model Q.

Wheel Layout

The obvious visible difference between the earlier Model L version and the later Model Q was the switch from three wheels to four. The design changes that did not show included a slightly bigger cylinder bore, but this did not affect the 12-20 power rating retained after the Q version was introduced. The later version of the engine had cylinders of 4.75in by 5.0in (12cm by 12.7cm) and a rated speed of 900rpm. On this example the muffler located below the engine compartment looks vulnerable to damage when traveling over rough ground.

The 12-20 Model Q remained in Emerson-Brantingham's tractor range until 1928, when the company lost its individual identity as part of the J. I. Case organization.

Above: *The four-wheel layout identifies this tractor as the later Model Q version of the Emerson Brantingham 12-20 instead of the earlier three-wheeler version.*

SAWYER-MASSEY
✲ 1917 Hamilton, Ontario, Canada

SAWYER-MASSEY 11-22

Although the first tractors built by Sawyer-Massey were aimed at the medium to heavyweight end of the market, some of their later models were smaller, reflecting the changing sales pattern in the market. The real lightweight in the range was the little 11-22 model. It was announced in about 1917, and it was still available in the early 1920s when the Sawyer-Massey company decided to pull out of the tractor market.

Below: Although smaller and lighter than previous Sawyer-Massey models, the 11-22 retained the same layout, with a rear-mounted engine and the cooling system at the front.

Right: Sawyer-Massey used a vertical four-cylinder engine to power the 11-22 tractor, its entry into the lower horsepower sector of the market.

Specifications

Manufacturer: Sawyer-Massey
Location: Hamilton, Ontario, Canada
Model: 11-22
Type: General purpose
Power unit: Four-cylinder engine
Power output: 22hp (16.3kw)
Transmission: N/A
Weight: N/A
Production started: 1917

Among the special design features claimed for the big Sawyer-Massey tractors was the position of the engine, and this was a design feature of the smallest model as well.

Engine

The engine was a vertical four-cylinder, and it was mounted well toward the rear of the chassis, where most of the weight would be over the driving wheels.

In fact Sawyer-Massey's sales publicity claimed a 75/25 percent weight distribution, with the 75 percent figure helping to increase the driving wheel traction for jobs such as plowing where drawbar pull was important.

The more intense competition and the price-cutting that hit the tractor market in the early 1920s affected smaller models such as the 11-22 rather than the heavyweights, but the tractor market generally was losing its attraction for Sawyer-Massey, and the company stopped making equipment for the agricultural market in order to concentrate on road-making and construction machinery instead.

HAPPY FARMER
1916 Minneapolis, Minnesot

HAPPY FARMER

American tractor sales boomed starting in about 1914 and many new companies began making tractors. But some of the newcomers disappeared as rapidly as they started, and the Happy Farmer company is an example.

Happy Farmer Tractor Co. of Minneapolis, Minnesota, was established in 1915 and started selling the 8-16 tractor in the following year. With no manufacturing facilities, the Happy Farmer company bought its tractors from two companies in La Crosse, Wisconsin, and one of these, La Crosse Tractor Co., had close financial and other links with the Happy Farmer company.

Engine

The 8-16 was equipped with a horizontal two-cylinder engine with 750rpm rated speed linked to a gearbox with single speeds forward and in reverse. The cooling system was a radiator mounted transversely to avoid blocking the driver's forward view, and a single steel tube provided a simple, low-cost chassis.

A New Model

By the end of 1916 the Happy Farmer company had disappeared. La Crosse took over, although the Happy Farmer name was retained until the early 1920s. A new model based on the 8-16 layout with a 24-hp (17.8-kw) engine arrived in 1920, available as the Model F with a single front wheel; the Model G was the four-wheel version. Production ended in about 1922.

Above: *The Happy Farmer Tractor Co. was to be a short-lived venture.*

Specifications

Manufacturer: Happy Farmer Tractor Co.
Location: Minneapolis, Minnesota
Model: 8-16
Type: General purpose
Power unit: Two-cylinder horizontal engine
Power output: 16hp (11.8kw)
Transmission: Single-speed gearbox
Weight: N/A
Production started: 1916

WALLIS
✕ 1916 Racine, Wisconsin

WALLIS CUB JUNIOR

In the early years of tractor development the standard design was a steel-girder frame on which the engine and other major units were mounted. This arrangement produced a number of problems, and it was the Wallis Cub tractor that provided the first practical alternative in 1913.

Above: *The Wallis Cub Junior was famous for the curved steel plate under the engine and gearbox.*

Specifications

Manufacturer:	Wallis Tractor Co.
Location:	Racine, Wisconsin
Model:	Cub Junior
Type:	General purpose
Power unit:	Wallis four-cylinder engine
Power output:	25hp (18.5kw)
Transmission:	Two-speed gearbox
Weight:	N/A
Production started:	1916

The Cub design team made a curved structure of rolled steel plate to replace the steel-girder frame, providing an immensely strong, rigid "spine" for the tractor. As well as the structural strength, another advantage of the curved structure was that it provided the underside of the engine and gearbox with protection from dirt and also made it waterproof.

Engine and Gearbox

The curved steel plate of the Wallis Cub supported the engine and gearbox, and it was an important step forward in tractor development. When the company introduced the Cub Junior tractor in 1916 it improved the design by extending the plate to support the final drive as well, bringing all the main mechanical components on one enclosed structure.

Popular Choice

The Cub Junior was a popular tractor, powered by a four-cylinder vertical engine with 25-hp (18.5-kw) rated output. Maneuverability was helped by the single front wheel topped by the distinctive Wallis bear emblem showing the driver which way the wheel is facing. Letting in the clutch with the front wheel at right angles could damage the steering mechanism.

SQUARE TURN

✜ 1917 Norfolk, Nebraska

SQUARE TURN

The Square Turn was one of the weird and wonderful designs that flooded onto the American tractor market during World War I, many of them rushed into production with inadequate testing and little or no parts or service backup. As the customers were usually first-time tractor buyers who previously farmed with horses or mules, some of them were easy victims for a slick salesman with inflated claims about power and performance.

Left: *This rear view of one of the few surviving Square Turn tractors shows the hand-operated levers that raised and lowered mid-mounted implements carried beneath the tractor's main frame.*

One result of the situation was the Nebraska test scheme, protecting tractor buyers by providing an independent source of performance data and also helping to ensure that manufacturers provided adequate after-sales support for their tractors.

The history of the Square Turn tractor started in Nebraska in 1915, four years before the test scheme became law. There is no evidence to suggest that it was better or worse than most of its competitors, but it had a checkered history as the company changed hands three times in less than three years.

Unconventional Design

It was also an unconventional tractor. The big driving wheels were at the front with a single steering wheel at the rear, and the design also included sufficient underside clearance to carry mid-mounted implements that were raised or lowered by a hand-operated lever. The engine was a four-cylinder Waukesha with 30-hp (22.2-kw) output, but this was later replaced by a four-cylinder Climax, increasing the output to 35hp (25.9kw).

Steering

The Square Turn's steering system was highly unconventional, and it was the feature that gave the tractor its name. Special clutches allowed the drive to one of the front wheels to be reversed while the other wheel continued driving forward, and as the single rear wheel could turn at a 90° steering angle the Square Turn could swivel round in its own length. Good maneuverability was obviously useful, but the ability to spin around on the spot had limited value in what was obviously a field-work tractor, and the power-operated steering system is likely to have caused expensive wear and tear on the steering clutches.

Some farmers must have been impressed by the Square Turn because it appears to have achieved some sales success, and it remained on the market much longer than some of its rivals. Production ended in about 1923 and the Square Turn Tractor Co. ceased trading in 1925.

Specifications

Manufacturer: Square Turn Tractor Co.	**Transmission:** N/A
Location: Norfolk, Nebraska	**Weight:** 7,400lb (3,360kg)
Model: 18-30	**Production started:** 1917
Type: Rowcrop	
Power unit: Waukesha four-cylinder engine	
Power output: 30hp (22.2kw)	

Below: There was sufficient clearance under the Square Turn to carry mid-mounted implements and its steering system offered good maneuverability.

WATERLOO BOY
✕ 1917 Waterloo, Iowa

WATERLOO BOY
MODEL N

The Waterloo Gasoline Engine Co. was established in 1895 as an engine manufacturer following problems encountered when selling a production version of John Froelich's 1892 tractor. The engine business was a success, and in 1912 the company moved back into tractor production to provide an additional outlet for its engines.

For their 1912 tractor the designers had chosen a four-cylinder engine, but this was replaced by a horizontal two-cylinder design when the Waterloo Boy L and R models arrived in 1914. The two-cylinder engine was probably more reliable and cost less to produce than a four-cylinder; it was also the start of America's best-known tractor engine series.

The engine for the Model R had 5.5-in (13.9-cm) bore and 7-in (17.7-cm) stroke, but 0.5in (1.3cm) was added to the bore in 1915, with a further 0.5in (1.3cm) in 1917 when the new Model N arrived. The Model N was also equipped with a two-speed gearbox instead of

Above: *The twin-cylinder horizontal engine on later versions of the Waterloo Boy tractor was adopted for John Deere tractors.*

the single speed on earlier versions, and another improvement was fitting roller bearings instead of the plain bearings used previously.

Ferguson and Deere & Co.

Both the Model R and the later Model N were successful, and they had an unexpected influence on future developments in the tractor industry. Waterloo Boy tractors were exported to Britain during the war years, where they were known as the Overtime, and the distributor for what is now Northern Ireland was a Belfast garage-owner named Harry Ferguson. Ferguson personally supervised some Overtime demonstrations, and this may have influenced the ideas that produced his Ferguson System of implement attachment and control.

Waterloo Boy tractors also attracted the interest of Deere & Co. At that time Deere was a highly successful machinery manufacturer with ambitions to move into the fast-expanding tractor market, but its attempts to develop a new John Deere tractor had met with little success. Purchasing an existing tractor company offered a shortcut into the market with an established product, and buying the Waterloo Boy company would give Deere & Co. its own engine facilities as well.

The takeover was completed in 1918 when Deere paid $2.35 million for the whole Waterloo company. The Model N tractor remained in production with minor modifications and still carrying the Waterloo Boy name until 1923.

Specifications

Manufacturer: Waterloo Gasoline Engine Co.

Location: Waterloo, Iowa

Model: N

Type: General purpose

Power unit: Two-cylinder horizontal engine

Power output: (rated) 25hp (18.5kw)

Transmission: Two-speed gearbox

Weight: 6,183lb (2,807kg)

Production started: 1917

Left: *The final drive on the Waterloo Boy tractors was exposed to dust and mud, but this did not prevent the tractors from establishing a reputation for reliability.*

Left: *The Waterloo Boy badge on the fuel tank was removed from tractors exported to Britain, where they were sold under the Overtime name.*

FORDSON
⚒ 1917   Dearborn, Michigan

FORDSON MODEL F

Although Henry Ford's first experimental tractor was completed in 1906 or 1907, the project remained a low priority for a few years because the success of his cars filled most of his time.

More experimental models emerged from time to time, proving that Ford had not abandoned his idea of developing a mass-produced tractor that small farms could afford, but it was World War I that put more urgency behind the development work.

Separate Tractor Company
In 1915 Henry Ford formed a separate company in Dearborn, Michigan, to develop the tractor project. It was called Henry Ford & Son and it employed some of Ford's most talented engineers, and by 1916 Ford gave the go-ahead for a batch of about 50 pre-production prototype tractors to be built for evaluation. Two were shipped to Britain at the request of the government to test their suitability for the wartime plowing campaign.

The tractors arrived in January 1917, and experts who observed the tests liked their

Above: The Model F was the biggest-selling tractor ever built, helped by Henry Ford's price-cutting policy, which put many rival manufacturers out of business.

performance and light weight. The fact that these were the first tractors designed specifically for mass production to reduce production costs also attracted the British government, and it asked Henry Ford to supply 6,000 tractors to Britain as quickly as possible.

Although Ford wanted to do more development work, he agreed to the British request and started preparations for production. The tractor was the Fordson Model F, and the production total reached 254 by the end of the year, peaking at more than 100,000 per year in the mid-1920s. More than 700,000 Fordsons were built in Dearborn before production was switched to Ireland in 1928.

Design Features

The most advanced design feature of the Model F was the way the housings for the engine, transmission and differential were brought together to form a fully enclosed, rigid unit that eliminated the need for a separate frame. Power

was provided by a four-cylinder engine with a water-washer air cleaner, a worm gear provided the final drive, and there were no brakes on the early versions.

The huge production volumes were helped by bulk orders from the new Communist government in Russia. With an urgent need to increase the amount of mechanization on Russian farms in order to boost food production, the Russians imported more than 26,000 Fordsons and also built an unknown number under license in Russia. Henry Ford's price-cutting policy also boosted Model F sales. The Fordson list price in America was $750 in 1918, but this was cut repeatedly to reach $395 in 1922.

Specifications

Manufacturer: Henry Ford & Son
Location: Dearborn, Michigan
Model: F
Type: General purpose
Power unit: Four-cylinder engine
Power output: 18hp (13.3kw)

Transmission: Three-speed gearbox
Weight: 2,710lb (1,230kg)
Production started: 1917

Below: *This side view shows how the Model F engine, gearbox, and back axle were joined together in one rigid dirt-proof structure.*

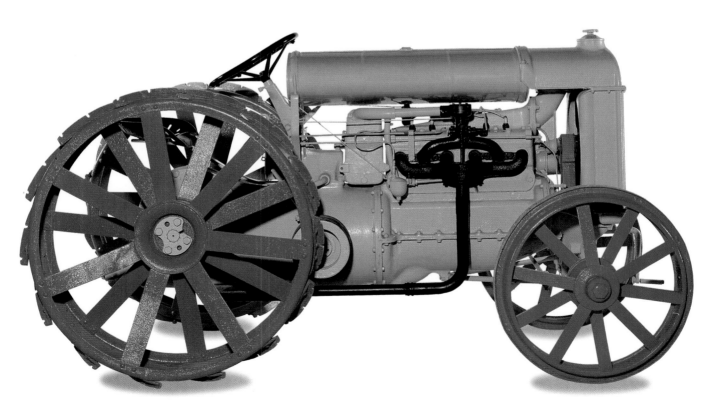

GARRETT

✹ 1917 Leiston, Suffolk, England

GARRETT SUFFOLK PUNCH

The Garrett company began making horse-drawn implements in Leiston, Suffolk, in 1782, and by the time it celebrated its first centenary it had already adopted the latest technology and was building agricultural steam engines.

Garrett became one of the biggest manufacturers of steam engines in Britain, with a successful export business, and when tractors provided the next power-farming revolution, it responded to the challenge in an unusual way.

Many of the old-established steam-engine companies tried to ignore the threat posed by the new competitors, but some adopted a more progressive approach and switched to making tractors. Garrett decided to redesign the traditional steam-traction engine and turn it into a new steam-powered tractor. It called it the Suffolk Punch after a well-known heavy horse breed—not, perhaps, the most suitable image for a tractor designed for the future—and it was developed to eliminate some of the disadvantages of the traditional traction engine.

Above: The Suffolk Punch steam tractor was Garrett's ambitious attempt to modernize the steam-traction engine, but it could not compete with low-cost tractor power.

Design Features

The driver was moved from his usual platform at the rear to a seat at the front, with a big improvement in forward visibility. The boiler was moved to the rear, putting the weight over the driving wheels to aid traction, and this also reduced the weight over the steering wheels at the front, allowing a more precise, driver-friendly Ackermann steering mechanism to replace the traditional chain-operated steering gear. There was also a suspension system over the tractor's rear axle.

As well as moving the boiler to the rear, the design team also located an auxiliary water tank over the rear axle to put additional weight on the driving wheels. This was because the tractor was designed to pull plows and other implements in the field instead of providing stationary power for threshing or for a cable-operated plowing system. It was a major step forward because steam-powered direct traction for cultivations was extremely unusual in Britain, where the soil is often heavy and easily damaged by a heavy traction engine.

Engine

The Suffolk Punch power unit was a double-crank compound engine fueled by coal and producing 40hp (29.6kw), and the first plowing tests in 1917 were encouraging. There was plenty of optimism about the steam tractor's future, but this turned to concern, according to one report, when performance and cost figures arrived for the new Fordson tractor.

Although the Suffolk Punch was comfortably ahead on plowing performance, the economic advantage heavily favored the Fordson. Garrett built eight of the Suffolk Punch tractors, and the sole survivor is in a museum in the factory where it was built.

Specifications

Manufacturer:	Richard Garrett & Sons
Location:	Leiston, Suffolk, England
Model:	Suffolk Punch
Type:	Steam tractor
Power unit:	Double-crank compound steam engine
Power output:	40hp (29.6kw)
Transmission:	N/A
Weight:	N/A
Production started:	1917

Below: *Garrett engineers redesigned the traditional traction engine, placing its driver at the front and the boiler at the rear of the Suffolk Punch.*

INTERNATIONAL HARVESTER
1917 Chicago, Illinois

INTERNATIONAL HARVESTER 8-16

International Harvester's commitment to the lightweight sector of the tractor market took a big step forward with the launch of the 8-16 or Junior model in 1917. It was built at the Chicago factory, the home of the I.H. Mogul series tractors, but I.H. had already taken the decision to phase out the Mogul and Titan names, and the 8-16 was simply sold as an International Harvester tractor.

The 8-16 arrived at a time when tractor design was progressing rapidly, and the new model had a number of advanced features. One of these was the sharply downward slope of the hood, ensuring good forward visibility from the driver's seat for increased steering accuracy. To achieve this downward slope the International Harvester engineers had to move the radiator from its traditional location at the front of the tractor to a new position behind the engine, a layout that was also adopted on the French-built Renault tractors at that time. Another 70 years

Above, top: International Harvester used what was then a more modern four-cylinder engine for the 8-16.
Above: To achieve the sloping hood line of the 8-16, the radiator was moved behind the engine.

were to pass before the sloping hood line was generally adopted by the tractor industry.

I.H. chose a four-cylinder engine for the 8-16, a step up from the twin-cylinder power unit in the earlier Mogul 8-16 and the 10-20 Titan available at the same time. The bore and stroke measurements of the new engine were 4.0in and 5.0in (10.1cm and 12.7cm), and the rated speed was 1,000rpm.

Another feature that put the 8-16 ahead of its rivals was the power takeoff shaft. This was not an I.H. invention, as the Scott tractor from Scotland was equipped with a similar device in 1904, but it was International Harvester with its 8-16 tractor that established the power takeoff as an important permanent addition to tractor versatility and efficiency.

Sales Success

Its small size and light weight, plus the addition of a power takeoff, made the 8-16 one of the most versatile and advanced tractors available, and its sales success extended to the United Kingdom where some of the tractors had been imported to help with the wartime plowing campaign. They were well suited to UK conditions and established a good reputation for performance and reliability.

Although the 8-16 design included some advanced features, the exposed chain-and-sprocket final drive with no protection from dirt and mud was becoming outdated by 1917. It was certainly out of date by 1922 when International brought the 8-16's five-year production run to an end.

Specifications

Manufacturer: International Harvester
Location: Chicago, Illinois
Model: 8-16
Type: General purpose
Power unit: Four-cylinder engine
Power output: 16hp (12kw)
Transmission: Three-speed gearbox
Weight: 3,660lb (1,662kg)
Production started: 1917

Left: *A metal seat mounted on a piece of spring steel was typical of the driver comfort provided on early 1920s tractors.*

HUBER
1917 **Marion, Ohio**

HUBER LIGHT FOUR

The Huber company of Marion, Ohio, was one of the tractor industry's early pioneers, with production starting in 1898, but its first big success did not arrive until 1917 when it introduced the Light Four model.

Below: *Huber was never among the top-selling makes in the United States, but its Light Four model remained in production for more than 10 years.*

The power unit for the Light Four was a four-cylinder engine made by Waukesha. The L-head engine was mounted transversely on the frame, midway between the front and rear axles, and the cooling system was based on a sideways-facing radiator with a belt-driven fan. The vertical cylinders had 4.0in by 5.75in (10.1cm by 14.6cm) bore and stroke, and the rated output at 1,000rpm was 25hp (18.5kw) on the belt pulley and 12hp (8.9kw) at the drawbar.

Transmission

In spite of choosing an up-to-date engine design, the Huber company relied on a more dated transmission to transfer the power to the Light Four's wheels. There were just two forward speeds with a sliding selector mechanism, and the final drive to the rear wheels was by fully exposed ring gears, a design that had already established a reputation for wear and tear. In spite of its name, the Light Four was not a real lightweight, with 5,500lb (2,497kg) recorded when the tractor was tested at Nebraska in 1920.

Light Four production continued until about 1928, helped by a reputation for sturdy design, and Huber remained in the tractor market until the early 1940s.

Specifications

Manufacturer: Huber Manufacturing Co.
Location: Marion, Ohio
Model: Light Four
Type: General purpose
Power unit: Four-cylinder engine
Power output: 25hp (18.5kw)
Transmission: Two-speed gearbox
Weight: 5,500lb (2,497kg)
Production started: 1917

SAMSON
1918   Stockton, California

SAMSON MODEL M

Although the Samson Sieve Grip tractor from Stockton, California, achieved some local success, on a national scale it was never among the big players. In spite of this it was the surprise choice when General Motors wanted a quick way into the tractor market.

Right: *General Motors, it seems, made the move into the tractor market to challenge the success of its great rival, Henry Ford, and his Model F tractor.*

Specifications

Manufacturer: General Motors

Location: Stockton, California

Model: M

Type: General purpose

Power unit: Four-cylinder engine

Power output: 19hp (14.06kw) (maximum)

Transmission: Two-speed gearbox

Weight: 3,300lb (1,497kg)

Production started: 1918

Exactly why in 1917 the General Motors car and truck company felt an urge to make tractors is not clear. One theory is that the decision was influenced by the launch of the Fordson. General Motors and Ford were well-established rivals in the car industry in 1917, and news that Henry Ford planned to add a tractor to his product list may have encouraged General Motors to do the same.

Price War

GM's offer to buy the Samson company was accepted, and the little Sieve Grip remained in production until a new model called the Samson Model M arrived in December 1918. The M was an obvious rival for the Fordson, and in the Nebraska test results for both tractors the Samson comprehensively outperformed the Fordson.

In the brief battle for sales, however, it seems that price mattered more than performance. Henry Ford, with no shareholders to consider, was quite willing to lose money as he made further cuts in his tractor prices, but General Motors presumably expected to make a profit from the Samson. By 1923 disappointing Samson sales forced General Motors out of the tractor market, and in the same year Henry Ford sold more than 100,000 Fordsons.

✂ 1918 Minneapolis, Minnesota

GRAY 18-36

The Gray Tractor Co. was established in Minneapolis in 1914, and the tractors were based on several experimental models designed and built by a fruit grower. Some of the design features introduced for orchard work survived on the later general-purpose models.

Above: *The unconventional design of the Gray 18-36 included a transversely mounted Waukesha engine and a chain-and-sprocket drive to the rear roller wheels.*

Specifications

Manufacturer: Gray Tractor Co.

Location: Minneapolis, Minnesota

Model: 18-36

Type: General purpose

Power unit: Waukesha four-cylinder engine

Power output: 36hp (26.6kw)

Transmission: Two-speed gearbox

Weight: 6,500lb (2,951kg)

Production started: 1918

One of the features of the Gray tractors was the low height, which may have been a result of their orchard origins. They were also designed with two wide rear wheels that were close together, working almost like a split roller, and this was known as the Gray Drum-Drive. The idea of fitting a roof to cover the engine and the rear wheels—but not the driver, who was fully exposed to the weather—was also inherited from the farm-built tractors.

Design Features

The most successful model in the Gray range was the 18-36. Production started in 1918 using a Waukesha four-cylinder engine, with the vertical cylinders arranged in two pairs. The engine was mounted transversely across the frame, with an enclosed chain-and-sprocket drive to the rear wheels.

According to the manufacturers, the advantage of the Drum-Drive feature was more efficient traction with less wheel slip, and this was an important sales point for the tractors. Unfortunately the traction theory was not confirmed when the Gray 18-36 was tested at Nebraska, and the traction efficiency indicated by the official wheelslip figures recorded in the drawbar pull tests was worse than average.

Above, left: *The Drum-Drive roller-type rear wheels and the roof over the engine and rear wheels were distinctive features of the Gray Tractor.*

AVERY

1919 Peoria, Illinois

AVERY 12-20

Most tractors in the Avery range followed a distinctive styling theme that started with the large circular cooling tower at the front and included the mid-mounted engine and the cab. The model that introduced the "Avery look" was the 20-35 built in 1912, and the 12-20 was one of the models that carried the same styling into the early 1920s.

Right: *The cylindrical cooling tower mounted on the front of the chassis was a distinctive design feature of Avery tractors such as the 12-20.*

Above: *Avery offered the 12-20 tractor from about 1919 until the company was overtaken by financial difficulties and stopped building tractors in 1924.*

Specifications

Manufacturer: Avery Co.

Location: Peoria, Illinois

Model: 12-20

Type: General purpose

Power unit: Four-cylinder horizontal engine

Power output: 24hp (18kw) (maximum)

Transmission: Two-speed gearbox

Weight: 5,500lb (2,497kg)

Production started: c. 1919

Avery introduced a number of new models during the four years from 1916, and these included the 12-20 available from about 1919. As well as the easily recognizable styling, the 12-20 also inherited the company's heavyweight approach to tractor design at a time when smaller, . lighter models were gaining a significantly bigger share of the market. The 1920 version of the 12-20 weighed 5,500lb (2,497kg), much heavier than most of its rivals in the 20-hp (14.-8kw) sector of the market.

Engine

The horizontal engine layout was another traditional Avery feature that was retained on the 12-20. The four cylinders were opposed to provide smoother running, and the bore and stroke measurements were 4.4in x 6.0in (11.2cm x 15.2cm).

Rated engine speed was 800rpm, but the Nebraska test figure at this speed was 24.26hp (18kw), comfortably ahead of the rated power, and the maximum drawbar pull figure was also well ahead of the 12hp (8.9kw) rated figure, with 17.58hp (13.1kw) recorded in bottom gear.

The early 1920s brought new, more up-to-date designs to the Avery range, but the company was already in financial difficulties, and tractor production ended in 1924.

MASSEY-HARRIS

c. 1919 Weston, Ontario, Canada

MASSEY-HARRIS NO. 3

When Massey-Harris signed an agreement to build the Parrett tractor at its factory near Toronto, it was the company's second attempt to move into the lucrative and fast-expanding agricultural tractor market.

An earlier agreement to distribute the Big Bull tractor in Canada ended when the American manufacturer failed to make delivery of the tractors because of production problems. For their next attempt Massey-Harris decided to control production as well as sales, and the tractor it chose was designed by the Parrett brothers in Chicago.

The agreement was signed in 1918, with production starting the following year, and the tractors carried the Massey-Harris name and were sold in Canada through the extensive Massey-Harris dealer network.

Big Wheels

A distinctive feature of the Parrett was the 4-ft (1.2-m) diameter front wheels, and the Parrett brothers had plenty of reasons why big wheels were better than small ones, even if they did look frail. Large-circumference wheels rode more easily over obstructions, and they also spread the weight of the tractor over a bigger area to reduce soil compaction, the Parretts claimed.

Wheel bearings also lasted longer, they said. This is partly because a big wheel rotates more slowly than a small one when the tractor is moving, and the bearings are also further from

Above, top: *The spacious platform had all of the controls within easy reach of the operator. The steering wheel was connected by a chain-and-sprocket device to the front end.*

Above: *Large-diameter front wheels inherited from the original Parrett design were an important selling feature for the new Massey-Harris tractor.*

the ground and away from the damaging effects of dust and mud.

Sales of Massey-Harris–built Parrett tractors made an encouraging start, but it is not clear if Canadian farmers were impressed by the sales pitch for the big wheels or were simply reassured by the familiarity of the Massey-Harris brand name.

Versions

Massey-Harris offered three versions of the Parrett tractor. Numbers 1 and 2 were basically similar with a 12-25 power rating—(12hp) 8.9kw at the drawbar and 25hp (18.6kw) on the belt pulley—and the radiator on both was sideways facing. Both featured a two-speed gearbox allowing speeds of 2.4mph and 4.0mph (3.8km/h and 6.4km/h), but this was considered too fast and the maximum speeds were reduced to 1.75mph and 2.4mph (2.8km/h and 3.8km/h) when the third model was introduced.

Other changes on Massey-Harris No. 3 included increasing the cylinder bore and stroke to 4.5in and 6.5in (11.4cm and 16.5cm), respectively, to boost the power rating to 15-28, and the radiator was turned through 90° to the more conventional forward-facing position.

Meanwhile shrinking demand for tractors together with intense competition plus Henry Ford's price-cutting policy were causing problems in the industry. The Parrett company stopped building tractors in about 1922 and Massey-Harris ended its tractor production in the following year.

Specifications

Manufacturer: Massey-Harris	**Transmission:** Two-speed gearbox
Location: Weston, Ontario, Canada	**Weight:** N/A
Model: No. 3	**Production started:** c. 1919
Type: General purpose	
Power unit: Four-cylinder engine	
Power output: 28hp (20.72kw)	

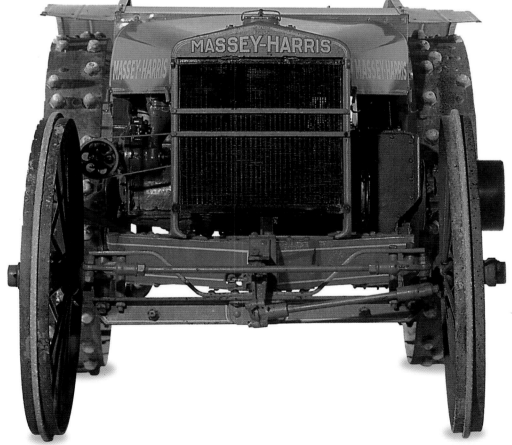

Left: *One of the distinguishing features of the No. 3 tractor was the forward-facing radiator, unlike the sideway-facing position on the Massey-Harris 1 and 2 models.*

TWIN CITY
⚒ **1919 Minneapolis, Minnesota**

TWIN CITY 16-30

Twin City was the principal tractor brand name of Minneapolis Steel and Machinery Co. (MSM), based in Minnesota. Production started in about 1910, and the Twin City tractors were soon well established in the heavyweight sector of the market.

Above: *An engine with twin overhead camshafts and four valves per cylinder helped to give the 16-30 tractor its sports car image.*

Specifications

Manufacturer: Minneapolis Steel and Machinery Co.

Location: Minneapolis, Minnesota

Model: 16-30

Type: General purpose

Power unit: Four-cylinder engine with 16 valves

Power output: 30hp (22.2kw)

Transmission: N/A

Weight: N/A

Production started: 1919

Although the emphasis on big tractors continued, the company was aware of the increasing popularity of smaller, lighter models, and these were added to the Twin City range. They included the distinctively styled 16-30 tractor announced in 1919. It was presumably the marketing team at MSM who came up with the idea of giving the 16-30 an upmarket image, using technical features from the automobile industry. The engine was a four-cylinder unit with an upmarket specification including twin overhead camshafts and four valves per cylinder.

Even the styling was reminiscent of a sports car, as the advertising emphasized, with a low overall height and a fully enclosed engine compartment with plenty of cooling louvers.

Design Features

The design included a fully enclosed transmission and final drive to reduce the risk of damage caused by dust and water, the cooling system was based on a honeycomb radiator of the type then used in cars, but with increased capacity, and all the gears and transmission shafts were made of forged steel.

Unfortunately for the 16-30, farm tractors were still expected to have a strictly working image, and with the agricultural industry facing increasing financial problems there were not enough farmers who were willing to pay a premium price for the special features of the 16-30. Sales of the tractor were disappointing, and production ended in 1920.

Above, left: *American farmers in the early 1920s were apparently unwilling to pay a premium price for a tractor with upmarket features such as those seen on the 16-30.*

CASE CROSSMOUNT
1919 Racine, Wisconsin

CASE CROSSMOUNT 22-40

Experimenting with different ideas was an important feature of the American tractor industry during the period from about 1915 until the early 1920s, and a number of companies decided to mount the engines transversely across the frame in some of their tractor models.

Right: *Distinctive styling and a transversely mounted engine helped to establish the Case cross-mount tractor series among the classics of the early 1920s.*

Specifications

Manufacturer: J. I. Case Threshing Machine Co.	
Location: Racine, Wisconsin	
Model: 22-40	
Type: General purpose	
Power unit: Four-cylinder engine	
Power output: 40hp (29.6kw)	
Transmission: Two-speed gearbox	
Weight: 9,940lb (4,512kg)	
Production started: 1919	

It was an idea that had been tried previously by several tractor manufacturers, but the company that promoted the transverse engine design most effectively was the J. I. Case Threshing Machine Co. Most of the new models they introduced during the 10 years from 1916 followed the transverse engine layout, forming a distinctive and successful series known as the Case Crossmount tractors.

Reliability

Although the advantages of mounting the engine across the frame are not obvious, the Case Crossmount models were popular, and they established a reputation for long-term reliability. An unusual and notable feature of some of the smaller Crossmount tractors was the cast-iron main frame, but this was replaced by a more traditional steel-girder frame for the 22-40 model introduced in 1919, when the success of the Crossmount models was helping Case to survive in an increasingly competitive tractor market.

The Crossmount 22-40 was equipped with a four-cylinder Case gasoline/paraffin engine, with the cylinders cast in pairs. The bore and stroke measurements were 5.5in and 6.75in (13.9cm and 17.1cm), respectively, the rated engine speed was 850rpm and the power was delivered through a two-speed gearbox.

AVERY
✖ **1919 Peoria, Illinois**

AVERY MODEL C

Six-cylinder engines were a rarity in the tractor market before the 1930s—and even 30 years after that they were still uncommon, and on modern tractors they are unusual on tractors producing less than 100hp (74kw). The Avery company decided to use a six to power its new Model C tractor in 1919, and it has the distinction of being the first six-cylinder tractor tested at Nebraska.

Specifications

Manufacturer: Avery Co.	
Location: Peoria, Illinois	
Model: C	
Type: General purpose	
Power unit: Six-cylinder engine	
Power output: 14hp (10.4kw)	
Transmission: Three-speed gearbox	
Weight: 3,164lb (1,436kg)	
Production started: 1919	

The engine was an Avery design with vertical cylinders of 3.0-in (7.6-cm) bore and 4.0-in (10.1-cm) stroke, and the rated operating speed was 1,250rpm at a time when the majority of tractor engines were rated at less than 1,000rpm.

It was probably a very good design, but it is surprising that Avery should choose what was presumably a relatively expensive engine to power a small tractor with an output of just 14hp (10.4kw) at the belt pulley and a modest 8.6hp (6.4kw) at the drawbar.

Transmission

A small tractor and a complicated and expensive engine make an odd mixture, particularly at a time when price competition was becoming increasingly intense, and there were some surprises in the transmission as well. The gearbox with three forward speeds was enclosed, but the final drive was by fully exposed ring gears with no protection from damage by dirt and stones. Avery was heading for financial problems in the mid-1920s when the Model C disappeared from the product line.

Above: Avery made a major break with tradition when it introduced the new Model C rowcrop tractor powered by a six-cylinder engine.

FIAT
✖ 1919 Turin, Italy

FIAT 702

When World War I ended in 1918 tractors were urgently needed to increase Europe's food production, and in Europe, this brought a big batch of new companies into the industry.

Above: *Fiat was one of the big European car and truck companies that decided to move into tractor production after the end of the war.*

Right: *Fiat 702 drivers had the luxury of a transverse leaf-spring suspension over the front axle, a feature that was probably borrowed from Fiat cars and trucks.*

Specifications

Manufacturer: Fiat	
Location: Turin, Italy	
Model: 702	
Type: General purpose	
Power unit: Four-cylinder engine	
Power output: 25hp (18.5kw)	
Transmission: Three-speed gearbox	
Weight: 5,720lb (2,600kg)	
Production started: 1919	

Fiat was one of the first big companies to begin tractor production in Europe. The Fiat car- and truck-making history stretches back to 1899, but tractor production did not start until 20 years later when the 702 model arrived. It was available as a standard agricultural version, and there was also an industrial version equipped with solid rubber tires.

Design Features
Fiat chose a four-cylinder gasoline/paraffin engine for the 702. It developed about 25hp (18.5kw) and the power was delivered through a three-speed gearbox that also provided three driving speeds for the belt pulley. The pulley was mounted at the rear, close to the driver's seat, which was offset to allow better forward visibility. An unusual feature was the transverse leaf spring over the front axle to give a smoother ride.

This was probably a result of Fiat's experience with designing other vehicles—suspension systems to improve driver comfort were standard equipment on cars and commercial vehicles almost 100 years before they were widely available on farm tractors.

The 702 was replaced in about 1921 by the 703 model with an improved transmission, and 702 owners were offered an update kit to bring their old tractors up to the latest specification.

RENAULT

⚒ **1919 Billancourt, France**

RENAULT GP

The list of European companies moving into the tractor market for the first time in the postwar period includes Citroën, Peugeot, and Renault, all of the big three companies in the French motor industry. It was Renault that had the biggest advantage initially because it was able to base the design of its first tractor on a small tank it had developed during World War I for the French army.

Below: Renault based the design of the GP crawler tractor on a light tank it had built for the French army during the war.

The new crawler tractor arrived in 1919 and was known as the GP. The power unit was a four-cylinder gasoline engine developing about 30hp (22.3kw); the transmission had a cone clutch linked to a three-speed gearbox.

A distinctive design feature inherited from the tank was the sloping hood line that helped to give improved forward visibility from the driver's seat. This was achieved by positioning the radiator between the engine and the driver, with the fuel tank mounted above the radiator. Another feature inherited from the wartime Renault tank was the tiller steering to change the direction of the tractor by controlling the drive to the tracks. When an improved version of the GP, known as the H1, was introduced in about 1920, the tiller steering was retained, but the addition of a pair of bicycle-style handlebars made the tiller easier to operate.

Indications for Future

The GP tracklayer was aimed at the top sector of the French market and was not a big-selling tractor, but it achieved sufficient success to encourage Renault to develop new crawler and wheeled models based on the same design.

Specifications

Manufacturer: Renault

Location: Billancourt, France

Model: GP

Type: Tracklayer

Power unit: Four-cylinder engine

Power output: 30hp (22.3kw)

Transmission: Three-speed gearbox

Weight: N/A

Production started: 1919

AUSTIN
⚒ 1919 Birmingham, England

AUSTIN

Austin was one of Britain's leading car manufacturers when it started building tractors in 1919, joining other leading European car and truck manufacturers (including Benz, Citroën, and Renault) also diversifying into the tractor market.

Above: Austin designed its new tractor to share the 26-hp (19.3-kw) engine it had developed to power a new Austin car.

Right: Demand for the Austin tractor was much stronger in France than in Britain, and production was eventually transferred from the British factory to France.

Specifications

Manufacturer: Austin Motor Co.
Location: Birmingham, England
Model: N/A
Type: General purpose
Power unit: Four-cylinder engine
Power output: 23.7hp (17.5kw) (paraffin)
Transmission: Two-speed gearbox
Weight: 3,129lb (1,422kg)
Production started: 1919

One of the attractions was the opportunity to use basically the same engine to power both the tractor and a new Austin car, improving the profitability by spreading the costs over a bigger production volume. The four-cylinder engine was available in a gasoline-only version for both the car and the tractor, and there was also a gasoline-paraffin version for the tractor only. Maximum power output was 26hp (19.3kw) for the gasoline version and 23.7hp (17.5kw) on paraffin.

Export Sales
The tractor, built at the Austin car plant in Birmingham, was more successful in France than in its home market. During its first appearance in France at the 1919 international trials it achieved both excellent results and plenty of publicity. This success encouraged the company to build a tractor factory in France, using engines supplied from Birmingham, and production started in 1920.

When Birmingham production ended in about 1925, tractors for the UK market were imported from France, and at this stage the French version was improved by adding a three-speed gearbox instead of the two-speed, which had been provided on the original British-built tractor. An attempt to relaunch the French-built Austin in Britain in 1930 achieved little success, and the French factory closed in about 1932.

GLASGOW

🔧 **1919 Cardonald, Glasgow, Scotland**

GLASGOW

Tractor production in Scotland has never achieved much success. The Scott tractor failed because it was years ahead of its time, the Leyland tractor plant at Bathgate produced excellent tractors but was starved of capital for new product development, and the Glasgow tractor failed partly because it could not match the low price of the Fordson.

The plans for the Glasgow project were certainly ambitious. The factory was on a 25-acre (10-hectare) site at Cardonald, the project was financed by a consortium of companies, and an agreement was signed with a London-based company offering distribution facilities throughout the UK and the colonies. A press announcement claimed production was scheduled to reach 5,000 tractors a year.

On the early version some of the styling, including the oval-shaped fuel tank, the radiator side panels, and the header tank, may have been influenced by the Fordson Model F, although it was altered after just a few months. The construction of the tractor, using a series of castings to link and enclose the engine and transmission, also appears to have been Fordson-inspired.

Above: In spite of its unconventional layout the Glasgow tractor attracted enthusiastic praise for the performance of its three-wheel drive system.

Original Features

In spite of the similarities, the Glasgow had plenty of its own original features, and the most unusual of these was providing three-wheel drive through equal-diameter front and rear wheels. Also, instead of using a differential to compensate for different wheel speeds while turning a corner, the Glasgow design team decided to use a series of ratchets to do the same job.

Eliminating the differential helped to increase traction on steep or slippery surfaces, the makers claimed, and testimonials quoted by the company suggest that customers were impressed by the Glasgow's pulling power in difficult conditions.

A four-cylinder Waukesha engine developed 27-hp (20-kw) rated output and powered a two-speed gearbox with a cone clutch, and the transmission—including the final drive—was fully enclosed.

Demand for the Glasgow was disappointing, and the tractor's production figures never even approached the promised 5,000 per year, leaving the project facing serious financial problems. Price was one of the problems, and a reduction from £450 to £375 did little to tempt customers away from the imported Fordson, which at one time was priced at £120, or less than one-third of the reduced Glasgow price.

End of Production

Production of the Glasgow tractor ended in about 1923 and the company stopped trading in 1924. A later attempt to revive the company under the Clyde Tractors name, with additional finance and new management, made little progress and was soon abandoned.

Specifications

Manufacturer: Wallace (Glasgow) Ltd.	**Transmission:** Two-speed gearbox
Location: Cardonald, Glasgow, Scotland	**Weight:** 4,023lb (1,829kg)
Model: Glasgow	**Production started:** 1919
Type: General purpose	
Power unit: Four-cylinder engine	
Power output: 27hp (20kw)	

Below: *The similarities between the fuel tank and radiator side-panel design of the Glasgow and the Fordson may have been coincidence.*

IH STEAM TRACTORS
⚒ **1920 Chicago, Illinois**

I.H. STEAM TRACTOR

Sales of agricultural steam engines were falling dramatically in the early 1920s, and some of the big companies from the age of steam faced serious financial problems as the farming industry switched increasingly to tractor power.

New developments in steam technology had been available since the early 1900s, but these were generally ignored by the manufacturers of portable and traction engines, and it was not until the early 1920s that serious attempts were made to develop a new generation of steam engines for agriculture.

Experimental Tractors
One of the companies working with the latest steam technology was International Harvester.

In 1920 I.H. had only recently lost its number-one place in the American tractor market to Henry Ford and his Model F tractor, and the steam tractor project may have been part of the search for new products that would restore I.H. to the top of the sales charts.

Between 1920 and about 1923 I.H. built at least two experimental steam tractors. Heat for raising steam was produced by a burner using a liquid fuel such as paraffin, and this offered a number of important advantages. The fuel

Above: *This archive photograph from the early 1920s shows one of the experimental steam tractors built by International Harvester engineers.*

occupied much less space than coal or firewood, feeding the firebox with a shovel was eliminated, there was no ash and clinker to remove, and—the biggest potential benefit of them all—it was easy to increase or reduce the flame in order to control steam production.

Design Features

Another feature was the tubular boiler. With a much smaller volume than the old-fashioned traction-engine boiler, there was a significant weight reduction, and the reduced water volume allowed steam pressure to be raised in just a few minutes after a cold start. The tubular boiler was also safer, as the relatively small volume of high-pressure steam would cause less damage if the boiler exploded. Another essential feature was the radiator-type condenser to recirculate the water and reduce the volume used.

Surviving photographs from the I.H. archives show that the experimental steam tractors were about the same size as an ordinary 25-hp to 30-hp (18.6-kw to 22.3-kw) tractor, and the power output has been estimated at about 20hp (14.9kw). The project was abandoned in about 1922, and this may have been to release resources for the new Farmall tractor.

Sadly, all the experimental steam tractors were scrapped, and very little technical data about the tractors or their performance has survived.

Specifications

Manufacturer: International Harvester Co.
Location: Chicago, Illinois
Model: N/A
Type: Experimental
Power unit: Twin-cylinder steam engine
Power output: N/A

Transmission: N/A
Weight: N/A
Production started: 1920

Below: Another of the original photographs, all that survive from an attempt to use new technology to update the agricultural steam engine.

CLETRAC

1920 Cleveland, Ohio

CLETRAC MODEL F

Cletrac was the brand name chosen for tractors made by the Cleveland Tractor Co. of Cleveland, Ohio. The company was established by Rollin White, a prominent businessman and a member of the White steam-car family, and he had been closely involved with the development of a new steering mechanism for crawler tractors.

The new mechanism was known as the controlled differential steering system, and the obvious advantage was that it was operated by a steering wheel instead of the levers used on most tracklayers, and using a steering wheel is likely to be more familiar to the majority of drivers than a pair of levers.

The Cletrac system used the action of the steering wheel to slow down the drive to one of the tracks, and this automatically made the other track turn faster. It was the system that was used on all Cletrac tracklayers, and it was also adopted by other manufacturers for various tracked vehicles, including tanks.

Above: *This original publicity photograph shows the Model F tractor working like a motor plow, with a set of extended controls.*

Production of the Model F started in 1920. It was a lightweight crawler tractor and it was available as a standard model, a narrow version for vineyard, nursery, and fruit applications, or a high-clearance model for rowcrop work. Additional versatility was available on the high-clearance Model F, which could be used as a conventional tractor or, with the steering wheel and other controls extended, as a motor plow.

Engine

A four-cylinder, side-valve engine was developed for the Model F and built by the Cleveland company. At that time Rollin White had started a new company to build the Rollin car, and the car was designed to share the same engine as the Model F tractor.

The operating speed of the engine was 1,600rpm, the rated output of the paraffin-fueled tractor version was 16hp (12kw) on the belt pulley, and the car version was designed to run on gasoline.

Track Design

An unusual feature of the Model F was the track design. The drive on each side was through a sprocket positioned near the rear of the track and high enough to give the track a triangular outline.

Under the main drive track on each side there was a second track consisting of steel rollers, and these had no driving function. They did, however, provide a low-friction surface for the main tracks to run on. The main problem with the roller tracks was that dirt and small stones caused a high wear rate, a definite negative when it came to attributes, and the idea did not appear on other Cletrac models.

Below: This side view of the Cletrac Model F shows the steering wheel and the dual track design that was supposed to reduce friction.

Specifications

Manufacturer: Cleveland Tractor Co.

Location: Cleveland, Ohio

Model: F

Type: Tracklayer

Power unit: Four-cylinder side-valve engine

Power output: 16hp (12kw)

Transmission: Single-speed gearbox

Weight: 1,920lb (872kg)

Production started: 1920

MINNEAPOLIS

1920 Hopkins, Minnesota

MINNEAPOLIS 22-44

The Minneapolis Threshing Machine Co. or MTM of Hopkins, Minnesota, was one of the companies that joined forces to form Minneapolis-Moline, but that was in 1929. In 1920, it was still making its own tractors with styling and features that were becoming outdated.

Below: Many of the design features on the Minneapolis 22-44 tractor, including the chain-operated steering mechanism, were already outdated when production started in 1920.

It was in 1920 that the Minneapolis 22-44 model arrived. At a time when tractor design was making rapid progress, the 22-44 seems to have missed out on many of the advances and its styling was similar to tractors built 10 or 12 years earlier. The chain-operated steering, dating back to steam-traction engine technology, was already old fashioned and was not easy to operate on a big tractor, and at almost six tons the 22-44 was firmly in the heavyweight sector.

Engine
The Minneapolis power unit was a four-cylinder engine with 6.0-in (15.2-cm) bore, 7.0-in (17.7-cm) stroke, and 700rpm rated speed. The maximum load test in Nebraska produced 46hp (34.3kw) on the belt, just ahead of the manufacturer's figure, but the MTM rating of 22hp (16.4kw) for drawbar pull was easily exceeded by the 33hp (24.6kw) shown in the test.

An unusual feature was two separate clutches, one controlling the power to the wheels and the other operating the belt pulley. This presumably gave the same sort of flexibility as the independent drive to the power takeoff on a modern tractor, but it is probably less useful on a belt pulley, which can only be operated when the tractor is stationary.

Specifications

Manufacturer: Minneapolis Threshing Machine Co.

Location: Hopkins, Minnesota

Model: 22-44

Type: General purpose

Power unit: Four-cylinder horizontal engine

Power output: 44hp (32.5kw)

Transmission: N/A

Weight: 12,410lb (5,634kg)

Production started: 1920

PETER BROTHERHOOD
✖ 1920   Peterborough, Cambridgeshire, England

PETERBRO'

Peterbro' is an abbreviation of Peter Brotherhood Ltd., the Peterborough-based engineering company that designed this high-specification tractor and produced it in small numbers throughout the 1920s, with most of the production being exported to Australia and other empire markets.

Right: A Ricardo-designed engine on the Peterbro' tractor featured tiny bleed holes in the cylinder walls to prevent unburned paraffin from diluting the sump oil.

Specifications

Manufacturer: Peter Brotherhood

Location: Peterborough, Cambridgeshire, England

Model: Peterbro'

Type: General purpose

Power unit: Four-cylinder engine

Power output: 31hp (23kw) (maximum)

Transmission: Three-speed gearbox

Weight: N/A

Production started: 1920

Peter Brotherhood already had a long history in railroad and marine engineering when the decision was taken to diversify into the tractor business. Production started in 1920, and the company announced the Peterbro' at that year's Royal Show. It also entered the new tractor in the 1920 national tractor trials near Lincoln, where it took second place in the class for 25 to 30hp (18.5 to 22.2 kw).

Design Features
By British standards the Peterbro' was a big tractor, powered by a four-cylinder engine developing up to 31hp (23kw). The engine was designed by Ricardo and, like most tractor engines at that time, it started on gasoline and

ran on paraffin. An unusual, and presumably expensive, feature was a series of tiny bleed holes drilled through the cylinder walls to remove some of the unburned paraffin that seeps past the piston rings and would otherwise dilute the sump oil. Other manufacturers accepted that sump oil dilution was inevitable and recommended frequent oil changes

Although British sales were disappointing, the Peterbro' proved more popular in New Zealand and Australia. A half-track version was introduced in 1928, but disaster struck two years later when an engine failure forced the Peterbro' entry out of the prestigious and highly publicized 1930 World Tractor Trials, and production ended soon after.

LANZ
1921 **Mannheim, Germany**

LANZ HL BULLDOG

When the first of the Lanz Bulldog tractors arrived in 1921 it was the start of what was to become one of the longest and most influential tractor series Europe has produced.

Specifications

Manufacturer: Heinrich Lanz
Location: Mannheim, Germany
Model: HL Bulldog
Type: Designed for belt work
Power unit: Single-cylinder hot bulb engine
Power output: 12hp (9kw)
Transmission: Single-speed gearbox
Weight: N/A
Production started: 1921

Above: *The classic designs of tractor history come in all shapes and sizes, including the little HL Bulldog tractor from Lanz, the first of a long line of Bulldog tractors.*

The Heinrich Lanz company was based in Mannheim, where it started making farm machinery during the 1860s. Production started with a range of stationary equipment, such as straw choppers and small threshing machines, and these were followed later by steam engines. But it was the introduction of the Bulldog tractors that had the biggest impact on the company's future development.

Design Features

The engineer who designed the first of the Bulldog tractors was Dr. Fritz Huber, who had joined the company in 1916. The HL Bulldog was his first production tractor, based on a single-cylinder semidiesel engine mounted on a self-propelled chassis. The engine output was 12hp (9kw), and the lack of ground clearance and the relatively small-diameter wheels show that the Bulldog was designed to power stationary equipment rather than do field work itself. Solid rubber tires were offered as an option, and the standard specification included foot-operated brakes with wooden blocks acting on both rear wheel rims.

Sales of the HL Bulldog during the eight-year production run totaled just over 6,000, but by 1956 the production total for Bulldogs of all models had reached more than 200,000, and large numbers of Bulldog lookalikes had been built in other European countries under various licensing agreements.

CASE

1922 **Racine, Wisconsin**

CASE 12-20

Case Crossmount series tractors with their transverse engine layout covered a wide range of power outputs, including the little 12-20 model, which was available starting in 1922. It was a classic Crossmount tractor, complete with a sturdy one-piece cast-iron frame; however, the pressed steel front and rear wheels were a distinctive 12-20 feature.

Right: *Case's 12-20 shared most of the Crossmount design features, but the pressed-steel front and rear wheels appeared only on the 12-20.*

Above: *This rear view of the little 12-20 shows the offset driving position—it also suggests that a repair job is overdue to deal with the damaged exhaust stack.*

Specifications

Manufacturer: J. I. Case Threshing Machine Co.
Location: Racine, Wisconsin
Model: 12-20
Type: General purpose
Power unit: Four-cylinder engine mounted tranversely
Power output: 22.5hp (16.7kw) (maximum)
Transmission: Two-speed gearbox
Weight: 4,450lb (2,020kg)
Production started: 1922

Case introduced the 12-20 as a replacement for the 10-20 three-wheeler model, and it remained in the range until about 1929. By that time Case had changed its system of model identifications, using letters of the alphabet instead of the rated power figures, and when the 12-20 ended its production life it was known as the Model A.

Engine Features

The cross-mounted engine was designed and built by Case and was a four-cylinder vertical design with overhead valves. Cylinder bore was 4.1in (10.4cm) with 5.0-in (12.7-cm) stroke. The rated speed was 1,050rpm, and a special feature of the engine design was the use of replaceable cylinder sleeves to simplify maintenance. The maximum engine power when the 12-20 was tested in Nebraska was 22.5hp (16.7kw), but this reduced to 20.17hp (15kw) when the engine was tested at its rated speed.

The 12-20 was one of the last of the distinctively styled Case Crossmount tractors, and when the replacement models arrived they were designed with the engine in the normal lengthwise position.

MINNEAPOLIS

1921 **Hopkins, Minnesota**

MINNEAPOLIS 17-30 TYPE A

The Minneapolis 17-30 tractor was built by the Minneapolis Threshing Machine Co., the company which, confusingly, merged with the Minneapolis Steel and Machinery Co. to form the Minneapolis-Moline tractor company.

Above: *Although this is the Type A version of the 17-30, only an expert would be able to recognize the small features that distinguish it from the later Type B.*

Specifications

Manufacturer: Minneapolis Threshing Machine Co.
Location: Hopkins, Minnesota
Model: 17-30 Type A
Type: General purpose
Power unit: Four-cylinder engine
Power output: 31.9hp (23.6kw)
Transmission: Two-speed gearbox
Weight: 6,000lb (2,724kg)
Production started: 1921

Above, left: *The Minneapolis Threshing Machine Co. was one of the smaller American-based tractor companies, one that was eventually to disappear in a merger.*

There is also plenty of confusion surrounding the 17-30 tractor. It was available in basically similar A and B versions, and although it was introduced as a Minneapolis Threshing Machine or MTM product it remained in the Minneapolis Moline or M-M range for several years after the merger.

Versions

Why the manufacturers went to the expense of producing two very similar versions of the same tractor is not clear. The A version, which first became available in early 1922, was equipped with a cross-mounted four-cylinder engine with 4.75-in (12-cm) bore and 7-in (17.7-cm) stroke, but when the 17-30 B arrived in 1926 the bore was increased by just 0.13in (3mm) and the rated speed was increased by 10 percent to 825rpm. Although this was not enough to alter the power rating quoted by the manufacturer, maximum power figures recorded for both tractors showed that the B had an advantage of less than 3hp (2.2kw) in both drawbar pull and flywheel figures.

Other differences included an extra 10in (25.4cm) added to the B version wheelbase. There was also a 700-lb (317-kg) difference in the weight of the two versions—the B type was heavier—and the B version list price was $100, or about 10 percent more expensive, than the A.

RENAULT

1922 Billancourt, France

RENAULT H0

Renault's move into the tractor market with the tank-based GP tracklayer and the improved H1 model did not produce big sales volumes, but the success was sufficient to justify further development work. The next addition to the range was the H0 wheeled tractor in 1922.

Right: *Renault moved into the wheeled-tractor market with the H0 model—still an obvious descendant from the wartime tank, but with a smaller engine.*

Specifications

Manufacturer: Renault
Location: Billancourt, France
Model: H0
Type: General purpose
Power unit: 194cubic-inch (3.2-liter) gasoline engine
Power output: 20hp (14.8kw)
Transmission: Three-speed gearbox
Weight: 4,708lb (2,140kg)
Production started: 1922

The H0 was based on the H1 and shared the same front-end design with the radiator positioned at an angle at the rear of the engine. They were both built on a massive steel girder frame, but the new wheeled tractor was smaller than the tracklayer and, at 4,708lb (2,140kg), it was much lighter.

Engine

The H0 specification also included a more compact Renault-built four-cylinder gasoline engine developing 20hp (14.8kw) output at 1600rpm, instead of the 30hp (22.3kw) produced by the previous models.

Renault had identified the need for a less powerful model, as the original 30-hp engine was probably too big to attract volume sales in a country with mainly small farms.

Like the tracked models, the H0 was designed with a reversible front-mounted belt pulley at right angles to the tractor. This would have made it easy to align the belt correctly, but maneuvering the tractor to tension the belt correctly must have been a much more complicated operation as a result.

Between them the distinctively styled GP, H1, and H0 family of tractors established Renault as the leading French tractor manufacturer, and they continued to demonstrate the styling influence of the Renault light tank until a completely new model from the company arrived in the late 1920s.

chapter 3

The First Diesel Tractors

Diesel engines took the lead in the tractor market in the late 1940s and early 1950s, but the first diesel tractors were available in the 1920s, when they attracted little interest. Some potential customers were probably discouraged by the price of the early diesel engines and by the often complicated starting arrangements. However, the fuel efficiency figures showed that diesels used significantly less fuel than their spark-ignition rivals.

Above: *Hart-Parr was one of the once-great companies that lost its identity in the huge merger that created the Oliver group.*

Left: *The first tractors designed and built by Deere & Co. arrived in the 1920s with the horizontal twin-cylinder engine that became almost a John Deere trademark.*

The list of tractor developments to appear during the 1920s also included the first John Deere tractors with their distinctive two-cylinder horizontal engines. The first special rubber tires for tractors arrived in the early 1930s, and the Allis-Chalmers Model U became fast and famous as the tractor at the center of a spectacular campaign to promote the new tires.

Another of the notable 1920s arrivals was the first of the Farmall rowcrop tractor series from International Harvester. Many important crops are grown in rows, and the development of a general-purpose tractor with special features that were ideal for work in between rows was a huge step forward that other American manufacturers were forced to follow.

It was also a period of structural change in the tractor industry. Mergers and takeovers have always been a feature of the industry—just as they are today—but in the 1920s the need for consolidation produced a whole series of important mergers. In Britain some of the companies that formed the ill-fated Agricultural and General Engineers group were destroyed in the organization's financial collapse—but one of the few AGE achievements was to produce the most advanced diesel tractors in the world.

INTERNATIONAL HARVESTER

⚒ 1923 Chicago, Illinois

I.H. MCCORMICK-DEERING 10-20

During a 10-year period from 1914 the engineers at International Harvester produced a whole series of excellent tractors, and the McCormick-Deering 10-20 was certainly one of the best of them.

The 10-20 was available starting in 1923, and apart from being smaller, lighter, and less powerful than the previously introduced 15-30, the two models shared similar styling and were also mechanically similar. They were both powered by a gasoline-paraffin burning four-cylinder engine with a valve-in-head design

and a rated speed of 1,000rpm, and an advanced design feature was the use of ball bearings for the main crankshaft bearings.

Design Features
Cylinder size for the early versions of the 10-20 was 4.25-in (10.7-cm) bore and 5.0-in (12.7-

Above: This McCormick-Deering 10-20, waiting for a new owner at an auction sale in England, has been equipped at a later date with nonstandard rubber tires.

cm) stroke, and the measurements for the 15–30 engine were slightly bigger at 4.5in and 6.0in (11.4cm and 15.2cm). A three-speed gearbox provided a 4-mph (6.4-km/h) top gear maximum for both models.

After four years the 10–20 tractor was given a design update that included increasing the rated engine speed to 1,025rpm, and the top speed on the road was raised slightly to 4.25mph (6.8km/h).

Other 10–20 developments included a narrow version with the overall width reduced from 60in to 48in (1.5m to 1.2m). There was also an orchard model with extra cladding and a modified air intake and exhaust stack for working close to trees, and a crawler version of the 10–20 arrived in 1928. Rubber tires were added to the options list in the late 1930s.

Power Takeoff

Having provided a power takeoff as an option on the 8-16 Junior model, the same feature was included in the standard specification for the 15–30 and 10–20 tractors, giving them the distinction of being the first tractors to be equipped in this way.

Because the power takeoff was still a novelty in the early 1920s, I.H. obviously realized that many farmers would not understand its function, and this is why it used a sales leaflet published in 1924 to explain that a power takeoff "consists of a shaft attached to the rear of the transmission. The 10–20 transmits power in much the same way as a propeller shaft of an automobile or truck and is used to drive the mechanism of the puller machine."

Production

Production of the three-plow 15–30 model started in 1921 and ended in 1934 when the sales total had reached 156,000. The annual production figures for the 10–20 model peaked at 34,742 in 1929, and the total reached an impressive 215,000 by 1939.

Specifications

Manufacturer: International Harvester Co.
Location: Chicago, Illinois
Model: McCormick-Deering 10-20
Type: General purpose
Power unit: Four-cylinder valve-in-head engine.
Power output: 20hp (14.8kw)
Transmission: Three-speed gearbox
Weight: 4,010lb (1,820kg)
Production started: 1923

Below: *The McCormick-Deering name plate on the radiator header tank of a nicely restored 15-30 tractor can be seen here.*

HOLT

⚒ **1923   Stockton, California**

HOLT 2 TON

The 2 Ton model was added to the Holt tractor range in 1923. At that time the merger between the Holt and Best companies was still two years away, and Holt was still a fully independent company with Caterpillar as its brand name.

Specifications

Manufacturer: Holt Manufacturing Co.

Location: Stockton, California

Model: 2 Ton

Type: Tracklayer

Power unit: Holt four-cylinder gasoline engine

Power output: 25hp (18.5kw)

Transmission: Three-speed gearbox

Weight: 4,040lb (1,834kg)

Production started: 1923

The Caterpillar 2 Ton tractor was the baby of the Holt range, and at 4,040lb (1,834kg) it was also unusually light for a tracklayer. The power unit was a Holt four-cylinder gasoline engine with a valve-in-head design and an overhead camshaft.

Engine

The cylinder bore and stroke measurements of the Caterpillar 2 Ton were 4.0in and 5.5in (10.1cm and 13.9cm), respectively, and the rated engine speed was 1,000rpm. Power output measured in performance tests averaged 25.4hp (18.9kw) at the rated speed. A three-speed gearbox provided a maximum forward speed of 5.23mph (8.4km/h).

Merger

The merger in 1925 brought together the two leading tracklayer manufacturers. Holt was the bigger partner, and Holt's Caterpillar brand name was chosen for the new company. Holt also provided three of the five tractors selected from the two ranges to form the new Caterpillar line, and one of these was the 2 Ton model.

Following the merger, production of the new Caterpillar 2 Ton continued until 1928 without major mechanical changes, but there were minor changes to the appearance of the tractor. One of these was having the model identification, "2 TON," cast into the radiator side plates, bringing it into line with the other models in the Caterpillar range.

Above: The 2 Ton tractor was a Holt product, introduced two years before Caterpillar was formed by the merger with Best. Production of the 2 Ton continued after the merger.

BENZ-SENDLING
✴ 1923 Gaggenau, Baden, Germany

BENZ-SENDLING

Below: This is an original studio shot from the Mercedes-Benz archives of the tractor that brought the diesel engine into power farming.

Daimler and Benz, two of Germany's leading vehicle manufacturers, joined forces in 1926 to form Daimler-Benz, one of the world's most successful companies and the manufacturer of the Mercedes-Benz range of vehicles.

Specifications

Manufacturer: Benz & Co.
Location: Gaggenau, Baden, Germany
Model: Benz-Sendling
Type: Motor plow
Power unit: Twin-cylinder diesel engine
Power output: 27.5hp (20.4kw)
Transmission: N/A
Weight: N/A
Production started: 1923 (diesel version)

The Benz part of the partnership had been building tractors in small numbers since 1919, and in 1921 the company had started making a two-cylinder diesel engine at its factory in Mannheim.

The diesel was used initially as the power unit for a Benz truck, but from 1923 it was to replace the gasoline engine as the standard power unit for the Benz-Sendling tractor.

First Diesel Tractor

Benz-Sendling production started in 1919 with a gasoline engine, but the diesel version was almost certainly the world's first production tractor with diesel power. The diesel engine is

the Benz-Sendling's only claim to fame. It was an unconventional three-wheeler, designed as a motor plow, with one big driving wheel at the rear, and the final drive was through an enclosed chain and sprockets.

One of the reasons for the success of the Benz diesel engines was their early use of a precombustion chamber. The diesel engines were made by Benz at its factory in Mannheim, and the twin-cylinder version used for the Benz-Sendling tractor had a 15:1 compression ratio and an 800rpm rated speed. The cylinder bore and stroke measurements were 5.3in and 7.9in (13.5cm and 20cm), and the rated output was 27.5hp (20.4kw).

JOHN DEERE
1923   Waterloo, Iowa

JOHN DEERE MODEL D

After taking over the Waterloo Boy company, Deere & Co. continued to build Model N tractors with just a few minor improvements, and it also continued to use the Waterloo Boy name.

Waterloo Boy engineers were already working on the replacement for their Model N tractor in 1918 when their company was taken over, and the project continued under the management of the new owners.

When the replacement arrived in 1923 it was known as the Model D, and it was the first tractor to carry the John Deere name and to sell in significant numbers.

New Features
Almost every feature of the old Waterloo Boy design was replaced on the new Model D, but

the principle exception to this was the tractor's two-cylinder horizontal engine.

There was an increase in the maximum power at 30.4hp (22.5kw) compared with the Model N version's 26hp (19.4kw), and the engine speed was given a 50rpm boost to 800rpm for the new tractor, but the bore and stroke measurements of the Waterloo Boy engine were retained on the new version.

The new design swept away the old steel-girder frame and the exposed final drive, and replaced them with unit construction and a fully enclosed transmission. The Model D was

Above, top: A spoked flywheel identifies this tractor as an early version of the John Deere Model D, the tractor that replaced the Waterloo Boy series.

Above: This sideways view shows the position of the twin-cylinder horizontal engine, probably the most famous engine series the tractor industry has produced.

shorter than its predecessor, and it was also much lighter, weighing 4,260lb (1,934kg) compared to the Model N's 6,200lb (2,812kg).

For John Deere two-cylinder enthusiasts the flywheel of the Model D is of particular interest. When production started the engine had a 26-in (66-cm) diameter spoked flywheel, but this was reduced to 24in (61cm) after the first 900 tractors had been built.

Flywheel

Another change came when the production total reached 5,755, and at this stage the spoked flywheel was replaced by a solid version. Model D tractors with a spoked flywheel, known to enthusiasts as "spoker Ds," are particularly prized by collectors because they date from the early production years.

Other changes introduced on the Model D included an increase in the cylinder bore to 6.75in (17.1cm) in 1928, and this plus other engine modifications introduced during the next few years raised the power output to 41.6hp (31kw) in 1935.

The original two-speed gearbox was replaced by three speeds in 1935, and the Model D was given new styling in 1939. Production continued in various versions until 1953.

Trail Blazer

The Model D was the first in a new line of rugged, reliable tractors that helped to establish John Deere as one of the most successful tractor companies in the United States, and it also contributed to the long-running success of the John Deere two-cylinder engine series.

Specifications

Manufacturer: Deere & Co.
Location: Waterloo, Iowa
Model: D
Type: General purpose
Power unit: Two-cylinder horizontal engine
Power output: 30.4hp (22.5kw)
Transmission: Two-speed gearbox
Weight: 4,260lb (1,934kg)
Production started: 1923

Below: *Model D tractors in various versions and with steadily increasing power outputs were to remain in production for 30 years.*

INTERNATIONAL HARVESTER

1924 Chicago, Illinois

I.H. FARMALL

The original Farmall was one of the most important developments in tractor history. While most of the design teams in the industry were developing new general-purpose tractors, International Harvester aimed the new Farmall specifically at farms growing crops in rows.

Above, top: *The rowcrop front wheel arrangement on the Farmall meant that the I.H. engineers had to develop a special steering mechanism.*

Above: *While the Farmall was designed as a rowcrop tractor, it could also handle other types of equipment.*

The Farmall was the last in a long line of outstanding I.H. tractors introduced between 1914 and 1924. It was a time when International Harvester employed what was almost certainly the best team of designers in the industry, including Bert R. Benjamin who produced the design for the original Farmall. Benjamin was "a very talented, far-sighted, and prolific inventor" according to one historian, and his Farmall was the first tractor to meet the specific needs of rowcrop farmers.

Rowcrop Tractor

Within a few years of the Farmall launch in 1924 most of the other leading tractor manufacturers in the United States had produced their own rowcrop models based on features Bert Benjamin had included in his original design. The imitations are clear confirmation of the influence and success of the Farmall, and further evidence of these two things comes from the production figures. In spite of tough competition and the economic downturn in the 1920s, more than 100,000 Farmalls had been built by 1930, and in the more favorable sales climate of the 1930s annual production figures reached more than 35,000 in a good year.

Rowcrop farmers liked the design of the Farmall because it provided plenty of clearance for straddling growing crop plants and to accommodate mid-mounted equipment. In addition to this, the Farmall's tricycle wheel layout with one wheel at the front ensured good maneuverability for making headland turns, helped by the differential or steerage brakes that could lock one of the rear wheels.

Design Features

Benjamin's original design also included unit construction linking the engine and transmission in a single rigid, dust-protected structure, and excess weight was avoided to minimize soil compaction risk. To provide the maximum versatility for handling a wide range of arable farm machinery, he also equipped the Farmall with a power takeoff and a belt pulley. A wide range of wheel-track adjustments to suit different row widths followed later.

The first preproduction Farmalls were completed in 1923 and worked in a field test program supervised by International Harvester engineers. Several problems were identified and dealt with, and the first production Farmalls were delivered during 1924. They featured a four-cylinder, valve-in-head engine delivering 18hp (13.3kw), 3.75-in and 5.0-in (9.5-cm and 12.7-cm) bore and stroke measurements, and a 1,200rpm rated speed.

Specifications

Manufacturer: International Harvester

Location: Chicago, Illinois

Model: Farmall

Type: Rowcrop tractor

Power unit: Four-cylinder valve-in-head engine

Power output: 18hp (13.3kw)

Transmission: Three-speed gearbox

Weight: 4,100lb (1,861kg)

Production started: 1924

Below: *An International Harvester four-cylinder engine with a valve-in-head layout powered the early Farmalls, with the power delivered through a three-speed gearbox.*

HART-PARR
✖ 1924   Charles City, Iowa

HART-PARR 12-24E

By the early 1920s the Hart-Parr company was making serious efforts to move away from its heavyweight-tractor image and compete in the small and medium sectors of the tractor market, and the 12-24E model was one of a new generation of lightweight tractors. Introduced in 1924, it weighed 4,675lb (2,122kg) and was one of the smallest models in the Hart-Parr range.

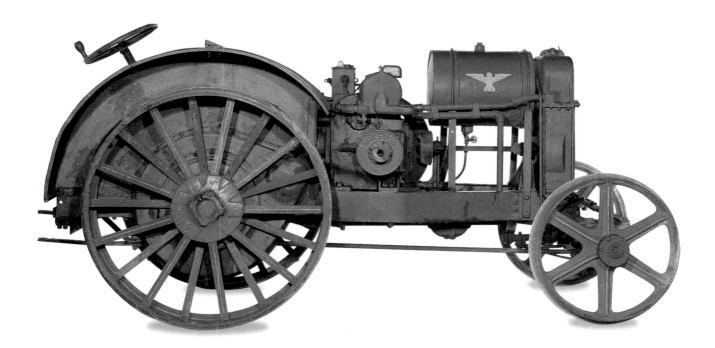

The power unit for the 12-24E was typical of a Hart-Parr design, based on a pair of horizontal cylinders, a valve-in-head layout, and an 800rpm rated speed. The bore and stroke measurements were 5.5in and 6.5in (13.9cm and 16.5cm), and the tractor's maximum output when the 12-24E was tested in Nebraska was almost 27hp (20kw).

Other Versions
The 12-24E was a development from the earlier 10–20 model, which was available in two different versions between 1921 and 1924. Both the 12-24 and the 10–20 shared basically the same engine, and the principal improvement to be found in the 12-24E model was a more up-to-date disk clutch to replace the previous model's band clutch.

The same engine, with an extra 0.25in (6mm) added to the cylinder bores, appeared once more in a new 12-24H tractor, available from 1928 as the replacement for the E.

The classic H version of the 12-24 was still in production when the Hart-Parr company lost its identity in the 1929 merger that formed the Oliver Farm Equipment Co., one of a series of mergers and takeovers that rationalized the tractor industry around that time.

Above: *Hart-Parr's efforts to attract smaller-acreage customers included the little 12-24E lightweight tractor.*

Specifications

Manufacturer: Hart-Parr Co.
Location: Charles City, Iowa
Model: 12-24E
Type: General purpose
Power unit: Two-cylinder horizontal engine
Power output: 27hp (20kw)
Transmission: Two-speed gearbox
Weight: 4,675lb (2,122kg)
Production started: 1924

HEIDER

1924 Rock Island, Illinois

HEIDER 15-27

An Iowa farming family started the Heider Manufacturing Co., which began building tractors in 1911. The tractors were popular, and within a few years the Heiders sold their business to the Rock Island Plow Co. of Rock Island, Iowa.

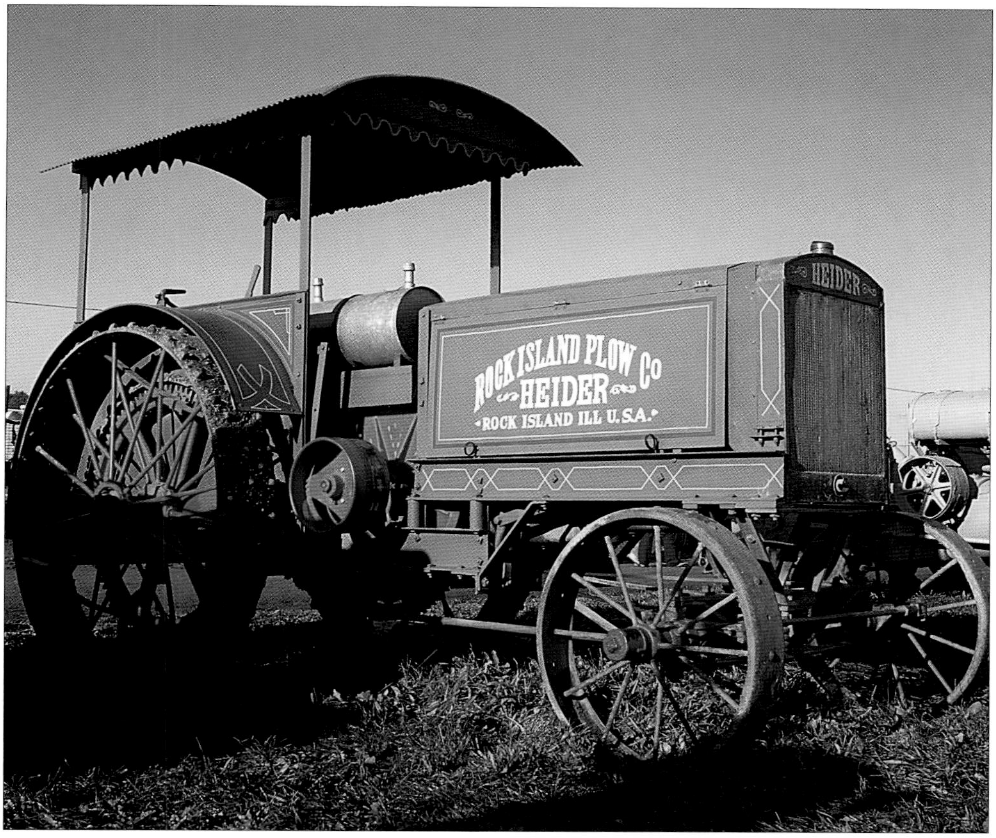

Right: *The Heider name was retained after the Rock Island Plow Co. bought the tractor business from the Iowa farming family that had designed the tractors.*

Specifications

Manufacturer: Rock Island Plow Co.	
Location: Rock Island, Illinois	
Model: Heider 15-27	
Type: General purpose	
Power unit: Waukesha four-cylinder engine	
Power output: 30hp (22.2kw)	
Transmission: Friction drive with infinitely variable travel speeds	
Weight: 6,290lb (2,856kg)	
Production started: 1924	

The new owners continued to base their tractors on the Heider design, and they also continued to use the Heider brand name and the distinctive trim along the sides of the canopy roof. They retained the Heider friction drive as well, another of the special design features. It provided an infinitely variable range of travel speeds, allowing the driver to match the engine and travel speeds more accurately to suit the working conditions and the equipment used.

Engine

When the Rock Island company introduced its new 15-27 tractor in 1924 it was still using both the Heider name and the existing friction drive. The Heider 15-27, like most Heider tractors, was equipped with a Waukesha four-cylinder engine. Cylinder measurements were 4.75-in (12-cm) bore and 6.75-in (17.1-cm) stroke, and the tractor's engine was positioned above the rear axle where the weight would assist the wheel grip.

The 15-27 remained in the Rock Island range for about three years and was one of the last tractors to carry the Heider brand name. The name was eventually dropped in the late 1920s, and the Rock Island Co. became part of the J. I. Case group in 1937.

HSCS

1924 Budapest, Hungary

HSCS PROTOTYPE

Clayton and Shuttleworth was one of Britain's leading manufacturers of agricultural steam engines during the nineteenth and early twentieth centuries, and the big farms and estates in Hungary provided one of the company's best export markets.

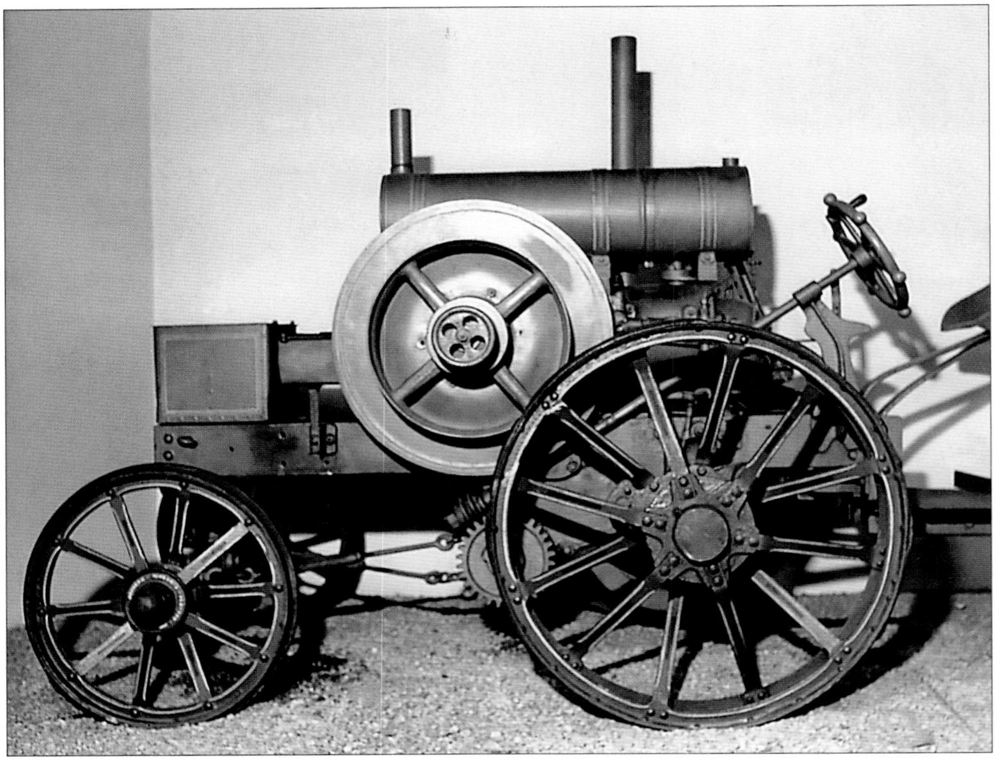

Left: *The original prototype tractor developed by the HSCS company still survives as an exhibit in the Hungarian Agricultural Museum.*

Specifications

Manufacturer: Hofherr-Schrantz Clayton-Shuttleworth
Location: Budapest, Hungary
Model: Prototype
Type: General purpose
Power unit: Single-cylinder hot-bulb engine
Power output: 15hp (11kw)
Transmission: Single-speed
Weight: N/A
Production: 1924

The switch from steam to tractor power caused serious problems for Clayton and Shuttleworth, and in 1912 it sold its Hungarian subsidiary. The buyer was a local farm-machinery manufacturer, and following the takeover the name was changed to Hofherr-Schrantz Clayton-Shuttleworth, or HSCS.

HSCS Tractors

The new company expanded, and by the early 1920s it had become Hungary's biggest manufacturer of stationary engines. It started its tractor development program in the early 1920s, and its first tractor powered by a semidiesel or hot-bulb engine was completed in 1924. It was a prototype model used for further development work, and it was powered by a single-cylinder two-stroke engine with 15-hp (11-kw) output, and it was capable of plowing between three and four acres at 7.5-in (19-cm) depth in a 10-hour day.

When the first HSCS production tractors arrived in 1925 they bore little resemblance to the prototype model. The single-speed transmission of the prototype was replaced by a three-speed gearbox, and the tractors' power output had increased to 20hp (14.9kw), but they still used a hot-bulb engine, which remained the standard power unit for HSCS tractors for more than 20 years.

CLETRAC
1925 Cleveland, Ohio

CLETRAC K-20

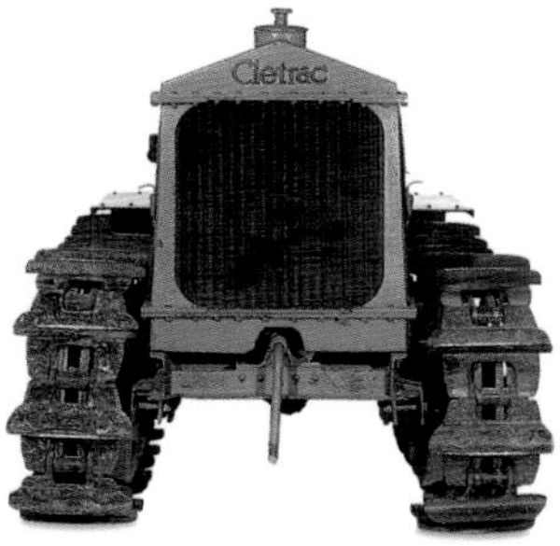

It may, of course, have been just a coincidence, but the first model in the Cleveland Motor Co.'s Cletrac range of crawler tractors was known as the Model R, its second was identified by the letter H and tractor number three was the Model W—and the letters RHW are the initials of Rollin H. White, who was the principle shareholder in the Cleveland company.

Above: *Cletrac's K-20 tractor arrived in 1925 to challenge the newly formed Caterpillar company in the crawler tractor market.*

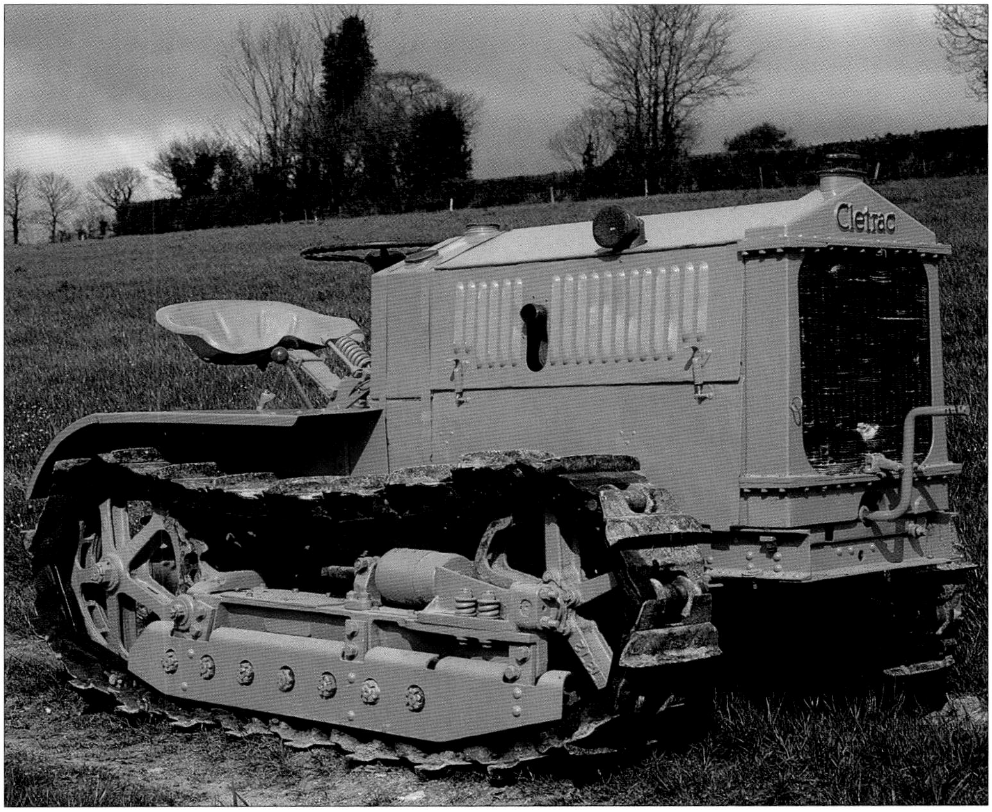

Right: *Adding a power-takeoff shaft to the Cletrac K-20 model was a significant step forward in crawler tractor design.*

Specifications

Manufacturer: Cleveland Tractor Co.
Location: Cleveland, Ohio
Model: K-20
Type: Tracklayer
Power unit: Four-cylinder engine with overhead valves
Power output: 24.5hp (18kw)
Transmission: Three-speed gearbox
Weight: N/A
Production started: 1925

After that the lettering appears to be completely random, with the Model F followed by the K-20, then the 30A. The K-20 arrived in 1925, featuring the Cletrac controlled differential steering, and it was based on the earlier R, H, and W models and shared their compact overall size.

Design Features

The engine was a Cleveland built four-cylinder overhead valve design with 4in by 5.5in (10.1cm by 13.9cm) cylinders and a 24.5-hp (18-kw) rated output, almost 5hp (3.7kw) more than the previous Model W. Possibly because of his previous automobile-industry background, Rollin White had a preference for high-speed engines for his tractors, and this was a feature of the K-20 engine with its 1,350rpm rated speed.

Principal improvements introduced on the K-20 were a belt pulley moved to the rear instead of the front of the tractor, and—a significant step forward in tracklayer design—it was also the first Cletrac to be equipped with a power takeoff.

VICKERS
⚒ 1925   Newcastle upon Tyne, UK

VICKERS-AUSSIE

The driving wheels were said to be the outstanding innovation when the British-built Vickers-Aussie tractor was introduced in 1925, although Australian drivers may have gained more benefit from the fancy sunshade on this tractor.

The wheels were developed by an Australian inventor, and the main advantage was that they could work effectively in a wide range of soil conditions, including a wet, sticky clay. The rim of each rear wheel was made in three sections with a 3-in (7.6-cm) gap between each section, and spring-mounted steel bars protruding into each of the gaps provided a self-cleaning action, knocking off any lumps of soil that were sticking to the wheel rims in order to prevent a buildup in wet conditions.

Reduced Soil Damage
Another benefit claimed for the triple-section rear wheels was reduced soil damage in wet conditions, and this was because the wheels were wider and, it was said, they had a larger contact area on the ground.

Above: The similarities between the Vickers tractor and the International Harvester 15-30 may have been the result of an agreement for Vickers to use the I.H. design.

Presumably the self-cleaning wheels would have been particularly beneficial in the United Kingdom, where there are large areas of clay that becomes sticky in wet weather; however, the Vickers tractor was designed for the Australian market. This is where much of the marketing effort was concentrated, and this also explains why the name Aussie was chosen for the new tractor.

Vickers

Apart from the nonstick wheels the Aussie bore more than a passing resemblance to the McCormick-Deering 15-30 tractor from International Harvester. The styling is certainly similar, and the Aussie engine has the same 30-hp (22.2-kw) rated output at 1,000rpm as the I.H. power unit.

Both models' engines also shared the same 4.5-in and 6-in (11.4-cm and 15.2-cm) bore and stroke measurements, both were an overhead valve design, and both were linked to a three-speed gearbox.

According to one theory the similarity between the British-built Vickers tractor and the I.H. 15-30 from the USA is more than a coincidence. I.H. is said to have signed an agreement allowing Vickers to build a version of the 15-30 under license, and this is why some of the components on both tractors are interchangeable.

Although the Aussie name was dropped at an early stage, Vickers continued to build the tractor for about five years and most of them were shipped to Australia and New Zealand. Two of the tractors—one carrying the Vickers-Aussie name and the other a later Vickers version—were on a return ticket, as they arrived back in the United Kingdom in 1970s to be restored at the Vickers factory where they had been built half a century earlier.

Below: *This is one of a pair of Vickers tractors that were returned to the United Kingdom in the 1970s to be restored and displayed at the Newcastle factory where they were built.*

Specifications

Manufacturer: Vickers Ltd.	**Transmission:** Three-speed gearbox
Location: Newcastle upon Tyne, UK	**Weight:** N/A
Model: Vickers-Aussie	**Production started:** 1925
Type: General purpose	
Power unit: Four-cylinder engine	
Power output: 30hp (22.2kw)	

RONALDSON-TIPPETT

✖ 1926 Ballarat, Victoria, Australia

RONALDSON-TIPPETT

The Ronaldson Bros. and Tippett company started building engines in 1903 in the town of Ballarat, Victoria, and within a few years it had expanded to become Australia's biggest engine manufacturer.

Its first tractor was built in about 1912 as an experimental model, but the project was abandoned and tractor development work did not start again until about 1924. The first production tractor was built in 1926, and Ronaldson-Tippett tractors were available in Australia, selling against mainly American competition, until about 1938.

American Engine

An American-built Wisconsin engine was chosen for the production tractor. It is not clear why it was decided to import an engine instead of using one from the company's own range, but it may have been an acknowledgment that Wisconsin already had considerable experience with building engines for tractors.

The engine chosen was a four-cylinder design with the cylinders arranged in two water-jacketed pairs, and the rated output was 30hp (22.2kw). Some of the tractors built during the first year or so suffered from an overheating problem, presumably due to working in very high temperatures. The

Above, top: Although Ronaldson Bros. and Tippett was a leading engine manufacturer, they imported their tractor engines from the United States.

Above: The flag and the pipe-smoking spectator suggest that this photograph was taken at a demonstration of a late version of the Ronaldson-Tippett.

problem was solved by increasing the capacity of the cooling system by fitting a larger header tank above the radiator, and this explains the unusual front-end styling on the later models.

Speed and Brakes

An unconventional feature of the tractors was the transmission. It was based on a simple two-speed gearbox, but customers could also buy alternative external pickoff gears that could be changed by hand to multiply the choice of available speeds, and the number of speeds could be doubled again by using the oversize 53-in (135-cm) diameter driving wheels instead of the standard 50-in (127-cm) size.

Making full use of the two-speed gearbox, the various external pickoff gears and the two wheel sizes provided 48 different forward speeds without adjusting the throttle setting. This sounds impressive, but as the maximum speed at the full throttle setting was only

6.6mph (10.6km/h) there must have been considerable overlap between adjacent gear settings. Also, changing pickoff gears is a messy job, which many drivers would prefer to avoid.

Another unusual feature was the brake, which was controlled by a foot pedal and operated on a drum attached to the belt-pulley shaft. This arrangement had serious limitations because the brake was effective only if the tractor was in gear. A gear change on a steep hill could be dangerous, the instruction book warned, because there was no way of stopping the tractor if it started to run down the hill between gears.

Specifications

Manufacturer: Ronaldson Bros. and Tippett
Location: Ballarat, Victoria, Australia
Model: 30hp
Type: General purpose
Power unit: Wisconsin four-cylinder engine
Power output: 30hp (22.2kw)

Transmission: Two-speed gearbox plus pickoff gears
Weight: N/A
Production started: 1926

Below: *A choice of cogs was available to fit on the outside of the gearbox to give a wider choice of gear ratios, but changing them was not easy.*

HART-PARR
✖ 1926   Charles City, Iowa

HART-PARR 18-36

The mid-1920s were a busy time for the engineers at Hart-Parr as they produced a steady stream of new and updated models for what was an increasingly competitive market. The new arrivals included the 18-36 tractor, introduced initially in 1926, then reintroduced as an improved H version just two years later in 1928.

Specifications

Manufacturer: Hart-Parr Co.	
Location: Charles City, Iowa	
Model: 18-36	
Type: General purpose	
Power unit: Two-cylinder horizontal engine	
Power output: 42.9hp (31.8kw) (maximum)	
Transmission: Two-speed gearbox (first version)	
Weight: 6,250lb (2,838kg)	
Production started: 1926	

The most important difference between the two versions of the 18-36 was the three-speed gearbox included in the H specification to replace the two-speed transmission of the previous version.

The maximum travel speed in top gear for the two-speed transmission tractor was a sedate 3mph (4.8km/h). This was a fairly typical top speed for tractors built in the mid-1920s, and it would presumably have been quite acceptable to those who had previously worked with horses.

Engine

Hart-Parr used its usual twin-cylinder horizontal engine design for the 18-36. The cylinder dimensions were 6.75-in (17.1-cm) bore and 7.0-in (17.7-cm) stroke, and the engine

developed its rated output at 800rpm. The maximum power output recorded in Nebraska was 42.85hp (31.9kw), comfortably ahead of the manufacturer's 36-hp (26.8-kw) rating, and the 32-hp (23.8-kw) maximum recorded at the drawbar was also well ahead of the rated figure.

Weight

The 18-36 weighed 6,250lb (2,838kg), which does not really justify calling it a lightweight model, and it remained in the Hart-Parr product range until after the 1929 merger that formed the Oliver company. The design changes aimed at reviving the company's fortunes in the 1920s were too little, too late, and the merger was a sad end to what had once been a success story of the American tractor industry.

Above: *Hart-Parr urgently needed some success in the 1920s, but the new 18-36 model introduced with a two-speed gearbox in 1926 did little to boost the sales figures.*

RUMELY
🔧 1927   La Porte, Indiana

RUMELY Y30-50

When the old 25-45 model was due for replacement, the engineers at the Rumely factory decided to squeeze another 95rpm from its engine in order to boost the rated power output. The result was an extra 5hp (3.7kw) on the drawbar power and 5hp (3.7kw) on the pulley.

Right: A set of cut-down rubber tires from a modern tractor helps to protect the wheel rims of this Canadian-owned Y30-50.

Specifications

Manufacturer: Advance Rumely Thresher Co.

Location: La Porte, Indiana

Model: Y30-50

Type: General purpose

Power unit: Twin-cylinder horizontal engine

Power output: 63hp (46.6kw)

Transmission: Three-speed gearbox

Weight: 13,025lb (5,913kg)

Production started: 1927

The new version was called the Y30-50, and it was available from 1927 to provide a popular choice for large-acreage farms in the United States and Canada. The new model easily achieved its 30- and 50-hp (22.3- and 37.2-kw) ratings when it was put through its paces in Nebraska. When the belt-pulley, or brake-horsepower, test results were published the maximum output was 63hp (44.6kw), beating the rated figure by almost 25 percent, and the 47hp (35kw) achieved in the drawbar pull test was more than 50 percent ahead of the rated output.

Horsepower

This was not the only example of a Rumely tractor with a very much understated power rating, and underselling its models' horsepower in this way may not have been the best marketing policy when competition in the tractor market was increasing.

Power was provided by a horizontal twin-cylinder engine with 7.75-in (19.7-cm) bore and 9.5-in (24.1-cm) stroke. The rated power of the previous 25-45 version was measured at a leisurely 540rpm, but this was increased to 635rpm for the new 30-50 model.

HART-PARR
✗ **1927 Charles City, Iowa**

HART-PARR 28-50

Hart-Parr's preference for two-cylinder engines continued when it introduced the big 28-50 model in 1927, but with no engine available to provide the necessary power output the Hart-Parr design team decided to use two of their standard two-cylinder engines and mount them side by side.

The 28-50 was not the first Hart-Parr tractor to feature the twin engine arrangement, which was a practical way to avoid the cost of developing a new high-horsepower engine likely to achieve relatively low sales volumes.

Engine
In this case, however, the 28-50 model was designed as the replacement for the previous 40 model, and the twin engines in the new tractor were essentially the same as those that were used to power the 40.

The two engines shared the same 6.5-in (16.5-cm) stroke, but the bore was increased by 0.25in (6mm) to 5.75in (14.6cm) to boost the power output. Although Hart-Parr had been concentrating on developing smaller, lighter models during the 1920s, the 28-50 was a big tractor. It was easily the most powerful model in the Hart-Parr line at that time, and at 10,394lb (4,719kg) it was also easily the heaviest.

Gears
The specification included a two-speed gearbox at a time when many manufacturers were offering three or more forward gears, but the fact that a cab was included on the options list is evidence that driver comfort was not completely ignored.

Above: *Using two small engines instead of developing a new large one was a cost-saving measure.*

Specifications

Manufacturer:	Hart-Parr Co.
Location:	Charles City, Iowa
Model:	28-50
Type:	General purpose
Power unit:	Two twin-cylinder horizontal engines
Power output:	64.5hp (47.7kw) (maximum)
Transmission:	Two-speed gearbox
Weight:	10,394lb (4,719kg)
Production started:	1927

CASSANI

⚒ 1928 Treviglio, Milan, Italy

CASSANI 40HP

Although Benz introduced the first tractor powered by a diesel engine in 1923, other manufacturers were in no hurry to follow its example and the next diesel model did not arrive until 1927, when an Italian engineer named Francesco Cassani built his first tractor.

Right: One of the earliest production models of the Cassani diesel tractor has pride of place in the SAME Deutz-Fahr group's headquarters in Italy.

Specifications

Manufacturer: Francesco Cassani

Location: Treviglio, Milan, Italy

Model: 40hp

Type: General purpose

Power unit: Twin-cylinder diesel engine

Power output: 40hp (29.6kw)

Transmission: Three-speed gearbox

Weight: N/A

Production started: 1928

Cassani was a self-taught engineer who learned most of his skills while helping his father to make and repair tools and implements for local farmers. He was 21 years old when he designed and built the first Cassani tractor, using a two-cylinder diesel engine with water cooling. When the tractor was demonstrated to local farmers it attracted sufficient interest to persuade Cassani to build more of the tractors, and he designed a 40-hp (29.6-kw) version of his diesel engine to power them.

Starting System
A special feature was the compressed-air system he developed for starting the engine. The air was stored in a tank above the engine, and a pump powered by the engine automatically maintained the necessary working pressure. Presumably some form of backup system was provided in case the compressed-air supply failed to start the engine.

Tractor production ended during the mid-1930s as Cassani concentrated on building marine and aircraft engines for the Italian government, but when the war ended in 1945 he started making tractors again. He established the SAME company, which later included the Lamborghini, Hurlimann, and Deutz tractor brands, and claims to be one of the top four tractor manufacturers worldwide.

RENAULT
⚒ 1927 Billancourt, France

RENAULT PE

The PE model was introduced as a replacement for the H0 tractor, and it was also the first Renault model to break away from a design that was based on the original Renault light tank.

A nother first for the PE was the addition of a manually operated implement-lift mechanism, and a push-button electric starter was available starting in 1933. The list of options also included solid rubber tires for the rear wheels, and it was also the first production tractor available with the new low-pressure inflatable tires introduced by Michelin in 1933.

Cooling System

Although the PE and the H0 look very different, one of the design features carried over from the previous model was locating the radiator behind the engine. On the PE model the radiator is upright instead of being slanted at an angle as on the previous tractors, and the vertical structure in front of the engine is an air cleaner with an enormous capacity.

The unconventional position of the radiator was not the only unusual feature of the PE cooling system. The PE's cooling fan was designed to form part of the clutch assembly in the base of the engine compartment, where it blew warm air out of the bottom of the

Above, top: In this photograph the side panels of the engine compartment have been removed, but their function was to force cooling air through the tractor's radiator.

Above: This Renault publicity shot shows a PE tractor equipped with the manually operated lift mechanism with a mounted plow.

compartment, drawing in cool air to replace it. Close-fitting steel panels enclosing both sides of the compartment ensured that most of the incoming air was drawn in through the radiator to cool the water.

The obvious advantage of placing the radiator at the rear of the engine is that it can allow a sloping hood line for improved forward visibility, as on previous Renault models, but this was not a feature of the PE.

The Renault design team may have realized that the cooling system was unnecessarily complicated because on later versions of the PE it scrapped the back-to-front arrangement, moving the radiator to the front of the engine, where it replaced the unnecessarily large air cleaner. In addition, a fan was placed behind the radiator to draw air directly through the radiator grille from front to back.

Disappointing Sales

Later developments of the PE model also included a narrow version for vineyard work, with the overall width reduced to 3ft 9in (1.14m). In spite of the options and design improvements, sales of the PE remained disappointing. This was partly due to the general economic situation at the time and partly because of intense competition from American imports and from the French-built version of the British Austin tractor. PE sales totaled 1,771 between 1927 and the end of production in 1936, amounting to a modest average of fewer than 200 per year.

Specifications

Manufacturer: Renault	**Power output:** 20hp (14.8kw)
Location: Billancourt, France	**Transmission:** Three-speed gearbox
Model: PE	**Weight:** 3,960lb (1,800kg)
Type: General purpose	**Production started:** 1927
Power unit: Four-cylinder 127-cubic-inch (2.1-liter) engine	

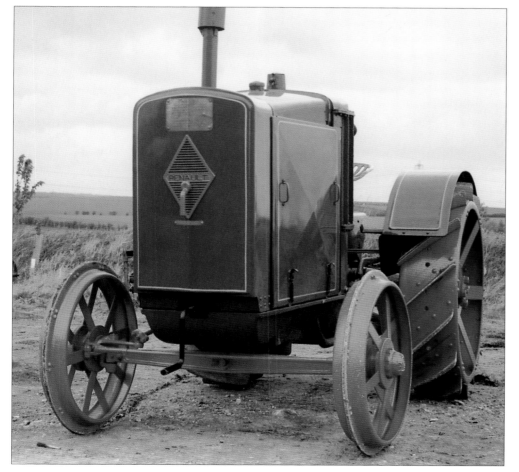

Left: *The large rectangular structure at the front of the PE's engine compartment is an enormous air cleaner for the engine.*

FOWLER

1927 Leeds, Yorkshire, England

FOWLER GYROTILLER

Fowler engines achieved worldwide success during the great days of agricultural steam power, but the switch from steam engines to tractor power brought serious financial problems, and by the mid-1920s there was an urgent need to find new products.

Above: *The initial success of the big Gyrotillers encouraged the Fowler company to develop a range of smaller models.*

For a while it looked as if the Gyrotiller would be the new success story that would restore the Fowler company's financial fortunes and fill the huge factory in Leeds. The Gyrotiller was a rotary cultivator invented by Norman Storey, an American who managed a sugar estate in Puerto Rico. It was a big, powerful machine, designed to cope with extreme conditions, and although it was designed specifically for sugar-cane production, it offered possibilities for other farming systems.

John Fowler Ltd. had established its success by making big machines and selling them throughout the world, and it signed an agreement that gave it exclusive rights to manufacture and market the Gyrotiller. That was in 1924, and the first of the Fowler Gyrotillers was built in 1927.

Engine

Even by Fowler standards the first Gyrotiller was big, with an overall length of 26ft (7.9m) and weighing 23 tons (22.6 tonnes). The power unit was a 225-hp (166.5-kw) Ricardo gasoline engine developed originally to power British tanks during World War I. Fuel consumption when operating at full throttle could be as high as 14 gallons (63.6 liters) per hour. The powered cultivator mounted on the rear consisted of two horizontal rotors covering a 10ft (3m) working width up to 20in (50.8cm) deep, said to be able to turn undisturbed soil into a tilth ready for planting in just one operation.

Fowler engineers later switched to a more modest 150-hp (111.8-kw) MAN diesel engine, and this was followed by a 170-hp (126.7-kw) Fowler diesel. There was also a smaller self-propelled model using an 80-hp (59.6-kw) Fowler diesel, and Fowler also designed smaller cultivator units for mounting on the 30- and 40-hp (22.3- and 29.8-kw) Fowler crawler tractors.

Failure

Early reports were favorable, and sales to the Caribbean sugar estates expanded rapidly, while British farmers and contractors welcomed the Gyrotiller as a form of minimum cultivation. The Gyrotiller was soon generating almost 50 percent of Fowler turnover with the prospect of further growth still to come. However, the happy ending failed to materialize, and production ended in 1937.

The problems included high warranty costs, partly because of faults on some of the diesel engines. On top of this, financial problems forced many of the sugar estates to cut back on their machinery investment, and there were complaints from UK farmers who found that excessive use of the Gyrotiller could seriously damage their soil structure.

Specifications

Manufacturer: John Fowler Ltd.

Location: Leeds, Yorkshire, UK

Model: Gyrotiller

Type: Self-propelled powered cultivator

Power unit: Ricardo gasoline engine

Power output: 225hp (166.5kw)

Transmission: N/A

Weight: 51,744lb (23,491kg)

Production started: 1927

Below: *Problems with some of the big diesel engines resulted in expensive warranty claims that helped to turn the Gyrotiller project from success to financial failure.*

RUSHTON
⚒ 1928 Walthamstow, London, UK

RUSHTON

The success of the Fordson Model F attracted several attempts to produce a direct rival, and one of them was the British-built Rushton. It was announced in 1927 with the backing of AEC, the company that built London's famous double-decker buses.

AEC was persuaded to support the project by George Rushton. Rushton's aim was to build what was basically a copy of the Fordson, but with extra features to justify a higher selling price. The company had spare factory capacity in Walthamstow, in London, and this was used for tractor production. AEC also allowed its General brand name to be used on the tractors; however, this was later replaced by the Rushton name.

Rushton and Fordson

Although the styling of the two models differed, the Rushton and Fordson tractors were so similar mechanically that some components

fitted both. One theory is that this allowed some Fordson parts to be used in the early stages of Rushton production before the correct Rushton parts were available.

When the two rivals competed on level terms at the 1930 World Tractor Trials near Oxford, England, the Rushton emerged victorious. One of the two Fordsons had to pull out of the trials because of a cracked cylinder block, and the paraffin version of the Rushton produced 23.9hp (17.7kw) against the Fordson's 20.8hp (15.5kw).

In the sales battle it was a different story, however, and financial problems ended Rushton tractor production in about 1934.

Above: *Britain's Rushton tractor was built at a London bus factory and was a fairly blatant copy of the Fordson Model F.*

Specifications

Manufacturer: Rushton Tractor Co.
Location: Walthamstow, London, UK
Model: Standard
Type: General purpose
Power unit: Four-cylinder engine
Power output: 23.9hp (17.7kw) (paraffin version)
Transmission: Three-speed gearbox
Weight: 3,950lb (1,793kg)
Production started: 1928

OLIVER

1930 **Chicago, Illinois, USA**

OLIVER 28-44

Above: *The Hart-Parr name lived on for a while after the merger that formed the Oliver company, but this was soon altered simply to Oliver, without the Hart-Parr.*

Takeovers and mergers have always played an important part in shaping the tractor industry, and the Oliver Corp. was the result of a merger that took place in 1929 when four middle-ranking American farm-equipment companies agreed to join forces.

Right: *Design changes introduced on the new Oliver 28-44 included a new four-cylinder engine instead of the twin-cylinder units used by Hart-Parr.*

Specifications

Manufacturer: Oliver Farm Equipment Co.
Location: Chicago, Illinois
Model: 28-44
Type: General purpose
Power unit: Four-cylinder engine
Power output: 49hp (36.3kw) (maximum)
Transmission: Three-speed gearbox
Weight: 6,415lb (2,912kg)
Production started: 1930

It was the Hart-Parr company that contributed most of the expertise in tractor design and production to the new group, and tractors built in the immediate aftermath of the merger carried the Oliver-Hart-Parr name, although this was later simplified to Oliver.

Developments

One of the significant tractor developments following the merger was the decision to replace the familiar twin-cylinder horizontal Hart-Parr engines with a new range of four and six-cylinder vertical power units.

The Oliver-Hart-Parr 28-44 was among the first tractors with an engine from the new range, featuring a four-cylinder valve-in-head version with 4.75-in (12-cm) bore and 6.25-in (15.8-cm) stroke. The engine produced its rated power at 1,125rpm, was available in both gasoline- and paraffin-fueled versions, and the specification included a pressure lubrication system. Maximum output when tested at Nebraska was 49hp (36.3kw).

Production of the 28-44 started in 1930 and continued until 1937, including a standard-tread agricultural model and an industrial version. A three-speed gearbox provided a top speed of 4.33mph (6.9km/h) for agricultural models, increasing to 7mph (11.3km/h) for the industrial version on high-pressure tires.

ALLIS-CHALMERS
✗ 1929 Milwaukee, Wisconsin

ALLIS-CHALMERS MODEL U

The Model U was the star performer in what was probably the most ambitious publicity program the tractor industry has ever known, and it helped to establish the new rubber tires that replaced traditional steel wheels and revolutionized tractor performance.

In 1929 the Model U tractor was built by Allis-Chalmers, but the marketing of the model was handled by the Chicago-based United Tractor and Equipment Co. of which Allis-Chalmers was a member. When the United group's financial difficulties became increasingly serious, Allis-Chalmers pulled out and took the tractor with it. The Continental engine fitted originally was replaced by an Allis-Chalmers four-cylinder power unit, and the Model U became just another typical mid-range American tractor.

Meanwhile some of the leading tire and tractor companies were looking for an alternative

Above: This original publicity photograph shows Barney Oldfield, a famous driver from the motor racing circuit, at the wheel of a high-speed Model U.

to the traditional steel wheels with lugs or cleats. These were reasonably good at gripping the soil, but the sharp lugs damaged road surfaces and manufacturers carefully restricted the speed of their tractors because of the risk of damage caused by bounce and vibration from the steel wheels.

The breakthrough came when tests were carried out with a Model U tractor fitted with a set of old aircraft tires. These had a low inflation pressure, allowing the carcase of the tires to mold itself to irregularities in the soil to produce efficient traction, but they also avoided damage to road surfaces and allowed faster travel speeds with a smoother ride.

Racing Tractors

Special tractor tires were soon available, and Allis-Chalmers offered them as an option on the Model U. The results were disappointing because of concerns about punctures and the durability of the new tires under farm conditions. A publicity campaign was needed, and Allis-Chalmers decided to focus on speed. It took a modified Model U tractor on rubber

tires to the race track at the Milwaukee Fair in 1933, and hired a local racing car driver to take it around the circuit at 35mph (56km/h).

At a time when the typical top speed for a tractor was 4mph (6.4km/h), the high-speed Model U was a local sensation. The next step was to form a Model U racing team including some of the best-known American racing drivers, and these performed at events throughout the United States during 1933. Some of the tractors were also used to set progressively faster world speed records, and these ended when Ab Jenkins, a driver with an international reputation, drove a Model U at 67mph (107.8km/h) on the Utah salt flats.

An estimated one million people saw the racing tractors in action during 1933, and by 1937 almost 50 percent of the new tractors sold in America were on rubber tires.

Specifications

Manufacturer: Allis-Chalmers
Location: Milwaukee, Wisconsin
Model: U
Type: General purpose
Power unit: Four-cylinder engine
Power output: 33hp (24.4kw)
Transmission: Four-speed gearbox

Weight: 5,140lb (2,334kg) (on rubber tires)
Production started: 1929

Opposite, top: Photographed, appropriately, on rubber tires is a 1930s version of the Allis-Chalmers Model U that helped to establish the new tractor tires.

Below: A sectioned view of an Allis-Chalmers Model U showing the standard four-cylinder engine and the four-speed gearbox.

chapter 4

The Ferguson System

Important tractor developments in the 1930s included the first commercially significant four-wheel drive model, the Massey-Harris General Purpose, and diesel engines were increasingly accepted on crawler tractors, but made little headway on wheeled models. A string of design improvements gave the Fordson Model F a new lease of life as the Model N, with production transferred to England after a brief stay in Ireland.

Above: *A fresh coat of bright orange paint requested by the American dealers helped to give the elderly Fordson a bright new image.*

Left: *Deere was one of the manufacturers that called in a professional stylist to give its tractors a new look with a more streamlined appearance.*

The most prominent name in the 1930s tractor industry was Harry Ferguson, a farmer's son from Northern Ireland who revolutionized tractor performance when he developed his hydraulically operated implement–attachment system with automatic draft control. Commercial development of the Ferguson System started in England with a production deal with David Brown, and it then moved to the United States where it was backed by the vast financial and manufacturing resources of Henry Ford.

Another important development was the new generation of tractors designed for smaller acreage family farms. It was a trend Henry Ford had started with the Fordson Model F, and Ford was at the forefront again when a new breed of small tractors arrived in the 1930s. His contribution was the Ford 9N Ferguson System tractor, but customers were also offered small tractors from other leading manufacturers. The late 1930s were also the time when styling became important, and leading American manufacturers hired professional stylists to give their tractors a new look. The result was a more streamlined appearance influenced by the car industry, with brighter colors to make their tractors more eye-catching.

FORDSON
⚒ 1929 Dagenham, Essex, England

FORDSON MODEL N

The decision to stop building Fordson Model F tractors in the USA in 1928 was surprising. According to the official explanation it was necessary to make factory space available for the new Ford Model A car, but other possible reasons included the slump in tractor sales plus increased competition.

Another factor in the equation is Henry Ford's pride in his Irish ancestry. A decision to switch production of a replacement model to a factory in the Irish Republic would have given Ford considerable satisfaction—even if it made little economic sense—as it brought investment and provided jobs in an area with high levels of unemployment. The production transfer was also an opportunity to update the original Model F, and the result was the Model N.

Design Developments

Design changes made during the development of the new Model N tractor included a bigger cylinder bore for the engine, raising the maximum power output to 23.24hp (17kw) on paraffin and 29.09hp (21.7kw) on gasoline. The tractor's front wheel design was strengthened and the front axle was redesigned. Although the new model performed well, the decision to build tractors in Ireland in the late 1920s

Above, top: *The water-washer air cleaner on the Fordson engine was retired in 1937, replaced by a more efficient oilbath version.*

Above: *As well as the orange paint, Fordson developments in 1937 included a higher compression ratio to boost the engine's power output.*

caused its own problems, including a shortage of skilled labor and the need to import virtually all the raw materials and export most of the finished tractors.

In 1932 the tractor line was on the move again, this time to the Ford complex at Dagenham in England, and in February 1933 the first English Model Ns arrived with a new blue paint finish plus a redesigned header tank and side panels for the radiator.

More design changes in 1937 included the first factory-built Fordson with a tricycle wheel arrangement. Known as the All-Around, it was built at the request of Ford's American dealers, and most of the tractors were sold in the United States. Other new developments for the standard Model N in 1937 included a change to orange paint, and an oilbath air cleaner instead of the old frost-vulnerable water-washer version. Increasing the compression ratio boosted the power output again, but it also brought reliability problems.

Wartime Paintwork

In 1939, with World War II looming, the Model N paint color changed once more—this time to green. One explanation is that green tractors were a less conspicuous target for enemy aircraft, but another theory is that the Ford factory had plenty of green paint available because of huge contracts to build equipment and vehicles for the British Army. The green Fordsons, which accounted for more than 90 percent of Britain's wartime tractor production, were the end of the line for the Model N, and the new E27N Fordson Major arrived in 1945.

Specifications

Manufacturer: Ford Motor Co.
Location: Dagenham, Essex, England
Model: N
Type: General purpose
Power unit: Ford four-cylinder engine
Power output: 23.24hp (17kw) (paraffin)

Transmission: Three-speed gearbox
Weight: 5,230lb (2,374kg)
Production started: 1929

Left: *During World War II the British Ford factory supplied large numbers of Model N tractors to the armed services, including this example in Royal Air Force colors.*

RUMELY
1930   La Porte, Indiana

RUMELY 6A

Rumely OilPull tractors were one of the outstanding success stories of the period before 1920 when heavyweight models were still popular for plowing the prairies, but when its 6A model was announced in 1930 the company was facing financial problems.

Specifications

Manufacturer: Advance Rumely Thresher Co.

Location: La Porte, Indiana

Model: 6A

Type: General purpose

Power unit: Waukesha six-cylinder engine

Power output: 48.37hp (35.8kw) (maximum)

Transmission: Three-speed gearbox

Weight: 6,370lb (2,892kg)

Production started: 1930

The 6A was a complete break from traditional Rumely design, and if it had been available a few years earlier it might have improved the company's prospects for survival. The slow-revving horizontal engine with two cylinders that had powered thousands of OilPull tractors was replaced on the 6A by a much more modern six-cylinder power unit from Waukesha.

New Engine, New Look

The new engine developed its rated power at a risk 1,365rpm instead of the 470rpm of the OilPull Z 40-60 tractor introduced in the previous year.

The new model was also lighter than earlier models, weighing 6,370lb (2,892kg) instead of the 9,440lb (4,281kg) of the X 25-40 model with comparable power output. The 6A model also looked different from previous versions, mainly because the old-fashioned rectangular tower of the OilPull cooling system had been replaced by an ordinary radiator and fan.

In 1931, the year after the start of 6A tractor production, the Advance Rumely company was taken over by Allis-Chalmers, but this was not the end of the 6A tractor story. During its first production year the 6A had proved to be a popular tractor, and Allis-Chalmers continued to sell it for another three years.

Above: *The 6A with its six-cylinder Waukesha engine and its new up-to-date styling was a bold attempt to restore Rumely's fortunes.*

GARRETT
1930   Leiston, Suffolk, England

GARRETT DIESEL

Below: This Garrett tractor set a world nonstop plowing record. It also helped to prove the fuel efficiency benefits of diesel power.

The 1930 World Tractor Trials held near Oxford, in England, provided the first opportunity to compare the latest diesel-powered tractors with their paraffin and gasoline rivals. The diesels easily won the fuel-efficiency stakes.

Specifications

Manufacturer: Richard Garrett & Sons

Location: Leiston, Suffolk, England

Model: Diesel

Type: General purpose

Power unit: Aveling & Porter four-cylinder diesel engine

Power output: 38hp (28kw)

Transmission: Three-speed gearbox

Weight: 7,300lb (3,314kg)

Production started: 1930

There were five diesel entries, including two from the Agricultural and General Engineers, or AGE group. AGE was formed when a large number of British farm-equipment manufacturers joined forces to match the marketing clout of the big North American companies such as International Harvester and Massey-Harris. It was an imaginative idea, but ended in a financial disaster that crippled some of the member companies.

Diesel Tractors

Probably the biggest AGE achievement was encouraging the development of the two most advanced diesel tractors of their day. They were built by Garretts of Leiston, a long-established steam-engine manufacturer, using four-cylinder engines designed by Blackstone and the Aveling and Porter (A & P) company. The A & P engine was started by an electric motor at a time when most tractor diesels used compressed air or a small gasoline engine, and it was also the most powerful diesel engine in the trials with a rated output of 38hp (28kw).

The A & P diesel-powered Garrett tractor won a silver medal at the 1931 Royal Show; it also established a new world record by plowing nonstop for 977 hours. In spite of these achievements sales figures were disappointing, and production ended in about 1933.

MASSEY-HARRIS

1930 **Racine, Wisconsin**

MASSEY-HARRIS GENERAL PURPOSE

The General Purpose was important because it was the first tractor designed and built by Massey-Harris, and it was also one of the first attempts by a big manufacturer to introduce the benefits of four-wheel drive.

Specifications

Manufacturer: Massey-Harris
Location: Racine, Wisconsin
Model: General purpose
Type: Four-wheel drive rowcrop tractor
Power unit: Hercules four-cylinder engine
Power output: 24.8hp (18.4kw) (maximum)
Transmission: Three-speed gearbox
Weight: 3,940lb (1,789kg)
Production started: 1930

Above: *Years ahead of its time, this Massey-Harris General Purpose tractor offered farmers the benefits of improved traction through the use of four-wheel drive.*

Two-wheel drive—the standard arrangement in the 1930s—is the least efficient way to convert the power of the engine into pulling power at the drawbar, especially in difficult working conditions. In terms of traction efficiency four-wheel drive is midway between two-wheel drive and crawler tracks, but although tracks are best for traction, the steel version available in the 1930s had a number of disadvantages.

Four-wheel Drive

Massey-Harris introduced the General Purpose tractor in 1930. It chose a Hercules four-cylinder engine with almost 25-hp (18.4-kw) maximum output, and electric starting was one of the options. As well as using four-wheel drive through equal-diameter front and rear wheels, Massey-Harris also designed its new tractor for rowcrop work, with 30in (72cm) of clearance under the axles and a generous selection of wheel track settings from 48–76in (116–186cm).

The sales figures were disappointing, probably because few farmers in the 1930s were aware of the benefits of four-wheel drive. An updated version introduced in 1936 and known as the Four-Wheel Drive, with a new vaporizer for burning paraffin and with rubber tires on the options list, did little to revive the flagging sales figures, and production ended in 1936.

INTERNATIONAL HARVESTER
1932 Chicago, Illinois

I.H. FARMALL F-20

The original Farmall Regular had been an outstanding success for the International Harvester company, and the F-20 model that replaced it was an even bigger success. Total deliveries during the seven-year production run starting in 1932 reached almost 150,000, reemphasizing the success of Bert Benjamin's original design.

Below: *The success of the International Farmall design continued during the 1930s with improved models such as the big-selling F-20.*

Specifications

Manufacturer: International Harvester

Location: Chicago, Illinois

Model: Farmall F-20

Type: Rowcrop

Power unit: I.H. four-cylinder engine

Power output: 23hp (17kw) (kerosene fuel)

Transmission: Four-speed gearbox

Weight: 4,545lb (2,063kg)

Production started: 1932

The F-20 was designed to take over from the original Farmall and was powered by basically the same four-cylinder engine with 3.75-in (9.5-cm) bore, 5.0-in (12.7-cm) stroke, and a 1,200rpm speed rating; but there were also significant design changes. These included a power boost of more than 10 percent, bringing the maximum output of the F-20 to 23hp (17kw) when burning paraffin or kerosene.

New Model

Ten years after the original Farmall tractor had been introduced, the new model featured a four-speed gearbox instead of the previous three speeds, and the new model had also put on weight, turning the scales at a total of 4,545lb (2,063kg) instead of the 4,100lb (1,859kg) of its forerunner.

There were also significant additions to the options list for the F-20. These included rubber tires, available from about 1934, and customers who chose this option could also specify alternative gears to provide a faster top speed. There were wide front-axle versions as well, and a power-operated rear implement lift was also introduced as an item at extra cost.

FERGUSON

⚒ **1933 Belfast, Northern Ireland**

FERGUSON BLACK TRACTOR

Harry Ferguson's childhood was spent on the family farm in what is now Northern Ireland, but he disliked the slow pace of working with horses and left home to live in the city of Belfast.

Specifications

Manufacturer: Harry Ferguson	
Location: Belfast, Northern Ireland	
Model: Black Tractor	
Type: General purpose	
Power unit: Hercules four-cylinder gasoline engine	
Power output: 18hp (13.3kw)	
Transmission: Three-speed gearbox	
Weight: N/A	
Production started: 1933	

City life obviously suited him, and he established a successful business repairing and selling cars, but he was also interested in tractor design and added a tractor franchise to his automobile business. Ferguson preferred to be personally involved in any demonstrations to potential tractor customers, and this experience made him aware that a tractor drawbar could be an inefficient way to drag implements through the soil.

The Ferguson System

Ferguson spent the next 15 years developing a new attachment system using hydraulic power and three hitch points. The result was the Ferguson System, still the basis for implement attachment and control on almost every modern wheeled tractor. In the early 1930s the Ferguson's implement attachment and control system was still a novelty, and to demonstrate its benefits he built a special tractor that was completed in 1933. It was the world's first Ferguson System tractor, and it was called the Black Tractor because of the paint finish.

A New Partnership

Harry Ferguson used a Hercules engine, and he bought other equipment from the David Brown Company. David Brown, managing director of the Yorkshire-based engineers, became increasingly interested in the new tractor, and he eventually formed a partnership, with his company building the tractors for Harry Ferguson's company to sell.

Above: *The Black Tractor was built by Harry Ferguson and his team to demonstrate the advantages of the Ferguson System, and it is now in the Science Museum in London.*

BRISTOL
1933   Bradford, Yorkshire, England

BRISTOL 10HP

The Bristol Tractor Co. was established in 1933 to build a small crawler tractor, and the name was chosen for the model because Bristol was where the company expected to build the tractors.

Right: Various 10-hp (7.4-kw) engine options, including a small diesel, were available for the little Bristol crawler tractor, which was equipped with a single-lever steering system.

Specifications

Manufacturer: Bristol Tractor Co.

Location: Bradford, Yorkshire, England

Model: 10hp (7.4kw)

Type: Tracklayer

Power unit: Various including a 10-hp (7.4-kw) Coventry Victor diesel engine

Power output: 10hp (7.4kw)

Transmission: Three-speed gearbox

Weight: 2,540lb (1,153kg)

Production started: 1933

In fact London or Bradford might have been more appropriate names because a last-minute change of plan meant the first tractors were built in London in 1933, followed two years later by a move to Bradford, Yorkshire.

The tractor was described as a 10-hp (7.4-kw) model, but four different engines were used during the 1930s. Production started with an air-cooled Anzani, which was replaced after about 12 months by a twin-cylinder engine made by the Jowett car and van company. Options available from 1935 included a four-cylinder Jowett car engine, and the Bristol company also offered the surprising choice of a small Coventry Victor diesel engine.

Tracks

Bristol chose rubber-jointed tracks, and these were powered through the front sprocket on each side. The steering was operated by differential brakes controlled by a single lever that also carried the twist-grip control for the throttle. The design included an implement lift at the rear of the tractor, and this was operated manually by using a ratchet system.

After the end of the war in 1945 the assets of the Bristol company were bought by one of the biggest distributors of Austin cars. They gave the company a new lease of life, providing much-needed investment and replacing the Jowett engine with a more powerful Austin unit.

FATE-ROOT-HEATH
1933   Plymouth, Ohio

SILVER KING

The Fate-Root-Heath company of Plymouth, Ohio, chose a lightweight model when it moved into the tractor market in 1933. It was the company's first tractor venture and it was named the Silver King. The power unit chosen was the popular Hercules IXA, a four-cylinder engine with a rated output of 20hp (14.8kw).

Left: *The Silver King offered many small-acreage farms an opportunity to make the change from horses or mules to tractor power.*

Specifications

Manufacturer: Fate-Root-Heath Co.	
Location: Plymouth, Ohio	
Model: Silver King	
Type: General purpose	
Power unit: Hercules four-cylinder gasoline engine	
Power output: 20hp (14.8kw)	
Transmission: Four-speed gearbox	
Weight: N/A	
Production started: 1933	

Many of the companies moving into tractor production for the first time misjudge the market and encounter serious problems, but the new Silver King tractor was a first-time success. There was a growing demand in the early 1930s for small, economical models to suit the thousands of farmers buying their first tractor to replace horses or mules, and the Silver King was a popular choice at a time when some of the leading manufacturers had still not developed their own lightweight tractors.

Tricycle Version
Silver King production started with the standard four-wheel model, and it was among the first tractors offered with the recently developed rubber tires.

A slightly bigger engine was fitted to the 1936 model, and at the same time a new tricycle version was introduced. The three-wheeler was tested in Nebraska, where it developed 19.74hp (14.7kw) in the brake test and achieved a top speed of 25mph (40km/h) in fourth gear.

The company's sales were hit by increasing competition as more manufacturers moved into the lightweight end of the market, and new models announced by Silver King in 1940 failed to recapture the company's earlier success. Production ended in the 1950s.

ALLIS-CHALMERS

1933 Milwaukee, Wisconsin

ALLIS-CHALMERS WC

The WC model was introduced by Allis-Chalmers to capture a share of the highly important rowcrop-tractor market in the United States and Canada, and it was a big success. It was announced in 1933, and the sales total had passed the 170,000 mark when production ended in 1948.

Above: *This front view shows the offset steering position, the dual front wheels, and the high clearance under the rear axle.*

Right: *The WC's profile shared some similarities with Allis-Chalmers Model B rowcrop tractor.*

Specifications

Manufacturer: Allis-Chalmers Manufacturing
Location: Milwaukee, Wisconsin
Model: WC
Type: Rowcrop
Power unit: Allis-Chalmers four-cylinder engine
Power output: 21hp (15.5kw)
Transmission: Four-speed gearbox
Weight: 3,190lb (1,448kg)
Production started: 1933

Allis-Chalmers also offered a WF version with a full-width front axle to give a standard wheel layout, but the WC rowcrop model outsold the WF by a 20 to 1 ratio, providing an example of how important the rowcrop-tractor market is in North America.

Two-Plow Tractor

The WC model was described as a two-plow tractor—designed to turn two furrows—and it was powered by an Allis-Chalmers–built four-cylinder engine. It was an unusual design because the piston bore and stroke were 4.0in (10.1cm), and an engine with this feature is sometimes described, misleadingly, as "square." The rated power output was just under 21hp (15.5kw), and when the WC was tested in Nebraska it reached 21.48hp (16.2kw) in the maximum-load test.

When the WC made its first appearance the front-end styling was flat, but in 1938 the Allis-Chalmers stylists introduced a more up-to-date streamlined appearance with a rounded grille in front of the radiator, and the tractor in the photograph here was built after the new look was introduced.

INTERNATIONAL HARVESTER
1934   Chicago, Illinois

I.H. MCCORMICK W-30

Under the International Harvester dual-range policy, the W-30 was the McCormick standard tread equivalent of the Farmall F-30 rowcrop model. Maintaining both the McCormick and the Farmall ranges with their own separate models was a policy that appears to have been successful during the 1930s. Both ranges achieved big sales volumes, helping to keep I.H. at the top of the sales charts in the USA and worldwide.

Left: *The W-30 was part of International Harvester's McCormick-Deering range; its engine was shared with the Farmall series F-30.*

Specifications

Manufacturer: International Harvester	
Location: Chicago, Illinois	
Model: W-30	
Type: General purpose	
Power unit: I.H. four-cylinder gasoline/paraffin engine	
Power output: 33.26hp (24.6kw)	
Transmission: Three-speed gearbox	
Weight: 5,575lb (2,531kg)	
Production started: 1934	

Although the W-30 was announced in 1932, production was delayed and did not start until 1934, and it peaked at 8,000 in 1937. The power unit shared by the W-30, and the F-30 was a four-cylinder engine with 4.25-in (10.8-cm) bore and 5.0-in (12.7-cm) stroke. The maximum output for the W-30 version when tested in Nebraska was 33.26hp (24.6kw).

Transmission
One important mechanical difference was the transmission, as W-30 customers had to make do with a three-speed gearbox while those choosing the Farmall model had the benefit of four speeds. This is, in fact, a logical arrangement because precise control over working speeds is usually more important for rowcrop work than for general arable work.

I.H. offered the W-30 in both standard and orchard versions. Rubber tires, electric lights, and a power takeoff were on the list of extra cost options, and customers who specified a power-takeoff shaft were charged an extra $14, which sounds like a bargain.

CATERPILLAR
✖ 1934   Peoria, Illinois

CATERPILLAR DIESEL FORTY

Diesel engines were a big success for the Caterpillar company, and by the mid-1930s it offered a wide choice of diesel-powered tracklayers alongside its spark ignition models. Production of the Diesel Forty lasted from 1934 to 1936, making it one of the rarer models, and a favorite among enthusiasts.

Above: Diesel engines achieved their biggest success with tracklayers, and Caterpillar offered the widest range of models by the mid-1930s.

Right: Fuel-consumption figures for Caterpillar's Diesel Forty model showed big gains in fuel efficiency when compared with the standard gasoline version.

Specifications

Manufacturer: Caterpillar Tractor Co.	
Location: Peoria, Illinois	
Model: Forty Diesel	
Type: Tracklayer	
Power unit: Three-cylinder diesel engine	
Power output: 56hp (41.44kw)	
Transmission: Four-speed gearbox	
Weight: 15,642lb (7,100kg)	
Production started: 1934	

The performance figure for the various engine types in the Forty model provide a good example of the extra economy available when burning diesel. The gasoline-powered Forty model, available at the same time, produced 48.57hp (36.2kw) at 1,000rpm in the one-hour maximum load test in Nebraska, using 5.94 gallons (22.6 liters) of fuel. Maximum output of the Diesel Forty in the same test was 56.05hp (41.8kw), but fuel consumption fell to only 4.14 gallons (14.4 liters). Data for diesel models tested in Nebraska seems to have done little to stimulate interest in diesel power for wheeled tractors.

Weight

The Forty series Nebraska test results also highlight another feature of diesel power. The weight of the gasoline-powered Forty was a hefty 13,625lb (6,180kg), but this figure increased to 15,642lb (7,100kg) for the Diesel, with the extra weight of the engine plus the additional gasoline-powered starter motor accounting for most of the difference.

The Forty and Diesel Forty were both equipped with a four-speed gearbox, and the power unit for both was a four-cylinder engine with, for the diesel version a bore and stroke of 5.75 x 8in (14.6 x 20.3cm).

SUPERLANDINI

🔧 **1934 Fabbrico, Italy**

SUPERLANDINI

Hot-bulb engines for tractors usually have a single horizontal cylinder with a low compression ratio. They operate on a two-stroke cycle, and the typical starting process is to heat the cylinder head with a blowlamp until it is hot enough to ignite the fuel. This action is followed by cranking the engine by turning the flywheel.

Above: *The SuperLandini model name was cast into the front of the radiator header tank on Italy's most powerful semidiesel tractor.*

Specifications

Manufacturer: Giovanni Landini & Figli

Location: Fabbrico, Italy

Model: SuperLandini

Type: General purpose

Power unit: Hot-bulb engine

Power output: 48hp (35.52kw)

Transmission: Three-speed gearbox

Weight: 8,030lb (3,650kg)

Production started: 1934

The complicated starting process, together with the high vibration levels and low power output, are disadvantages. But hot-bulb engines also have a number of significant attractions that made them long-term favorites in some European countries. They burn virtually any liquid fuel, including old cooking oil and waste sump oil, and their reliability is often good because there are few moving parts and no electrical systems to cause problems.

Power

Landini was Italy's leading hot-bulb tractor manufacturer and its most impressive model was the SuperLandini. Production started in 1934 when the 48-hp (35.52-kw) maximum output made it one of Europe's most powerful tractors, and 3,400 were built before the last SuperLandini left the factory in 1951.

Because of the poor efficiency of hot-bulb or semidiesel engines, the SuperLandini needed a single cylinder with a massive 740.5 cubic inches (12.2 liters) capacity to achieve its 48hp (35.52kw) at 620rpm.

This compares with 270hp (201kw) from the 455.25-cubic-inch (7.5-liter), six-cylinder diesel engine that powers the latest Canadian-built Landini Starland tractor.

Above, left: *With a single cylinder of 740.5 cubic inches (12.2 liters) capacity, the semidiesel engine on the SuperLandini was one of the biggest of its type.*

INTERNATIONAL HARVESTER
1934   Chicago, Illinois

I.H. MCCORMICK W-12

Demand for small tractors grew rapidly during the late 1930s, but competition also increased, and the little W-12 model from the International Harvester McCormick range was one of the tractors that lost out in the battle for sales.

Right: *This is the standard version of International Harvester's lightweight W-12 model, but it was also available in orchard and fairway or amenity versions.*

Specifications

Manufacturer: International Harvester

Location: Chicago, Illinois

Model: W-12

Type: General purpose

Power unit: I.H. four-cylinder engine

Power output: 17.65hp (13kw) (gasoline)

Transmission: Three-speed gearbox

Weight: 3,360lb (1,525kg)

Production started: 1934

The first W-12s arrived in 1934, and production ended after four years when only 3,617 of the standard version had been built. In addition the orchard model, known as the 0-12, accounted for almost 2,400 sales between 1935 and 1938, and the Fairway-12 model designed for golf courses and other amenity areas notched up 600 sales over the same period.

By International Harvester standards W-12 sales figures were poor, and they were dwarfed by the 120,000 sales achieved by the I.H. Farmall F-12 using the same engine.

The four-cylinder engine, available in gasoline- and paraffin-burning versions, had a 3-in (7.6-cm) bore and 4-in (10.1-cm) stroke. Top output figures when the W-12 was tested in Nebraska were 17.65hp (13kw) for the gasoline version and 15.28hp (11.4kw) on paraffin.

Speed

The W-12, equipped with a three-speed gearbox, is another example of manufacturers allowing faster travel speeds for tractors with rubber tires. The maximum travel speed for the standard model, which could be supplied in both steel-wheel and rubber-tire versions, was a sedate 4.25mph (6.8km/h), but this increased to 7.5mph (12km/h) for the orchard model, which was not available with steel wheels.

JOHN DEERE

⚒ 1934 Waterloo, Iowa

JOHN DEERE MODEL A

The John Deere Model A was a small tractor designed for rowcrop work, and it quickly became one of the most popular of all the John Deere two-cylinder models. The tractor was available in a wide range of versions to meet special crop requirements.

Production started in 1934, and the design included a number of features that put the Model A ahead of most of its competitors. It was the first production tractor available with a hydraulic lift to raise and lower implements, narrowly beating the Ferguson Model A—although the John Deere version lacked the all-important three-point linkage and draft control features included in Harry Ferguson's hydraulically operated lift system.

Wheel Settings

Another Model A feature was the splined rear axle to simplify altering the wheel settings, an important improvement for farmers growing a wide range of crops with different row centers. The transmission casing design was improved to give extra clearance when working with mid-mounted equipment, and the specification also included a four-speed gearbox instead of the three speeds on John Deere's earlier General

Above, top: The small fuel tank on the end of the main tank was for gasoline. Because kerosene would not burn in a cold engine, the tractor was started and warmed up on gasoline.

Above: Model A tractors, like this AR or "regular" model, were available with rubber tires, the first John Deere tractors to include this option.

Purpose or GP model. The A was also the first John Deere tractor to be offered with the choice of steel wheels or rubber tires.

The first production Model As were equipped with twin front wheels, but the AN version with a single front wheel and the AW with a wide, adjustable front axle were available during the second production year.

More special models followed, including the ANH and AWH high-clearance versions, both equipped with bigger diameter wheels to raise the axle height.

The AR, or "regular," version of the Model A with a standard four-wheel layout was introduced in 1935, and this model was also produced in an industrial, or AI, version and an orchard, or AO, specification.

Power Output

When the Model A made its first appearance at the Nebraska test center in 1934 the power output figures were 24.71hp (18.4kw) in the one-hour belt test with 16.31hp (12.2kw) developed at the drawbar in the 10-hour rated load test. At this time the twin cylinders of the A series engine had bore and stroke measurements of 5.5in (13.9cm) and 6.5in (16.5cm), respectively, but the capacity was later increased by adding 0.25in (6mm) to the stroke.

The first big external change for the Model A was the addition of styling in 1938, and this was followed by the addition of a new six-speed transmission using a three-speed gearbox with high and low ratios. The last Model A tractor rolled off the production line in 1952.

Specifications

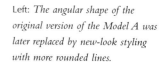

Manufacturer: Deere & Co.
Location: Waterloo, Iowa
Model: A
Type: Rowcrop
Power unit: John Deere two-cylinder horizontal engine
Power output: 25hp (18.5kw)
Transmission: Four-speed gearbox
Weight: 4,059lb (1,843kg)
Production started: 1934

Left: *The angular shape of the original version of the Model A was later replaced by new-look styling with more rounded lines.*

ALLIS-CHALMERS

1935 Milwaukee, Wisconsin

ALLIS-CHALMERS M

The American market for medium- and large-capacity crawler tractors during the 1920s and 1930s was dominated by Caterpillar and Cletrac, but there were also some smaller manufacturers that achieved success on a more limited scale, and these included the Monarch Tractor Co. of Watertown, Wisconsin.

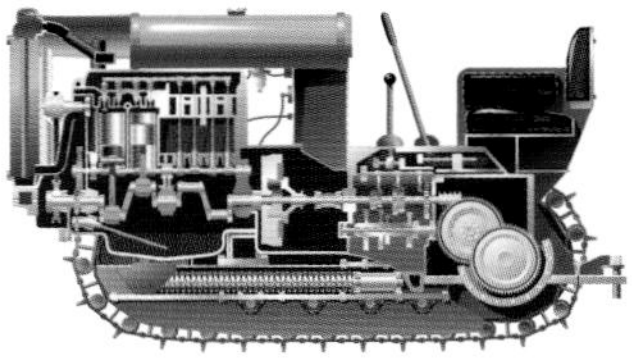

Above: *The engine in this sectioned picture of the Model M tracklayer is the same four-cylinder unit that powered the Model U tractor.*

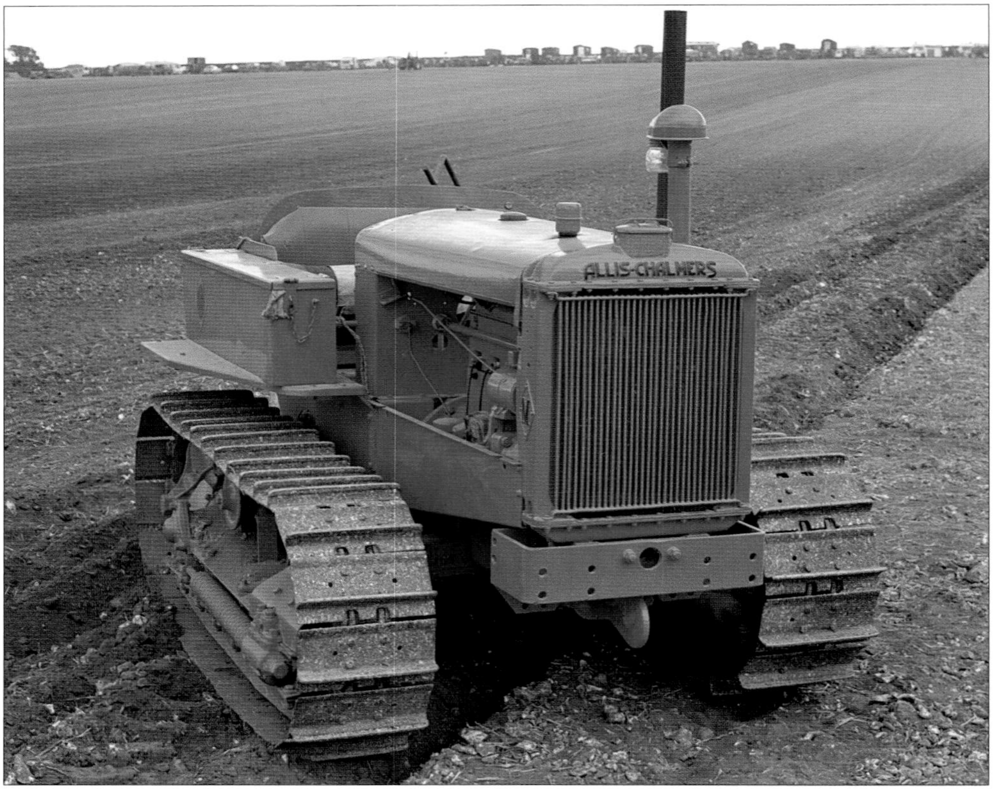

Above, left: *Buying the Monarch Tractor Co. in 1928 was an opportunity for Allis-Chalmers to expand into the lucrative crawler-tractor market.*

Specifications

Manufacturer: Allis-Chalmers
Location: Milwaukee, Wisconsin
Model: M
Type: Tracklayer
Power unit: A-C four-cylinder engine
Power output: 31.8hp (23.5kw)
Transmission: Four-speed gearbox
Weight: 6,855lb (3,108kw)
Production started: 1935

In spite of some successes and a good reputation in the crawler-tractor market, the company ran into increasing financial problems during the late 1920s. This was partly due to the general economic problems and a slump in tractor sales, and in 1928 the Monarch company was taken over by Allis-Chalmers. Under the new ownership, the Monarch line soon lost its separate identity, and the Monarch name above the radiator grille soon disappeared to be replaced by Allis-Chalmers.

As well as sharing the Allis-Chalmers name, some of the tracklayers introduced in the 1930s also used Allis-Chalmer engines, and the new model announced in 1935 was equipped with the same four-cylinder engine that also powered the Allis-Chalmers Model U tractors.

The rated engine output for the crawler model was 31.8hp (23.5kw), and the four-speed gearbox on the Model M provided a 4.15mph (6.7km/h) top speed.

Weight

The weight of the Model M was 6,855lb (3,108kg) compared with 5,030lb (2,281kg) for the similarly powered Model U on steel wheels, and it was the crawler model's running gear that caused most of the weight difference.

JOHN DEERE
1936 Waterloo, Iowa

JOHN DEERE MODEL AO STREAMLINED

John Deere's special orchard tractors were modified to provide a smoother outline to avoid snagging branches when working near trees, but the smoothest of all was the streamlined version of the Model A orchard model.

Right: *John Deere's Streamlined version of the Model A orchard tractor is one of the most distinctively styled tractors of the 1930s and remains very much a favorite with John Deere enthusiasts.*

Specifications

Manufacturer: Deere & Co.

Location: Waterloo, Iowa

Model: AO Streamlined

Type: Orchard tractor

Power unit: Deere two-cylinder horizontal engine

Power output: 25hp (18.5kw)

Transmission: Four-speed gearbox

Weight: N/A

Production started: 1936

Production of the AO Streamlined started in 1936 and continued for only four years, and because of the small production total plus the attractive and highly distinctive special styling it is a popular model with John Deere enthusiasts.

Streamlining
The smooth shape was emphasized in one memorable advertisement that portrayed the streamlined orchard tractor as a racing car. The shape was achieved by having a 53-in (1.35-m) maximum overall height and by eliminating the usual projections such as upright exhaust and air intake pipes above the engine compartment.

Overall width was less than 56in (1.42m), making the streamlined AO slim enough for working in a vineyard, the makers claimed.

The mechanical specification is similar to the early versions of the ordinary Model A, but this was the only engine used in the tractor because production of the Streamlined model ended before the standard tractor's bigger capacity engine became available in 1941. The Streamlined tractor also missed out on the six-speed gearbox introduced on the A range starting in 1940; however, customers were offered the option of choosing rubber tires or steel wheels on their orchard tractor.

FERGUSON

🔧 **1936   Huddersfield, Yorkshire, England**

FERGUSON MODEL A

This was the tractor that followed the agreement between Harry Ferguson and David Brown, and although its correct name is the Ferguson Model A it is often referred to as the Ferguson-Brown.

Under the terms of the agreement between the two, Harry Ferguson retained strict control over the design of the new tractor and the marketing program, while David Brown's company was responsible for its manufacturing. Ferguson based the design on the Black Tractor, but the color was changed to battleship gray, and this was the color he continued to specify for all the production tractors for which he retained control.

Design

Harry Ferguson's design included, of course, his three-point linkage attachment system for mounted equipment. The Ferguson name in its distinctive script appeared prominently on the casting above the radiator grille, while the David Brown company name was relegated to a small plate attached to the base of the grille. Production started in 1936, using a Coventry Climax E engine which developed up to 20hp

Above: Based closely on the design of the Black Tractor, the Ferguson Model A was the first production tractor to include the Ferguson System hydraulics and rear linkage.

(14.8kw) instead of the Hercules power unit used previously. After the first 500 tractors were built the Coventry Climax was replaced by a 122-ci (2,010-cc) engine designed and built by the David Brown company.

In spite of its compact size and modest power, the new tractor performed well, helped by the three-point linkage, which improved traction efficiency in difficult conditions by transferring more of the weight of a mounted implement on to the rear wheels.

Sales Problems

Unfortunately the sales figures did not match the Model A's performance in the field, and the factory was left with ever-mounting stock of unsold tractors.

Price was one of the problems. The price of a Ferguson in 1936 was £224, compared with the bigger, more powerful Model N Fordson, which was available for £140. Farmers who chose a Ferguson had to buy special implements to suit the three-point linkage, and these were priced at £28 each, but the Fordson could be used with standard equipment that was already available on many farms.

The light weight of the new tractor was also a problem because some farmers were skeptical that the Model A could be as durable as a conventional tractor.

David Brown wanted design improvements including more power and a four-speed gearbox, but Harry Ferguson rejected the request. The situation was resolved only when Harry Ferguson pulled out of the agreement and entered a new partnership with Henry Ford, leaving David Brown with a stock of unsold Model As.

Specifications

Manufacturer: David Brown Tractors
Location: Huddersfield, Yorkshire, England
Model: Ferguson Type A
Type: General purpose
Power unit: Coventry Climax four-cylinder engine
Power output: 20hp (14.8kw)
Transmission: Three-speed gearbox
Weight: 1,848lb (839kg)
Production started: 1936

Below: *At the time of writing the Model A pictured on this page and the previous page is in the Massey Ferguson Heritage Centre at the former Banner Lane factory, in Coventry, in England.*

CASE

⚒ **1936   Racine, Wisconsin**

CASE MODEL R

The Case company was quick to appreciate the importance of good styling, and the Model R is a fine example. The appearance is neat and well balanced, and the design of the radiator grille is distinctive and eye-catching, having been inspired by the shape of an ear of wheat, according to one theory.

Above: *The distinctive pattern on the Model R radiator grille is said to have been based on the shape of an ear of wheat.*

Specifications

Manufacturer: J. I. Case	
Location: Racine, Wisconsin	
Model: R	
Type: General purpose	
Power unit: Waukesha L-head engine	
Power output: 20hp (14.8kw)	
Transmission: Three-speed gearbox	
Weight: 4,140lb (1,880kg)	
Production started: 1936	

Later versions of the Model R also benefit from the new Flambeau Red paint color introduced by Case in 1939 to make its tractor range more eye-catching.

Case announced the Model R in 1936 to fill a gap at the lower end of the power scale. Lacking a suitable power unit of its own, Case's choice for the Model R was a gasoline engine supplied by Waukesha and developing about 20hp (14.8kw) at 1,400rpm. The power was delivered through a three-speed gearbox. Rubber tires were included on the options list for the Model R.

Versions

Three versions of the Model R were available. These were the standard-tread Model R, the RC with a tricycle-wheel layout, and an industrial model identified as the RI. The tractors were introduced at a time when the Case company was beginning to recover from financial difficulties and management problems, and the little R series tractors played their part in the recovery.

Production of the Model R continued until 1940, when it was phased out to make way for the new V-series tractors.

Above, left: *A standard-tread version of the Case Model R finished in the Flambeau Red paint finish adopted by Case in 1939 to give its tractors more visual appeal.*

RANSOMES
⚒ 1936 Ipswich, Suffolk, England

RANSOMES MG TRACKLAYERS

Ransomes was one of the leading manufacturers of agricultural steam engines during the nineteenth century, but its most notable success in the tractor market was on a much more modest scale.

Right: *Providing basic tractor power on a small scale, the little Ransomes MG crawler tractor was available in various versions for 30 years.*

Above: *The Ransomes decal on the front of the fuel tank of its MG series "motor cultivator," or market-garden tractor.*

Specifications

Manufacturer: Ransomes, Sims and Jefferies
Location: Ipswich, Suffolk, England
Model: MG
Type: Tracklayer
Power unit: Sturmey-Archer single-cylinder engine
Power output: 4.25hp (3.3kw)
Transmission: Single speed forward and reverse
Weight: N/A
Production started: 1936

The Ransomes MG was a mini-sized crawler tractor designed mainly for market gardens. The first production version, called the MG2, was available in 1936 powered by a 37-ci (600-cc) single-cylinder Sturmey-Archer engine. The design included a centrifugal clutch delivering the power through reduction gears, and a pair of crown wheels, one for forward travel and the other for reverse.

Tracks

The tracks were a Roadless design with rubber joints, and the width between track centers could be adjusted. For rowcrop work a set of crop dividers to push plants away from the tracks and minimize damage was on the options

list, and Ransomes also produced a wide range of special implements to suit the small size and modest power of the MG.

MG2 production continued until 1949 when the MG5 version arrived. The new model was powered by a 37-ci (600-cc) Ransomes side-valve engine producing up to 4hp (2.98kw), and this was followed by the diesel-powered MG40. Approximately 15,000 MG tractors were built during the 30-year production run, and, although most of them were used in small-scale crop production, others were used for a varied range of jobs including harvesting salt in East Africa, and some were exported to Holland where their small size allowed them to be ferried across drainage dykes on small boats.

HSCS

1936 **Budapest, Hungary**

HSCS R-30-35

Hungary's leading tractor manufacturer during the 1920s and 1930s was the Budapest-based company known as Hofherr-Schrantz Clayton-Shuttleworth. Fortunately the name was abbreviated to HSCS.

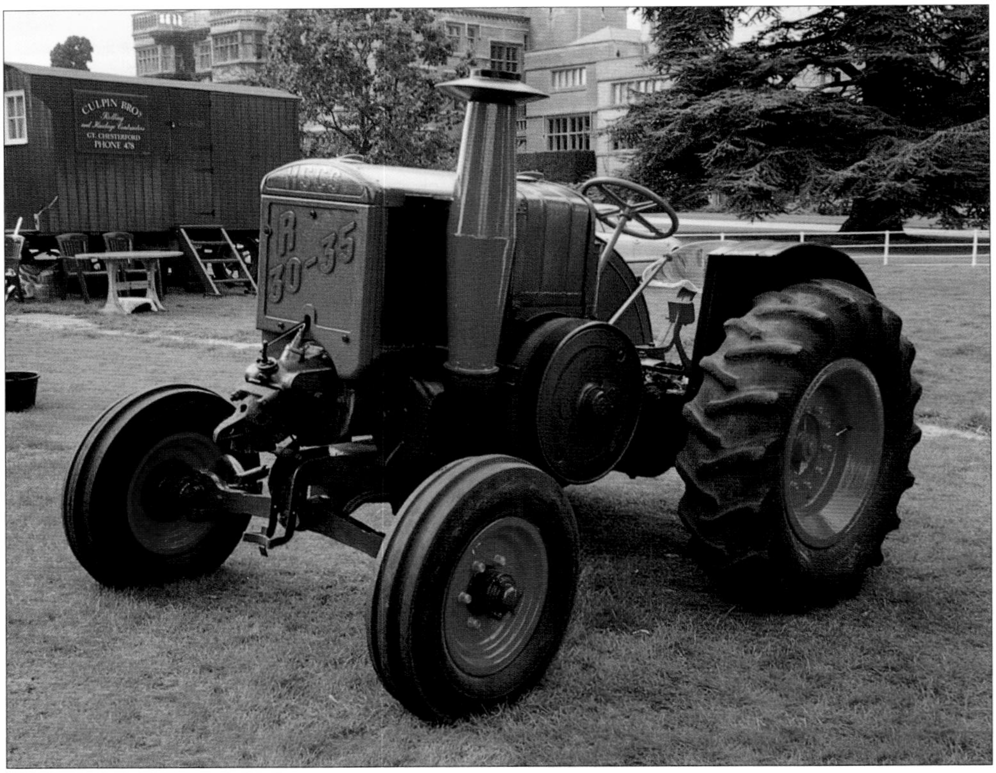

Specifications

Manufacturer: Hofherr-Schrantz Clayton-Shuttleworth
Location: Budapest, Hungary
Model: R-30-35
Type: General purpose
Power unit: Hot-bulb engine
Power output: 35hp (26kw)
Transmission: Three-speed gearbox
Weight: N/A
Production started: 1936

Above: *Like many of their German and Italian rivals, the HSCS company in Hungary specialized in semidiesel tractor production during the 1930s.*

The company, established in 1912, expanded from general farm-machinery production to building stationary engines. It built its first prototype tractor in 1923, and in 1924 it built what was the first in a long line of tractors with a semidiesel engine.

SemiDiesel Engine

The single-cylinder semidiesel engine with blowlamp starting was the type of engine that powered the K-35 series tractors. These were introduced in 1930 with a 35-hp (26-kw) version of the engine, and this was updated to produce the R-30-35 model, one of a batch of new models HSCS introduced in 1936. The R-30-35 was produced in both wheeled and tracklaying versions, and the 35-hp (26-kw) rated output made it a popular mid-range model. As well as producing sales in Hungary and other mid-European countries, HSCS achieved some success in other export markets, including Australia.

R-30-35 series tractors were available until tractor production was disrupted by the war in the early 1940s. Under the communist regime in Hungary the company name was changed to Red Star Tractor, perhaps because the original name was considered to have undesirable capitalist associations. In the late 1950s the brand name was changed once more, this time to Dutra—a somewhat unimaginative abbreviation of "dumper" and "tractor."

MINNEAPOLIS-MOLINE
1937 Minneapolis, Minnesota

MINNEAPOLIS-MOLINE Z SERIES

Minneapolis-Moline joined the 1930s fashion for bright colors with an eye-catching shade of yellow it called Prairie Gold, plus a bright shade of red for the wheels and radiator grille.

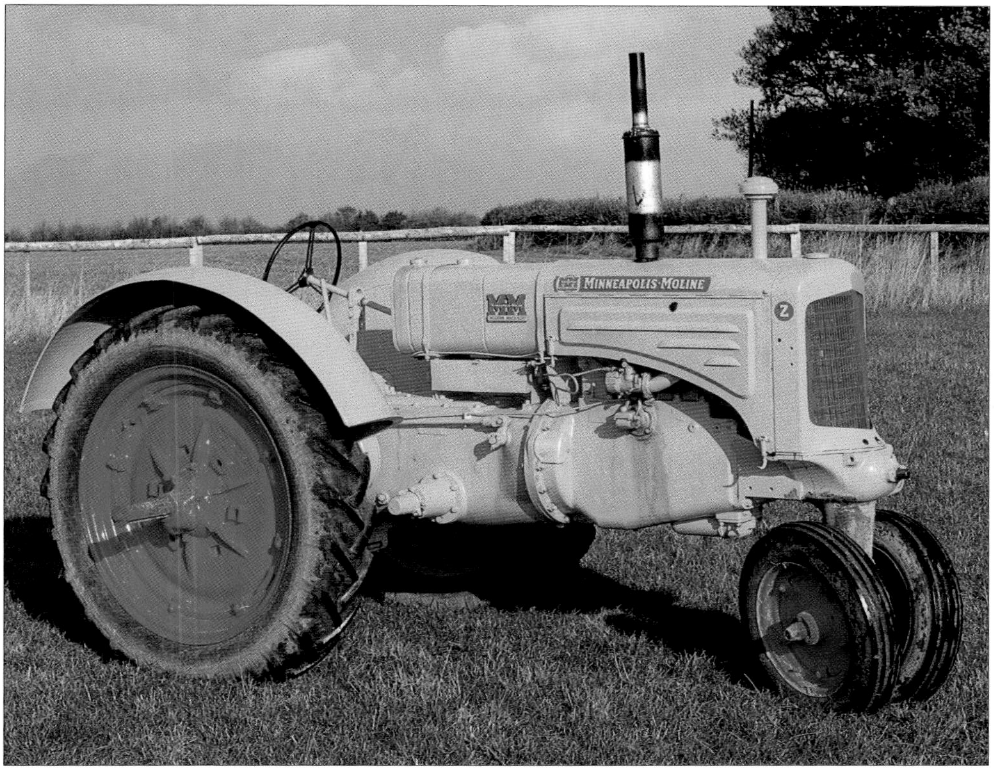

Right: *Minneapolis-Moline's new Prairie Gold color was the most conspicuous of the new paint finishes adopted by tractor manufacturers in the 1930s.*

Specifications

Manufacturer: Minneapolis-Moline
Location: Minneapolis, Minnesota
Model: Z series
Types: General purpose and rowcrop
Power unit: MM four-cylinder engine
Power output: 31hp (22.9kw)
Transmission: Five-speed gearbox
Weight: N/A
Production started: 1937

The Z series of tractors announced in 1937 featured the new Minneapolis-Moline colors, and the series also used an unusual engine designed by Minneapolis-Moline. This was a four-cylinder unit with the cylinders cast in two pairs, and part of the cylinder head could be adjusted in order to vary the compression ratio.

By altering the compression ratio the engine could be adjusted to burn fuels with different octane levels more efficiently, providing an ingenious answer to the wide variation in fuel quality that was causing considerable problems for farmers, particularly in the United States.

Unusual Features

Another unusual feature of the engine was the location of the inlet and outlet valves, which were both positioned horizontally in the block where they were operated by rocker arms.

The gearbox was another unusual feature, providing the choice of five ratios at a time when some manufacturers were still offering a basic three-speed box. The fifth gear on the MM Z series produced what was then an unusually fast top speed of 14.3mph (23km/h), but customers were warned that this was reserved for tractors equipped with rubber tires and should not be used with steel wheels.

ALLIS-CHALMERS

1937 Milwaukee, Wisconsin

ALLIS-CHALMERS MODEL B

The Allis-Chalmers entry in the late 1930s competition for small tractor sales was the popular Model B. It was a big success, with sales totaling more than 127,000 tractors during a 20-year production run starting in 1937, and the total included some Model B tractors built in England from 1947.

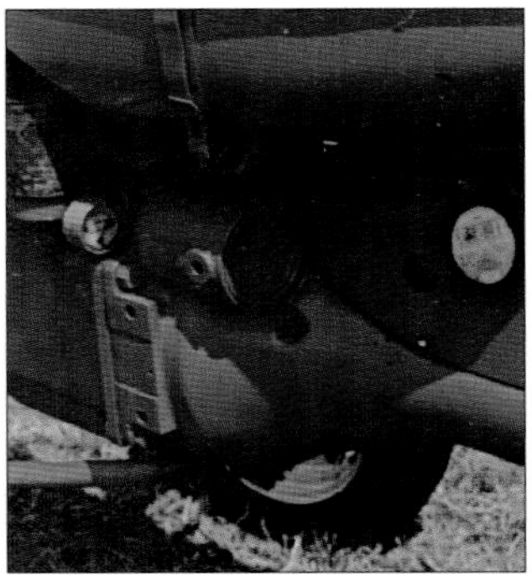

Above, top: *The Allis-Chalmers B starting handle was mounted under the rear of the fuel tank, where it was easily accessible when needed.*

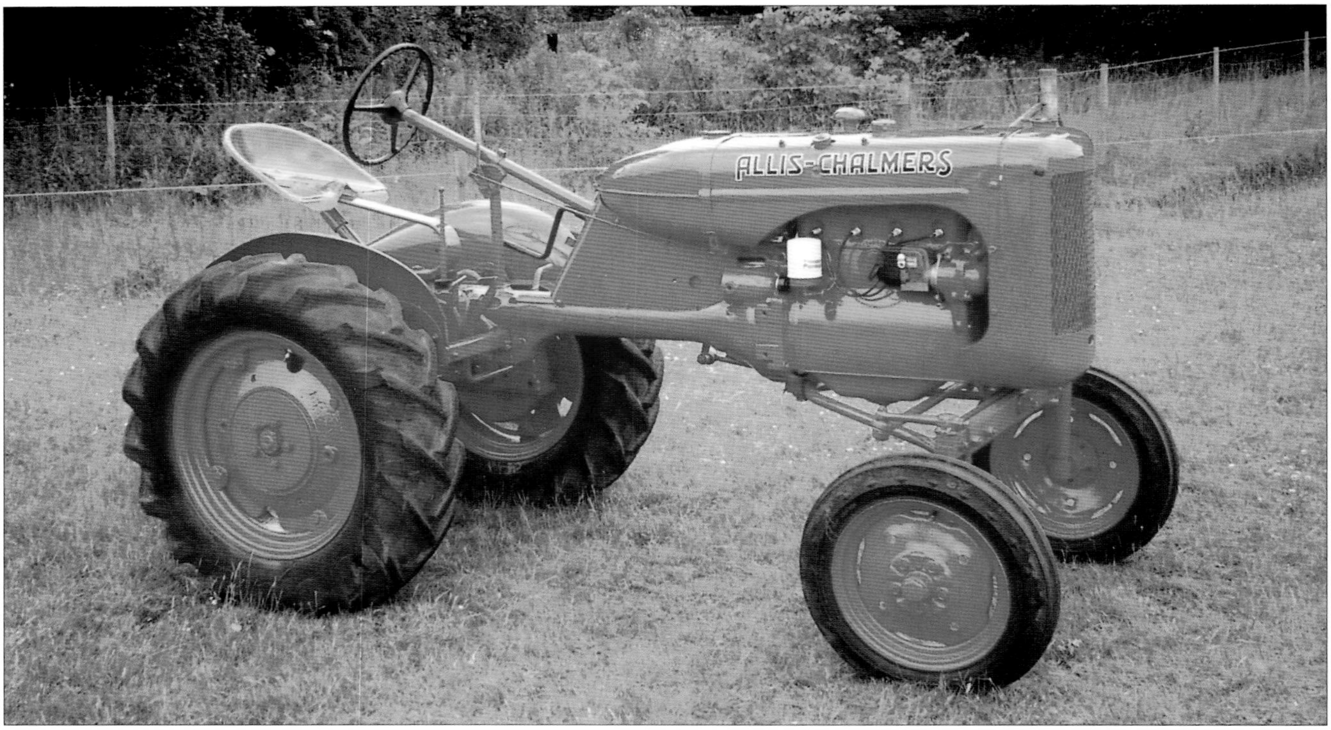

Above: *With its neat styling and good design features for rowcrop work, the Allis-Chalmers Model B was popular throughout the 1940s.*

Some of the Model B's success was due to its versatile design. It was a popular general-purpose tractor on livestock farms, with a turning circle of 7ft 8in (2.3m) to provide good maneuverability, but it was also designed for rowcrop work, and this was an important factor in its sales success.

The design included plenty of underside clearance to provide space for mid-mounted equipment such as inter-row hoes, and the distinctive slimline shape allowed the driver a good view for accurately steering between the crop rows. There was also a generous amount of wheel track adjustment with settings available from 40in to 52in (102cm to 132cm) to suit crops grown on different row widths.

Engine

Allis-Chalmers built a four-cylinder engine for the Model B, with a bore and stroke of 3.25in by 3.5in (8.3cm by 8.9cm) for tractors built before 1944. Engine capacity was increased slightly by using a wider cylinder bore for tractors built from 1944 until production of the Model B ended in 1957. Power output for the smaller engine was 14hp (10kw) at the 1,400rpm rated engine speed, but this was increased to 16hp (12kw) for the later version.

A three-speed gearbox provided a maximum travel speed of 7.75mph (12.5km/h) at the rated engine rpm, and driver comfort on later versions was improved by providing a fully padded seat cushion and backrest instead of the basic metal-pan seat mounted on a simple spring included in the earlier specification. As well as offering more power, later versions of the Model B were also equipped with additional features such as a hydraulically operated implement lift instead of the standard mechanical version, and electric lights were added to the options list.

UK Production

Model B popularity extended to British farms, where it sold so well that the Allis-Chalmers company joined other leading North American tractor manufacturers by setting up a UK assembly plant. Production started in 1947, and a diesel version powered by a Perkins P3 engine was available in the UK starting in 1953.

In addition to the diesel option, UK models were available with the choice of steel wheels or rubber tires, and the options list also included a three-speed belt pulley and a power-takeoff kit.

Specifications

Manufacturer: Allis-Chalmers
Location: Milwaukee, Wisconsin
Model: B
Type: Rowcrop
Power unit: Allis-Chalmers four-cylinder engine
Power output: 14hp (10kw) (early version)
Transmission: Three-speed gearbox

Weight: 2,620lb (1,189kg)
Production started: 1937

Below: An important feature of the Model B design was the space beneath the engine and transmission for carrying mid-mounted hoes and other inter-row equipment.

JOHN DEERE
⚒ 1937   Moline, Illinois

JOHN DEERE MODEL L

Horizontal twin-cylinder engines powered almost every John Deere tractor built before 1960, but there were just a few exceptions.

Specifications

Manufacturer:	Deere & Co.
Location:	Moline, Illinois
Model:	L
Type:	General purpose
Power unit:	Hercules two-cylinder vertical engine
Power output:	9hp (6.7kw)
Transmission:	Three-speed gearbox
Weight:	2,180lb (990kg)
Production started:	1937

The power unit for the mini-sized Model L tractor announced in 1937 was a twin-cylinder design, but this time the cylinders were vertical instead of horizontal and, when Model L production started, the engine was not a John Deere unit, but was bought in from Hercules. The cylinder dimensions were 3.25-in (8.25-cm) bore and 4-in (10.1-cm) stroke, and the power output was 9hp (6.7kw) with about 7hp (5.2kw) available at the drawbar. The water-cooled engine developed its rated power at 1,550rpm, but it could be modified to boost the rpm figure to 2,400 to give a 12-mph (19.3-km/h) road speed. Model L tractors built starting in 1941 until production ended in 1946 were powered by a John Deere engine that shared the same cylinder dimensions as the original Hercules unit.

Other Model L developments included a new "styled" model in 1938 with more rounded lines, and there was also an industrial LI model available from 1938. The LI, finished in a bright yellow paint color, sold mainly for grass-cutting jobs on roadside verges and amenity areas such as golf courses.

Above: Early versions of John Deere's Model L tractor were powered by a vertical two-cylinder Hercules engine instead of the usual John Deere horizontal design.

OLIVER
✂ **1937   Charles City, Iowa**

OLIVER 80 STANDARD

The rowcrop and standard versions of the 80 series tractor were added to the Oliver range in 1937, and both were based on the industrial and orchard models that were introduced originally in 1930.

Above: *By 1938 Oliver was offering the 80 Standard and Orchard models in steel wheel and rubber tire versions.*

Right: *A standard version of the Oliver 80 tractor powered by a four-cylinder spark ignition engine. The diesel version was introduced in 1940.*

Specifications

Manufacturer: Oliver Farm Equipment Co.
Location: Charles City, Iowa
Model: 80 Standard
Type: General purpose
Power unit: Oliver four-cylinder engine
Power output: 35hp (26kw)
Transmission: Four-speed gearbox
Weight: 8,145lb (3,698kg)
Production started: 1937

The power unit for the 80 series was an Oliver four-cylinder engine with an I-head valve layout and a 4.5-in (11.4-cm) by 5.25-in (13.3-cm) bore and stroke.

The power output recorded at the 1,200rpm rated engine speed in the 1938 Nebraska test was 35.2hp (26.2kw) for both versions, which were available with either steel wheel or rubber-tire options.

Diesel Version

Another option introduced for the 80 rowcrop tractor in 1940 was a diesel engine. This was still an unusual option in a mid-range wheeled tractor such as the 80 series, and the Oliver engineers chose a Buda-Lanova diesel engine, a highly unusual design based on the Acro injection system. This engine was later replaced on the 80 model by a diesel engine designed and built at the Oliver factory.

As well as taking a lead by offering the diesel option, Oliver also added to the list of improvements to the 1940 version of the 80 rowcrop and standard models by including a fourth gear, increasing the top speed from 4.33mph (6.9km/h) to 6.44mph (10.4km/h). There was an increase in engine power, boosting the output figure to 36hp (26.8kw).

JOHN DEERE

1938 Waterloo, Iowa

JOHN DEERE MODEL B STYLED

During the second half of the 1930s most of America's leading tractor manufacturers followed the fashion for rounded styling borrowed from the car industry, and they also chose brighter, more eye-catching colors.

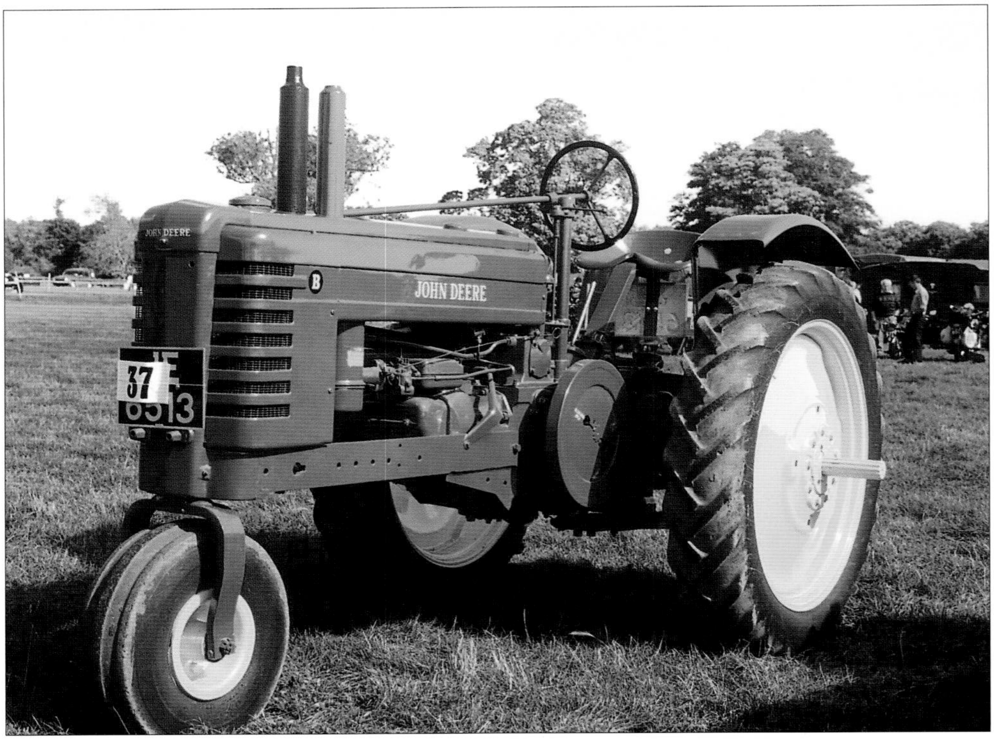

Specifications

Manufacturer: Deere & Co.
Location: Waterloo, Iowa
Model: B Styled
Type: General purpose
Power unit: Deere two-cylinder horizontal engine
Power output: 15.92hp (11.8kw) (maximum)
Transmission: Four-speed gearbox
Weight: N/A
Production started: 1938

Above: *Henry Dreyfuss, a leading industrial stylist, gave the John Deere tractor range a new look, and the Model B was one of the first tractors to feature the new styling.*

John Deere's green-and-yellow paint finish needed no improvement, but the company did hire one of the leading American design consultants, Henry Dreyfuss, to give its tractors a more up-to-date shape.

A Changed Appearance

The new rounded look arrived in 1938, and the first tractors to carry the Dreyfuss styling were the A series, plus rowcrop models from the B series. Other models followed later, and the new look continued to be an influence on John Deere tractor styling for more than 20 years.

The Model B had first appeared in unstyled form in 1934, powered by the two-cylinder horizontal engine that was almost a John Deere trademark. The output for the early versions was about 14hp (10kw) on the belt and 9hp (6.7kw) on the drawbar, and this was achieved at 1,150rpm, making the Model B the first John Deere tractor with an engine rated at more than 1,000rpm.

Developments

Model B developments included an extra 0.25in (6mm) on the engine bore and stroke in 1938, a lengthened frame to allow more space for mid-mounted equipment in 1937, and in 1940 replacement of the four-speed gearbox with a six-speed version.

MASSEY-HARRIS
1938 Racine, Wisconsin

MASSEY-HARRIS 101

The Massey-Harris design team made its final break from the old Wallis-inspired tractor features with the new 101 model introduced in 1938, and it also a chose a six-cylinder engine with an electric starter.

Above: The Twin Power feature available on some Massey-Harris tractors in the late 1930s provided a faster engine speed to boost the power output.

Right: A Chrysler six-cylinder engine was chosen as the upmarket power unit for the new 101 tractor from Massey-Harris.

Specifications

Manufacturer: Massey-Harris

Location: Racine, Wisconsin

Model: 101

Type: General purpose

Power unit: Chrysler six-cylinder engine

Power output: 36hp (26kw)

Transmission: Four-speed gearbox

Weight: 5,725lb (2,599kg) (rubber tires)

Production started: 1938

Gone was the old U-frame linking the underside of the engine and transmission, and the new rounded styling of the Massey-Harris 101 was far removed from the angular lines of the Wallis. The manufacturers also broke with tradition by fitting a Chrysler T57-503 series engine instead of relying on a Massey-Harris power unit.

Upmarket Features

The Chrysler engine was a six-cylinder design, and this helped to set the 101 apart from its mainly two- and four-cylinder rivals, by offering a smoother performance. The opportunity to drive a farm tractor powered by a six-cylinder Chrysler engine would have been a strong sales point, but it was not the only upmarket feature on the 101. The standard specification also included an electric starter

motor at a time when this was either an extra-cost option or simply not available on most mid-range tractors.

Engine Power

Rated output from the gasoline engine was 31.5hp (23.5km/h) at the relatively fast 1,500rpm engine speed, but for belt work the revs could be pushed up to 1,800rpm, using the Twin Power feature previously introduced on the Pacemaker.

This boosted the Massey-Harris 101's maximum power output to 36.15hp (26.9kw) for the standard model and to an impressive 38.65hp (28.8kw) for the rowcrop version. It was a simple device, and a similar arrangement is provided on some modern tractors where extra engine output is available when operating the power takeoff.

CATERPILLAR
1938   Peoria, Illinois

CATERPILLAR D2

Caterpillar was the first American manufacturer to offer diesel power in a production tractor, and the success it achieved had an important part to play in establishing diesel power for farm work.

One of the advantages of diesel engines compared with gasoline- and paraffin-fueled rivals is better fuel economy, and Caterpillar provided an example of this with its small D2 crawler tractor in 1938.

The D2 was powered by a four-cylinder diesel engine, and there was also a similar model called the R2 with the choice of paraffin- or gasoline-fueled engine. The D2 and R2 tractors were based on the same design, and so were the diesel and spark-ignition versions of the Caterpillar-designed power units.

Fuel Economy
The engines were based on the same size block and the same cylinder dimensions and cubic capacity, and they also shared the same 1,525rpm rated operating speed, but significant differences showed up in the tractors' performance figures. All three versions were taken to the Nebraska

Above: *Some D2 tractors were exported to Britain to boost the wartime plowing campaign, providing many British farmers with their first experience of diesel power.*

center and were tested consecutively. In the belt tests, to measure engine power, the maximum output of the diesel engine was 29.9hp (22kw), slightly ahead of the 28.95hp (21.5kw) for the gasoline version and the 27.78hp (20.7kw) developed on paraffin. The big differences were the amount of fuel burned to produce the power, and this is where the diesel engine scored.

The paraffin engine used 3.09 gallons (11.7 liters) of fuel to deliver its maximum output for one hour, the gasoline engine was even more thirsty with 3.56 gallons (13.5 liters) consumed in the same one-hour test, while the diesel engine scored an easy victory in the economy test by burning a modest 2.26 gallons (8.6 liters).

Other Factors

Obviously fuel efficiency is only one factor in a comparison between engine types. Diesels have better torque characteristics for tractor work,

and the absence of spark plugs and other electric equipment should give diesels a reliability advantage. The plus side for spark-ignition engines includes lighter weight, lower production costs, and, before the development of easy-starting diesels in the 1940s, avoiding the extra cost and complications of having a separate engine to start the diesel.

The D2 engine is an example. It was equipped with a 36-ci (587-cc) gasoline starter motor with twin horizontal cylinders and its own pull-cord starting. This must have added a significant amount to the production cost of the tractor, and it also complicated the fuel-management routine as both diesel and gasoline were necessary.

Specifications

Manufacturer: Caterpillar Tractor Co.
Location: Peoria, Illinois
Model: D2
Type: Tracklayer
Power unit: Four-cylinder diesel engine

Power output: 29.9hp (22kw)
Transmission: Five-speed gearbox
Weight: 7,420lb (3,369kg)
Production started: 1938

Left: *The gasoline-powered starter motor on the D2 tracklayer had two horizontal cylinders and was started manually by using a pull-cord.*

MASSEY-HARRIS
✗ **1938   Racine, Wisconsin**

MASSEY-HARRIS TWIN POWER PACEMAKER

The bright red paint and the curving shape at the front were among the new features introduced by Massey-Harris when it produced the updated version of its Pacemaker model in 1938.

The original Pacemaker, plus a new rowcrop model called the Challenger, arrived in 1936. Both models were based on the previous MH 12-20 model, and they inherited the more angular lines of the Wallis tractors that Massey-Harris had taken over from the J. I. Case Plow Works Co. in 1927. The old shape plus the previous dull gray paint finish disappeared when the new Massey styling arrived.

Design Features

The Pacemaker and Challenger also inherited the U-frame that had contributed to the success of the Wallis tractor since its original introduction in 1913, but they were the last M-H models to be equipped with this feature.

The four-cylinder engine in the Pacemaker was made by Massey-Harris and was an improved version of the power unit used in the

Above: Massey-Harris retained the old Wallis U-frame design when it introduced the Pacemaker and the rowcrop Challenger models in 1936.

old 12-20 model. The improvements boosted the output to more than 27hp (20kw) on the belt pulley at the 1,200rpm rated speed; however, there were more power developments still to come.

Beginning in 1938 the engine was also available in a Twin Power version. The Twin Power option was controlled by a lever positioned at the base of the gear-shift control, and it allowed the driver to select from two different power settings. With the lever switched to the low or standard setting the maximum engine speed was 1,200rpm to give 36.8hp (27.4kw) on the belt pulley, but switching the lever to the "high" position boosted the maximum engine speed to 1,400rpm and increased the power output to 42hp (31.3kw). The faster engine speed was recommended for belt work only, which is why the Twin Power Pacemaker was described in the sales literature as a three-plow tractor with four-plow performance on the belt.

Later Developments

Other developments introduced in 1938 on the improved Pacemaker included an optional powered-implement lift, and customers could also specify high-ratio gears that gave the tractor a top speed of 8.5mph (13.7km/h) instead of the 7.5mph (12km/h) available from the standard four-speed transmission.

The new Pacemaker enjoyed only a brief commercial life. Production of the 101 Senior model started at the Massey-Harris factory in Racine in 1938, and this was the model that replaced the Pacemaker. It was also the first model in a new range of tractors designed without the Wallis U-frame.

Specifications

Manufacturer: Massey-Harris
Location: Racine, Wisconsin
Model: Twin Power Pacemaker
Type: General purpose
Power unit: Four-cylinder engine
Power output: 42hp (31kw) (maximum)

Transmission: Four-speed gearbox
Weight: N/A
Production started: 1938

Left: *The new-look Pacemaker with the Twin Power feature to provide extra power when driving the belt pulley was soon replaced by the 101 Senior model.*

CLETRAC

1938 **Cleveland, Ohio**

CLETRAC GENERAL

The Cleveland Tractor Company was one of the leading specialist manufacturers of tracklayers, and it did not venture into the wheeled-tractor market until 1938 when it announced the General.

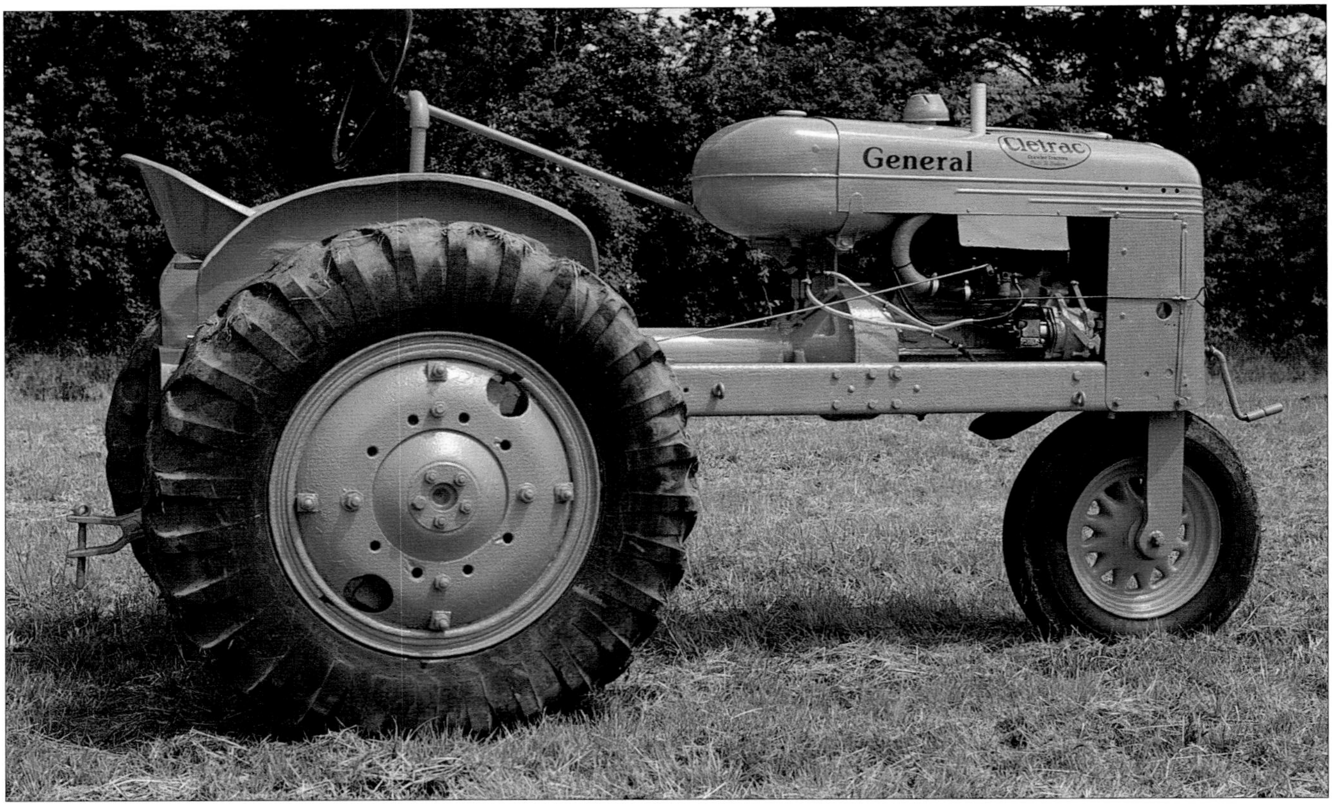

This was the smallest tractor to carry the Cletrac name, and it was available in both wheeled and tracklaying versions. On wheels it was known as the Cletrac General GG, but the crawler model was the Cletrac HG.

Both versions were equipped with a Hercules IXA four-cylinder engine developing 19hp (14kw) on the belt, but this was later increased to 22hp (16.4kw) by adding 0.5in (1.27cm) to the cylinder bore. A three-speed gearbox provided a top speed of 6.0mph (9.7km/h) for the GG tractor and 5.0mph (8km/h) for the crawler model.

A tricycle-wheel layout for the GG tractor and the high clearance for both versions made the small Cletracs suitable for rowcrop work. In order to expand the tractors' appeal in the rowcrop sector of the market, Cletrac arranged for the B. F. Avery Co. of Louisville, Kentucky, to build a range of implements specifically for the new tractors.

Wartime Work

This agreement was followed in 1941 by the news that Avery was taking over the production of the GG tractor, leaving the Cleveland company to concentrate on supplying the big crawler tractors that were needed by the U.S. Air Force and U.S. Army for urgent wartime construction work.

Above: *Cleveland Tractor Co.'s only venture into the wheeled-tractor market was the General, also available as a small tracklaying version.*

Specifications

Manufacturer: Cleveland Tractor Co.
Location: Cleveland, Ohio
Model: General GG
Type: Rowcrop
Power unit: Hercules four-cylinder engine
Power output: 19hp (14kw)
Transmission: Three-speed gearbox
Weight: 3,115lb (1,414kg)
Production started: 1938

JOHN DEERE

1938 Waterloo, Iowa

JOHN DEERE MODEL H

Unlike the Model L, the new H series tractor was a "real" two-cylinder model because it was powered by a "proper" John Deere engine with two horizontal cylinders. It was the smallest engine of its type in the John Deere range, with almost 15hp (11kw) available at the belt pulley.

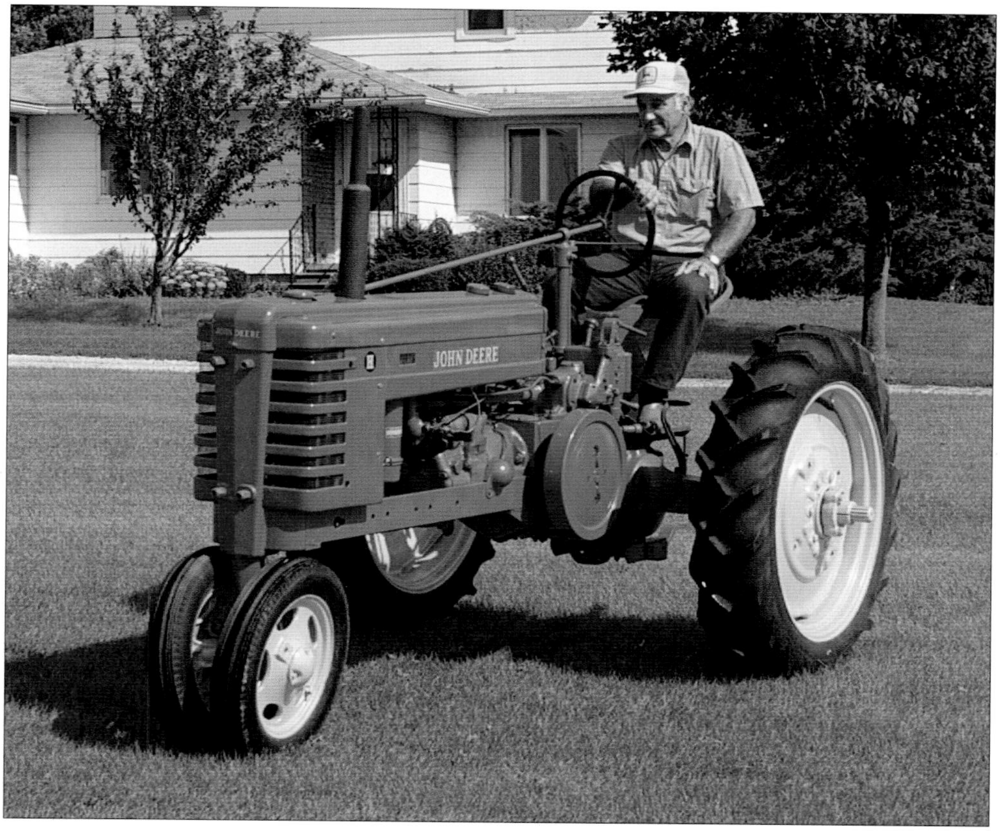

Right: *John Deere competed in the lightweight end of the rowcrop-tractor market with the Model H tractor, powered by a twin-cylinder engine with 15-hp (11-kw) output.*

Specifications

Manufacturer: Deere & Co.
Location: Waterloo, Iowa
Model: H
Type: Rowcrop
Power unit: Two-cylinder horizontal engine
Power output: 15hp (11kw)
Transmission: Three-speed gearbox
Weight: 3,035lb (1,378kg)
Production started: 1938

Another difference between the two small models is the fact that unlike the Model L, the H was a rowcrop-style tractor that slotted into the John Deere range below the B and the A.

Other Versions

The H was the first model to be launched with the new-look Dreyfuss styling. It was available initially as a regular four-wheeler, but the HN "narrow" version with a single front wheel followed in 1940. HWH and HNH models equipped with larger diameter rear wheels to increase the underside clearance and designed respectively with a wide front axle and a single front wheel were both built for just a short period, and both are now prized by collectors because of the low production numbers.

Special Features

The standard H specification included a three-speed gearbox with a hand-operated clutch. There was also a foot throttle enabling the driver to exceed the governed engine speed and increase the travel speed, but this was recommended only when the Model H was being used on the road.

FORD

⚒ **1939 Dearborn, Michigan**

FORD MODEL 9N

As the cracks began to show in the business relationship between Harry Ferguson and David Brown, Ferguson set sail for America to seek a new partnership, and the person he had in mind was Henry Ford.

It was a shrewd move. The Ferguson-Brown partnership had launched Ferguson's three-point linkage system and proved its significant advantages, but commercial progress was slow and Ferguson needed much bigger resources to achieve the international impact that he needed for his equipment.

Ferguson and Ford
Nobody in the 1930s tractor industry had bigger resources than Henry Ford, and he was actively looking for a new tractor design to replace the aging Model N Fordson from England. Henry Ford had spent many hours designing experimental tractors in the workshop at Fair Lane, the mansion he had built in Dearborn. However, when Harry Ferguson arrived in 1938, Ford was still looking for the right idea.

The meeting, held in the grounds of Fair Lane, had been arranged to give Ford an opportunity to see the Ferguson System in

Above: *The Moto-Tug was a special version of the 9N designed for working on wartime airfields, but later used as a small general-purpose industrial tractor.*

action. Harry Ferguson had brought one of his Model A tractors and some implements from England, and Ford arranged for a Fordson Model N and an Allis-Chalmers Model B to be brought from his own farm for comparison.

The Model A easily outperformed its rivals, and Henry Ford, a farmer's son, quickly appreciated the advantages. By the end of the demonstration he and Ferguson had agreed to form a partnership to design, build, and market a new Ferguson System tractor, with Ford providing much of the finance and the production facilities; Ferguson's responsibility was to set up a dealer network to market the tractors in North America.

New Tractors

Henry Ford's checkbook ensured that the project was completed quickly and efficiently. The new tractor, called the Ford 9N or Ford Tractor with Ferguson System, was ready for production only eight months from the original demonstration, and it was launched at a lavish party held on the Ford farm for 500 VIP guests.

The new tractor was powered by a Ford L-head engine, with the power delivered through a three-speed gearbox with a top speed of 6mph (9.6km/h) on the road. Rubber tires were standard equipment. The list of options included steel wheels, road lights, and a belt pulley. It was suggested—but perhaps not seriously—that as the engine was so quiet the 9N tractor might be equipped with a built-in radio.

Specifications

Manufacturer: Ford Motor Co.	**Transmission:** Three-speed gearbox
Location: Dearborn, Michigan	**Weight:** 3,375lb (1,532kg)
Model: 9N	**Production started:** 1939
Type: General purpose	
Power unit: Ford four-cylinder engine	
Power output: 23hp (17kw) (maximum)	

Below: When Harry Ferguson and Henry Ford formed a partnership to develop a new tractor, the result was the Ford 9N, the most advanced small tractor of its day.

JOHN DEERE
⚒ 1939 Waterloo, Iowa

JOHN DEERE LINDEMAN TRACKLAYER

The Model B was a popular tractor, and it was available in a wide range of special versions including the orchard, or BO, model.

Some fruit growers with orchards on steep land preferred the extra stability of crawler tracks instead of wheels, and this prompted the John Deere distributor based in a fruit-growing area the state of Washington to produce special tracklayer conversions of some of the John Deere orchard tractors to suit the needs of his local customers.

The company that carried out the tracklayer conversion work was Lindeman Brothers of Yakima, which started with a small number of John Deere General Purpose, or GP, orchard tractors. The demand grew rapidly when Lindeman offered a tracklaying version of the small BO tractor. Deere supplied about 2,000

BO skid units to be mounted on Lindeman tracks between 1939 and 1947.

Other Uses

Most of the demand was from fruit growers and other specialist farming operations on steep land, but there was also a demand for some of the Lindeman tracklayers to be equipped with a hydraulically operated blade for road leveling and general site work.

In 1947 the Lindeman company was taken over by John Deere, and it became the main source of technical expertise for developing and manufacturing a new and much wider range of John Deere crawler tractors.

Above: Most of the Model B-based tracklayers were used on farms, but some were equipped with a blade for small-scale earthmoving jobs.

Specifications

Manufacturer: Deere & Co.

Location: Waterloo, Iowa

Model: Model B Lindeman

Type: Tracklayer

Power unit: Deere two-cylinder horizontal engine

Power output: 15.9hp (11.8kw)

Transmission: Four-speed gearbox

Weight: N/A

Production started: 1939

INTERNATIONAL HARVESTER
1939 Chicago, Illinois

I.H. FARMALL MODEL A

The Farmall Model A was the International Harvester competitor in the expanding market for small tractors during the late 1930s. It was designed as a one-plow tractor, meaning that it would pull a single-furrow plow in most conditions.

Right: International Harvester's expertise in rowcrop design produced the Farmall A model with Culti-Vision and a high-ground clearance.

Above: The little Model A one-plow tractor carried the names of International Harvester, McCormick and Farmall.

Specifications

Manufacturer: International Harvester

Location: Chicago, Illinois

Model: A

Type: Rowcrop

Power unit: I.H. four-cylinder engine

Power output: 16.86hp (12.5kw) (gasoline)

Transmission: Four-speed gearbox

Weight: 3,570lb (1,621kg)

Production started: 1939

Production started in 1939, when the International Harvester red paint finish and the new rounded shape were already established, but the Model A was the first production tractor to feature Culti-Vision. This was the name chosen, presumably by someone in the I.H. publicity department, for the sharply offset position of the driver's seat and the controls that were designed to provide good forward visibility for precise rowcrop work.

Variants

Culti-Vision was very much in the Farmall tradition of catering for the needs of arable farms, and so was the generous underside clearance for straddling growing crops, but another Model A feature designed to meet the needs of customers with special crop requirements was the high clearance AV version with larger wheels and a modified front axle to give an extra 6in (15.2cm) of clearance above the ground. I.H. also introduced a Model B, effectively a Model A tractor with a tricycle-style wheel layout.

An International Harvester four-cylinder engine with 3-in (7.6-cm) bore and 4-in (10.1-cm) stroke powered both the A and the B models, producing just over 18hp (13kw) at the belt during the Model A's Nebraska test.

chapter 5

Diesel Power Takes Over

Tractor development came to a virtual halt during the wartime years of the early 1940s. Many of the factories were taken over to build military equipment and some European factories were destroyed in bombing raids. The end of World War II, however, was to bring a big surge in the demand for tractor power and attracted new companies into the market.

Above: *As an alternative to the standard spark-ignition engine, the International Harvester W-6 tractor was also available with a diesel engine that started on gasoline.*

Left: *Tool-carrier tractors, such as this Allis-Chalmers Model G, provided excellent visibility for inter-row cultivations in vegetables and other row crops.*

As tractor production increased again, the biggest technical development was a new generation of more user-friendly diesel engines that arrived in the late 1940s and early 1950s. The companies at the forefront of this development were British and included David Brown, the Ford plant in Essex, and Perkins. The engines they produced were easier to start, smoother running, and offered improved torque characteristics.

International Harvester's pioneering development of the Farmall tractor in the 1920s had brought big improvements to rowcrop mechanization, and this was followed in the late 1940s by the first of the new tool-carrier tractors. They consisted of an open framework on wheels, with the engine and driver at the rear and attachment points for underslung and rear-mounted equipment.

Developments in the tractor industry included the abrupt end of the Ferguson-Ford partnership in an acrimonious legal action. Meanwhile some of the leading North American companies established European assembly or production plants.

Most of these new plants were found in the United Kingdom, bringing Allis-Chalmers, International Harvester, Massey-Harris, and, very briefly, Minneapolis-Moline to join the long-established Ford factory.

INTERNATIONAL HARVESTER

1939 Chicago, Illinois

INTERNATIONAL HARVESTER T-6

The gasoline- and kerosene-powered T-6 TracTracTors and their diesel-engined stablemate the TD-6 became available in 1939, and when production ended 17 years later the combined sales total was approaching 40,000, a high figure for a crawler tractor.

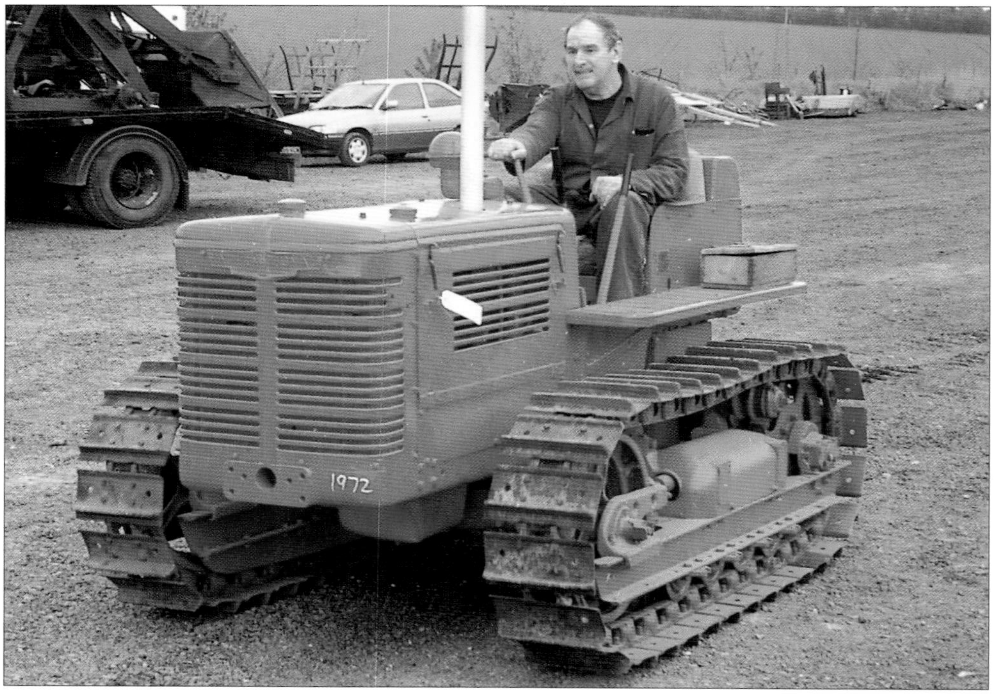

Specifications

Manufacturer: International Harvester
Location: Chicago, Illinois
Model: T-6 TracTracTor
Type: Tracklayer
Power unit: Four-cylinder engine
Power output: 36hp (26.6kw) (maximum)
Transmission: Five-speed gearbox
Weight: 7,420lb (3,369kg)
Production started: 1939

Above: *International Harvester's T-6 tracklayer and the diesel-powered TD-6 version were big-selling crawler tractors during World War II.*

Some of their success was due to the way they slotted into the popular mid-range sector of the tracklayer market, attracting a customer base that included farmers and the smaller end of the construction industry. It was also a time when International Harvester was one of the top names in the crawler-tractor market, offering a wide range of models that included the big TD-18 model delivering almost 100hp (74.5kw).

Design Features

The T-6 and TD-6 shared the same frame, transmission, and tracks, and even the spark ignition and diesel versions of the engine had the same 1,450rpm rated speed and the same bore and stroke measurements, but the differences were in the performance figures. All three models were tested in Nebraska, where the gasoline engine produced a maximum output of 36.06hp (26.8kw) compared with 34.22hp (25.5kw) for the engine burning paraffin or distillate, and 34.54hp (25.7kw) for the diesel. Still, as usual, fuel efficiency figures clearly favored the diesel.

Specification details for the T-6 family of tracklayers included a five-speed gearbox and a choice of track widths. The options list had a set of crop guards to cover the top of half of each track for protection when working in orchards.

MINNEAPOLIS-MOLINE
1939 Minneapolis, Minnesota

MINNEAPOLIS-MOLINE GT

Minneapolis-Moline announced a batch of new models during the late 1930s, and the biggest of the bunch was the GT tractor, which became available from 1939.

Right: *The four-speed gearbox for the Minneapolis-Moline GT provided a 9.4-mph (15.1-km/h) top speed, but this was only for tractors with rubber tires, drivers were warned.*

Specifications

Manufacturer:	Minneapolis–Moline
Location:	Minneapolis, Minnesota
Model:	GT
Type:	General purpose
Power unit:	Four-cylinder engine
Power output:	54hp (40kw) (maximum)
Transmission:	Four-speed gearbox
Weight:	9,445lb (4,288kg)
Production started:	1939

The GT was a real heavyweight, tipping the scales at 9,445lb (4,283.4kg) when it was tested in Nebraska, and this makes it one of the heaviest wheeled tractors available during the early 1940s. It was also the most powerful tractor in the Minneapolis-Moline range, recording almost 40hp (29.8kw) in the drawbar pull tests and producing a 54-hp (40-kw) maximum on the belt when tested in Nebraska.

Engine
Although the GT shared the Minneapolis-Moline new look with more rounded lines and the bright yellow Prairie Gold paint color, the engine was much less up to date. For several

years it was available as gasoline only, and the four cylinders were arranged in two separate blocks. The bore and stroke measurements were 4.63in and 6.0in (11.7cm and 15.2cm), and the rated power was developed at 1,075rpm. The four-speed gearbox for the GT was mounted transversely and provided a top speed of 9.4mph (15.1km/h), but the instruction book warned that this should only be used on tractors equipped with rubber tires.

GT production continued through the war years, when some were exported to Britain where farmers were no doubt impressed by its size and power. The replacement for the big GT was the new G model introduced in 1947.

CASE

1939 **Racine, Wisconsin**

CASE LA

When Case introduced the new LA tractor in 1939 it was an important event for the company. The tractor it replaced, the Case L, had built up an excellent reputation as one of the best tractors in its power range, and the design team for the new LA model must have realized it was a hard act to follow.

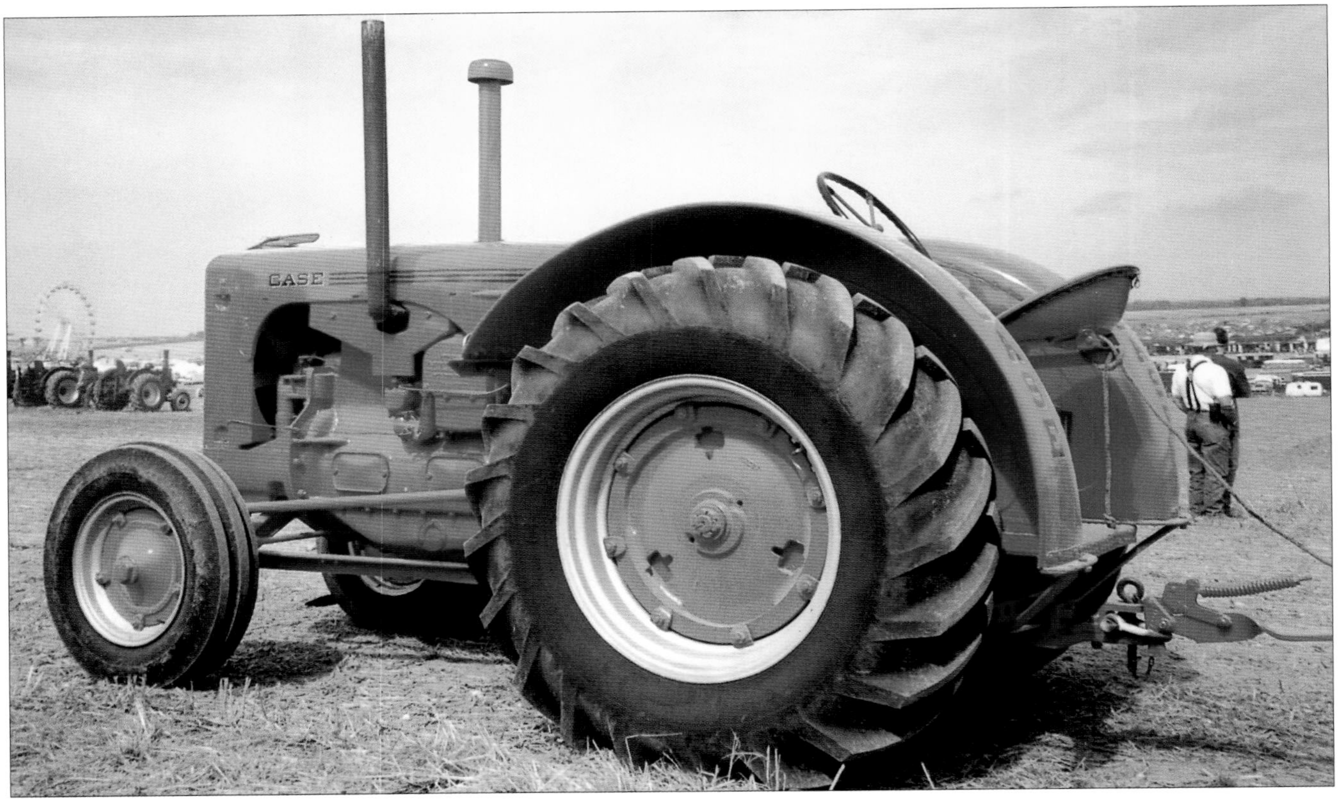

Above: *The four-cylinder engine for the Case LA tractor produced up to 48hp (35.5kw) and was an uprated version of the power unit in the previous Model L.*

To some extent the Case designers played safe and simply retained most of the mechanism of the L. The components that were carried over into the new model included the four-cylinder engine, a valve-in-head design with 400.6-ci (6.6-liter) capacity. When the engine first appeared in the L model the output had been about 40hp (29.8kw), but this was increased to almost 50hp (37.2kw) for the new LA tractor.

Transmission and Drive

The transmission was also based on the L model and was unconventional by 1940s standards. The clutch was controlled by a hand-operated lever instead of a foot pedal, and when the lever was moved into the "drive" position it forced a pair of metal plates together, sandwiching the clutch disk between them. Unlike a conventional clutch, the over-center action of the lever held the plates together without using compression springs, but there was a set of springs to push the plates away from the disk when the drive was disengaged.

The final drive was also unusual. It consisted of a pair of chains and sprockets to transfer the power from the gearbox to the rear axle. Although this was old-fashioned by the time the LA tractor was launched, it was also a simple, reliable arrangement that was easy to maintain and was already familiar to many farmers.

Styling

Although, apart from a few detailed improvements, the L and LA tractors shared basically the same mechanical features, and it was the styling that provided the obvious differences. The late 1930s were a time when the tractor stylists, particularly in the United States, were adopting brighter, more striking paint colors and borrowing rounded bodywork from the car industry, and the LA was an early example of the new look adopted by the Case company, including a bright orange color called "Flambeau Red."

Styling is obviously a matter of taste, and the rounded shape of the LA certainly attracted customers and continued to be fashionable throughout the 1940s. There are also those who think that the stylists who were responsible for the simple, clean lines of the old L tractor had produced one of the classic designs of the 1930s, and the shape of the LA was, perhaps, not an improvement.

Above: *An unusual design feature on the big LA tractor was the hand-operated lever to control the clutch.*

Specifications

Manufacturer: J. I. Case	**Power output:** 48hp (35.5kw)
Location: Racine, Wisconsin	**Transmission:** Four-speed gearbox
Model: LA	**Weight:** 5,940lb (2,700kg)
Type: General purpose	**Production started:** 1939
Power unit: Case four-cylinder engine	

Below: *This cutaway diagram shows the final drive of the LA tractor, using a chain and sprockets to deliver the power to the rear axle.*

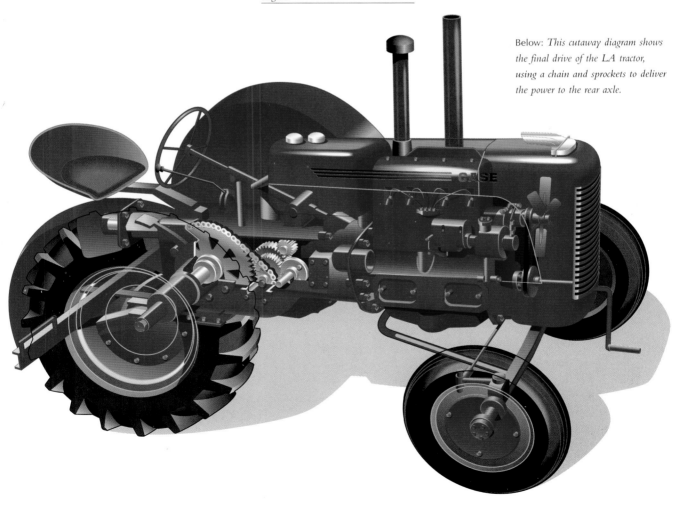

DAVID BROWN
⚒ **1939   Meltham, Yorkshire, England**

DAVID BROWN VAK 1

When Harry Ferguson formed a new partnership with Henry Ford it left David Brown, his previous partner, free of Ferguson's firm control over tractor design and development, but with a large stock of Ferguson Model A tractors that had to be sold at a substantial discount.

There were several design features of the Model A tractor that David Brown had wanted to change, but his requests had been vetoed by Ferguson. The end of the partnership provided the opportunity to design a totally new tractor based on Brown's own ideas. He was not able to use the complete Ferguson System for implement attachment and control because of patent restrictions, but David Brown engineers designed their own three-point linkage with hydraulic control that gave many of the benefits of using mounted implements, but did not infringe the Ferguson patents.

Extra Power
The new David Brown tractor was called the VAK 1, and production started in 1939. The design included the extra power and the four-

Above, top: *Because of patent restrictions, the first production tractor designed by David Brown did not use a full Ferguson System rear linkage.*

Above: *David Brown's engineers designed the VAK 1 tractor with some of the improvements Harry Ferguson had rejected for the Ferguson A.*

speed gearbox David Brown had wanted for the Ferguson A, and it was painted a bright red color called "Hunting Pink." The design also included a more rounded shape that was described in the sales literature as "streamlined," and an unusual feature was a seat for a passenger beside the driver.

When the new VAK 1 was launched at the 1939 Royal Show it attracted considerable interest and, the company claimed, orders for 3,000 tractors. It was certainly an encouraging start because this meant that the order book was more than the entire production total of Ferguson A tractors; however, the outbreak of World War II brought government restrictions and raw materials shortages. In the end, production of the tractor totaled 5,350 by 1945, when the VAK 1 was replaced by an updated version known as the VAK 1A.

Improvements

Although the VAK 1A and its predecessor were similar and shared basically the same 35-hp (26-kw) engine, there were still some important differences between the two.

The many improvements included a patented "hot spot" in the engine for a faster warmup for burning kerosene, and the engine lubrication was also greatly improved. A power takeoff was included in the standard specification for both tractors, and there was also a belt pulley added for improved efficiency. Steel wheels were also included in the basic specification for the VAK 1, with rubber tires listed as an option at extra cost.

VAK 1A production lasted just four years and averaged a little more than 1,000 tractors per year. It was replaced during 1947 by the first of the Cropmaster series tractors.

Specifications

Manufacturer: David Brown Tractors
Location: Meltham, Yorkshire, England
Model: VAK 1
Type: General purpose
Power unit: Four-cylinder engine
Power output: 35hp (26kw)
Transmission: Four-speed gearbox
Weight: 3,250lb (1,625kg)
Production started: 1939

Below: *The cushioned seat on the VAK 1 was wide enough for two people—as long as they were both reasonably slim.*

INTERNATIONAL HARVESTER

1940 Chicago, Illinois

INTERNATIONAL HARVESTER W-4

The various tractor families within the International Harvester range can be confusing, and the McCormick-Deering W-4 is an example. It is, in fact, an equivalent model to the Farmall H. Both tractors are mechanically similar, but the W-4 has a standard four-wheel layout instead of the Farmall's rowcrop design.

Above: *The W-4 was powered by a spark-ignition engine and lacked the diesel option, which was available with the bigger W-6 model.*

Above, left: *International Harvester introduced the McCormick W-4 in 1940 and replaced it 13 years later with the Super W-4 with a new five-speed gearbox.*

Specifications

Manufacturer: International Harvester
Location: Chicago, Illinois
Model: W-4
Type: General purpose
Power unit: Four-cylinder engine
Power output: 22hp (16.3kw)
Transmission: Four-speed gearbox
Weight: 5,690lb (2,583kg)
Production started: 1940

International Harvester introduced the W-4 model in 1940 and production continued until 1953. Powered by a four-cylinder engine, it was available in two versions: gasoline/paraffin and gasoline-only. Both were tested in Nebraska, and the top output was 22hp (16.3kw) for the paraffin- or distillate-fueled version; 24hp (17.8kw) for the gasoline model. The specification included a four-speed gearbox. Covered electric lighting and an electric starter were optional, as were rubber tires, but these were available at an extra cost.

Although production ended officially in 1953, the replacement model was basically a continuation of the W-4 with a few improvements. Known as the Super W-4, its most important design change was a new gearbox with five forward speeds.

INTERNATIONAL HARVESTER
1940 Chicago, Illinois

INTERNATIONAL HARVESTER W-6

The W-6 was effectively a bigger version of the McCormick-Deering W-4, and both models were introduced in the same year. The most significant difference between the two was the addition of a diesel-powered version of the W-6.

Right: *International Harvester's W-6 model was a popular mid-range tractor with spark ignition and diesel engine options producing about 35hp (26kw).*

Specifications

Manufacturer: International Harvester Co.
Location: Chicago, Illinois
Model: W-6
Type: General purpose
Power unit: Four-cylinder engine
Power output: 36hp (26.6kw) (maximum)
Transmission: Four-speed gearbox
Weight: 7,610lb (3,455kg)
Production started: 1940

It was an early example of a diesel engine in a mid-range wheeled tractor, and it showed that International was ahead of most of its competitors in this area of development. The diesel version of the W-6 was known as the WD-6, and the spark ignition and the diesel engines were both the same as those used in the International's T-6 and TD-6 crawler tractors and the Farmall M models. Both engine types were based on the same four-cylinder block with bore and stroke measurements of 3.87in and 5.25in (9.8cm and 13.3cm). The maximum output figure for the gasoline version was 36.15hp (26.9kw) for the W-6 gasoline engine and 34.75hp (25.9kw) for the diesel engine in the WD-6. Unsurprisingly, both figures are almost the same as those for the T-6 and TD-6 engines.

Starting System

A special feature of the diesel engine was the gasoline starting system. The engine was equipped with a carburettor and magneto for burning gasoline when starting from cold. When a suitable temperature was reached the fuel supply was switched to diesel and the gasoline equipment switched off.

A four-speed gearbox in the W-6 produced a rather sedate top speed of 5mph (8km/h), and the standard specification included steel wheels, with rubber tires available at extra cost.

MASSEY-HARRIS
✖ 1941 Racine, Wisconsin

MASSEY-HARRIS 81

The 81 and 82 tractors were part of the Massey-Harris wartime product line, and for the 81 model the war brought substantial orders for tractors to be used by the Royal Canadian Air Force for use as tow vehicles on military airfields (the photograph shows a batch of tractors ready for delivery to the RCAF).

Specifications

Manufacturer: Massey-Harris Co.	
Location: Racine, Wisconsin	
Model: 81	
Type: General purpose	
Power unit: Four-cylinder engine	
Power output: 26hp (19.24kw) (maximum)	
Transmission: Four-speed gearbox	
Weight: 2,895lb (1,314kg)	
Production started: 1941	

Production of the 81 model started in 1941, and this was a difficult time for Massey-Harris, as it was for other tractor companies in North America and Europe. As well as trying to maintain production levels for tractors and farm equipment, Massey-Harris factories were building a wide range of equipment for the armed services, including tanks, guns, wings for Mosquito aircraft, and 50,000 armored vehicle bodies for use by the British army in the North Africa campaign.

Design Features
The 81 was available with both regular and rowcrop wheel layouts. Massey-Harris chose a four-cylinder Continental engine with 3.0-in (7.62-cm) bore and 4.38-in (11.1-cm) stroke for the 81, and this produced 26hp (19.4kw) in the maximum-load test in Nebraska using gasoline as fuel. The maximum drawbar pull, an important factor for its air force work, was 2,898lb (1,314.3kg) measured in low gear. The maximum travel speed in fourth gear was 16mph (25.7km/h), reflecting the fact that rubber tires were included in the 81 tractor's standard specification.

Production of the 81 tractor continued through the war years and ended in 1948 when Massey-Harris was in the process of introducing a new range of tractors.

Above: *This Massey-Harris wartime publicity picture shows a neat row of model 81 tractors awaiting delivery to the Royal Canadian Air Force.*

OLIVER

⚒ **1944 Cleveland, Ohio**

OLIVER HG

When the Oliver company bought the ailing Cleveland Tractor Co. in 1944 it acquired the Cletrac range of tracklayer plus the little General tractor. The General GG was the first Cletrac tractor with wheels, but it was also available as a tracklayer under the HG label, and it was the HG version that appeared to interest the new owners.

Right: *A new paint color and decals brightened up the HG tracklayer when it became part of the Oliver range.*

Above: *The Oliver company continued to use a Hercules engine on the HG crawler tractor it took over when it bought the Cleveland Tractor Co.*

Specifications

Manufacturer:	Oliver Corpn
Location:	Cleveland, Ohio
Model:	HG
Type:	Tracklayer
Power unit:	Hercules four-cylinder engine
Power output:	24.7hp (18kw) (maximum)
Transmission:	Three-speed gearbox
Weight:	4,183lb (1,899kg)
Production started:	1944

Production of the Cletrac General and the HG had originally started in 1939, so both models were still relatively up to date when Oliver took over in 1944.

New Model

The new owners dressed the crawler model up in a smart new paint finish and marketed it as the Oliver HG, but in mechanical terms it remained basically similar to the later versions of the Cletrac HG, including a four-cylinder Hercules L-head engine. The engine had 3.25-in (8.2-cm) bore and 4-in (10.1-cm) stroke measurements, and the maximum power output was 24.7hp (18kw).

Weight

A three-speed gearbox with a top speed of 5mph (8km/h) was also inherited from the Cletrac version, but at some point in the transition from Cletrac to Oliver the HG had put on weight, increasing from 3,510lb (1,592kg) for the previous version to 4,183lb (1,899kg) when it appeared under the Oliver colors.

Exactly when the HG was dropped from the Oliver product line is not clear, but it was probably not there more than about three years. In spite of the Cletrac purchase, crawler tractors never became a major part of the Oliver range, and Oliver was taken over in 1960, when it became part of White Motors.

FORDSON

1945 **Dagenham, Essex, England**

FORDSON E27N MAJOR

Considering the E27N was just a stopgap model powered by an engine that was almost 30 years old, it was an extraordinary success. The engineering team at the Ford factory in Dagenham, Essex, was already working on a much more ambitious project, but this tractor was still several years away from production. Meanwhile the company needed a new model to fill the production line.

The answer was the Fordson Major with new styling and bigger diameter wheels that helped to make it bigger and more impressive-looking than the previous Fordsons. There was also another color change—this time from the green of the wartime Model N to a new dark blue color. Underneath the new look, however, there were close links between the new tractor and the more than 750,000 Model F and N Fordsons that had been built in the USA, Ireland, and England since 1917.

Engine

Although the engine was based on the 1917 Model F power unit, boosting the speed to 1450rpm helped to increase the rated power output to 28.5hp (21kw) for the gasoline/paraffin version. The biggest mechanical change on the Major was getting rid of the old worm-wheel final drive. This was an important improvement because the previous drive was expensive to build, while the new spur gear was more efficient and absorbed less power.

Above: *Many of the main components of the Fordson E27N Major were inherited from the Fordson Model N and ultimately from the Model F.*

A new single-plate clutch was also included on the Major, and the previous air cleaner was replaced by a more efficient cylindrical design. A glass sediment bowl made it easier to check for dirt in the fuel, and the engine was equipped with a ring gear to allow a starter motor to be fitted. Steering brakes were standard on all but the lowest-priced version of the Major.

Other Developments

Other important developments during the Major's production life included the addition of a hydraulically operated three-point linkage, and the Major also became the first Fordson to be equipped with a factory-fitted diesel engine. A Ford diesel engine was already under development, but it was not ready for the Major and so Ford specified a Perkins P6 engine with 45-hp (33.5-kw) rated output.

The new Fordson arrived at a time when the demand for tractor power was increasing rapidly, both in the United Kingdom and overseas, and the Major rapidly established a reputation for reliability.

Production peaked at more than 50,000 tractors in 1948, and the Fordson Major remained available until the launch of the New Major at the end of 1951.

Specifications

Manufacturer: Ford Motor Co.
Location: Dagenham, Essex, England
Model: Fordson E27N Major
Type: General purpose
Power unit: Four-cylinder engine
Power output: 28.5hp (21kw)
Transmission: Three-speed gearbox
Weight: 4,592lb (2,085kg)
(on steel wheels)
Production started: 1945

Left: *The Perkins badge became an increasingly familiar sight on the E27N as more customers chose the diesel version.*

Above: *The attractive cover picture for the original sales brochure published for the Fordson E27N Major.*

OPPERMAN

1946 **Borehamwood, Hertfordshire, England**

OPPERMAN MOTOCART

The Motocart was designed in 1945 by a farmer. He decided that a small rough-terrain load-carrying vehicle would outperform the horse and cart he was using for moving loads on the farm and for local transportation work.

A prototype built in the farm workshop was so successful that he took the idea to S. E. Opperman, an engineering company that was making special strakes or grips to fit over tractor tires for improved traction in difficult conditions. Opperman improved the basic design of the load carrier, called it the Motocart and started building it in 1946.

Design

The design was ingenious, with a single large-diameter wheel at the front to provide traction and for steering the vehicle, plus a small air-cooled engine actually attached to the offside of the front wheel. The small wheels at the rear were equipped with drum brakes, and the driver was positioned near the front of the vehicle, between the front wheel and the rear load compartment.

A single-cylinder four-stroke engine provided about 8hp (6kw) to drive the front wheel. The power was delivered by a chain and sprocket to a single-plate clutch and a compact four-speed gearbox providing a top speed of 11mph (17.7km/h) on the road.

The Motorcart's load capacity was 1.5 tons (1.52 tonnes) carried in a choice of fixed and tipping bodies, and the work rate for on-farm transportation work was said to be three times faster than that achievable by a horse and cart.

Above: *The initial idea of a transportation tractor for farms was adopted by the Opperman company in the Motorcart.*

Specifications

Manufacturer: S. E. Opperman
Location: Borehamwood, Hertfordshire, England
Model: Motocart
Type: Transportation tractor
Power unit: Single-cylinder air-cooled engine
Power output: 8hp (6kw)
Transmission: Four-speed gearbox
Weight: 3,300lb (1,500kg)
Production started: 1946

BEAN
⚒ 1946 Brough, Yorkshire, England

BEAN TOOL CARRIER

Below: A Yorkshire vegetable grower designed the Bean 8-hp (6-kw) tool carrier and a range of special implements for rowcrop work.

Not surprisingly, the Bean tool carrier was designed by a Mr. Bean, a vegetable grower from Yorkshire, England. His first machine was built for his own use in about 1945, and when this attracted interest from other growers he made more of the tool carriers to sell locally.

Specifications

Manufacturer: Humberside Agricultural Products
Location: Brough, Yorkshire, England
Model: Bean
Type: Tool carrier
Power unit: Ford four-cylinder engine
Power output: 8hp (6kw)
Transmission: Three-speed gearbox
Weight: 1,344lb (610kg)
Production started: 1946

As the demand continued to increase Mr. Bean arranged for Humberside Agricultural Products to take over the production in 1946, and it continued to build it for about 10 years.

Two Versions

The tool carrier was available in three- and four-wheel versions, but the three-wheeler was the most popular model. Both versions were based on a rectangular steel frame with two large driving wheels at the rear, and the tricycle version had a single wheel at the front with tiller steering. An 8-hp (6-kw) Ford industrial engine mounted over the rear wheels provided

the power, and this was linked to a three-speed Ford gearbox. The driver's seat was in front of the engine, providing an almost uninterrupted view of the ground in front of the tractor and of mid-mounted implements, and equipment such as hoes or light harrows could also be attached to the rear of the frame.

Bean tool carriers were used mainly for working in field-scale vegetable crops, but they were also popular for controlling weeds in sugar beet. As well as inter-row cultivators and hoes, the attachments list for the Bean included a sprayer, a six-row drill for sowing vegetable seeds, and a fertilizer distributor.

ALLIS-CHALMERS
✴ 1947 Milwaukee, Wisconsin

ALLIS-CHALMERS MODEL G

Most manufacturers aim to make their tractors as versatile as possible in order to create the maximum number of sales opportunities, but when Allis-Chalmers was developing the Model G the objective was to produce a machine designed for a very narrow and specific range of jobs.

Specifications

Manufacturer: Allis-Chalmers	
Location: Milwaukee, Wisconsin	
Model: G	
Type: Tool carrier	
Power unit: Four-cylinder engine	
Power output: 8hp (6kw)	
Transmission: Four-speed gearbox	
Weight: 1,400lb (636kg)	
Production started: 1947	

The Model G was a tool-carrier tractor, designed to work with mid- and rear-mounted hoes and other implements, usually in a rowcrop situation. The requirements to carry out this type of work included a high clearance to accommodate mid-mounted equipment and excellent visibility from the driver's seat to allow accurate steering between the plant rows, plus a light weight to minimize the risk of causing soil compaction.

Good Visibility
The Model G met all of these requirements, particularly when it came to the view from the driving seat. Forward visibility was helped by mounting the engine at the rear of the tractor,

and even the steering wheel rim was incomplete, with a gap to avoid creating a blind spot. At 1,400lb (636kg) it was certainly a lightweight, but it was also well equipped. The power output was only 8hp (6kw), but this was produced by a water-cooled four-cylinder gasoline engine, and the four-speed gearbox included a "special low" first gear giving a forward speed of 1.6mph (2.5km/h) for use with slow-speed precision equipment such as transplanters.

Another important design feature for rowcrop work is plenty of track adjustment for the tractor wheels, and the Model G tractor provided eight different width settings between 48in and 64in (1.21m and 1.62m) for the front and rear wheels.

Above: *Allis-Chalmers moved into the tool-carrier market with the Model G powered by an 8-hp (6-kw) engine and built in the United States and in France.*

DAVID BROWN

✖ 1947 Meltham, Yorkshire, England

DAVID BROWN CROPMASTER

Although the Cropmaster looked basically similar to the VAK 1A model it replaced, there were important differences between the two tractors. The differences included the production totals, amounting to 3,500 for the VAK 1A compared to almost 60,000 for the Cropmaster.

Right: *David Brown introduced its first diesel engine in 1949 and used it to provide the Cropmaster tractor with a 34-hp (25.3-kw) output.*

Above: *The first of the new Cropmaster series tractors was a major development in the David Brown range, replacing the previous VAK 1A model.*

Specifications

Manufacturer: David Brown Tractors
Location: Meltham, Yorkshire, England
Model: Cropmaster
Type: General purpose
Power unit: Four-cylinder engine
Power output: 35hp (26kw) (maximum)
Transmission: Six-speed gearbox
Weight: 3,304lb (1,500kg)
Production started: 1947

David Brown began building the Cropmaster series in 1947, offering a standard-specification model and the high-spec 4S version. The first production models were equipped with a David Brown gasoline/paraffin engine developing up to 35hp (26kw), but by 1949 the new David Brown diesel engine was added to the Cropmaster options list, providing a major boost to the tractor's popularity.

New Engine
The diesel engine was one of the new generation of easy-starting, high-speed tractor engines that were helping to revolutionize power farming in the United Kingdom. It had a 34-hp (25.3-kw) rated output at 1,800rpm and, like the rival engines from companies such as Perkins and Ford, it offered new standards of torque backup and fuel efficiency.

Sales Features
Another important sales feature on the new Cropmasters was the dual-ratio gearbox providing six forward speeds and two in reverse. It was described initially as an option, but within less than two years it had become standard equipment, and the specification also included an extra-wide seat for two people. Later versions of the Cropmaster included the 25 and 25D versions available from 1953.

FERGUSON
1946   Coventry, Warwickshire, England

FERGUSON TE-20

When the American-built Ford 9N tractor with its Ferguson System hydraulics and rear linkage proved to be an outstanding success, Harry Ferguson expected that Ford would extend production to its factory at Dagenham in England.

Exactly why this did not happen is not clear. It may have been due to the practical problems of changing production during the war years, but another suggestion is that the Ford directors at Dagenham were reluctant to involve Ferguson who, rightly or wrongly, had a reputation for being difficult to work with. Instead, when World War II ended they replaced the Model N tractor with the Fordson E27N Major.

Ferguson and Standard

Harry Ferguson realized that he would have to make his own arrangements to build a Ferguson System tractor in England, and he subsequently signed an agreement with the Standard Motor Company, a major car manufacturer. Standard was a good choice because it had plenty of space available at its factory in Banner Lane, Coventry, and it also had a good reputation for quality. The arrangement was somewhat similar

Above, top: The Ferguson System three-point linkage on the back of a TE series tractor from the Banner Lane factory.

Above: Ferguson tractors were built at the Banner Lane factory near Coventry under an agreement with the Standard Motor Co., which was responsible for production.

to Ferguson's previous agreements with David Brown and Henry Ford. Ferguson controlled the design and marketing, while his partner provided the factory and looked after the tractor's production.

Production

Small-scale production began at the end of 1946. The tractor was the Ferguson TE-20 and it closely resembled the American-built Ford 9N tractor, with both sharing the same battleship-gray paint finish and basically similar styling. The major differences included a four-speed gearbox in the new tractor, and the engine for the first two years of TE production was supplied by Continental and featured overhead valves, 1,179.6-ci (1,966-cc) capacity, and a maximum output of 24 hp (17.8 kw).

The replacement for the Continental power unit was an engine of approximately similar size and power built by the Standard company, and this engine was also adopted to power the Standard Vanguard car, pickup truck, and van.

When a diesel model was added to the TE series in 1951, Ferguson chose a new engine designed by Standard, and the tractor was called the TE-F20.

Developments

Other TE series developments included an agreement to build Ferguson tractors in France, where the locally built Ferguson rapidly overtook the Renault as the top-selling tractor in France. The biggest overseas project was in the USA, where Ford's decision to stop supplying tractors to Harry Ferguson's North American marketing company left him with a big dealer network and no tractors to sell. Ferguson was able to supply TE series tractors from England while he set up new production facilities in Detroit.

The American-built Ferguson was called the TO-20. Although it was based on the TE design, the TO-20 was equipped with a Continental engine and a number of other American-sourced components.

Specifications

Manufacturer: Standard Motor Co.
Location: Coventry, Warwickshire, England
Model: Ferguson TE-20
Type: General purpose
Power unit: Four-cylinder engine
Power output: 24hp (17.8kw) (maximum)
Transmission: Four-speed gearbox
Weight: 2,460lb (1,117kg)
Production started: 1946

Below: *This was the first TE series tractor to be built in the Banner Lane fatory. It was used as a light factory vehicle, but was later restored and moved into the museum at the factory.*

FERGUSON
1946   Coventry, Warwickshire, England

ANTARCTIC FERGUSONS

Most tractors spend their working lives on the fields of just a few farms, but the working life for three Ferguson tractors held more extreme challenges. They were part of a batch of 12 Fergusons shipped to Antarctica to be used for transportation work at the British and New Zealand bases in the 1950s.

Left: Cabs for the TE series Fergusons shipped to the Antarctic were made at the British base camp, to protect the drivers from the extremely low temperatures. One of the polar expedition tractors was later shipped back to the United Kingdom and is now on display at the Banner Lane factory, in Coventry, in England, where it was built.

Specifications

Manufacturer: Standard Motor Co.
Location: Coventry, Warwickshire, England
Model: Ferguson TE-20
Type: General purpose
Power unit: Four-cylinder engine
Power output: 28hp (20.7kw)
Transmission: Four-speed gearbox
Weight: 2,520lb (1,144kg)
Production started: 1946

Part of the 1957/58 program of research and exploration involved a 1,200-mile (1,931-km) journey to the South Pole by a team led by the New Zealander Sir Edmund Hillary. As well as the three Fergusons, the team also used vehicles developed for traveling over ice and snow, but these were abandoned due to mechanical problems, and it was the three tractors that completed the journey through some of the harshest conditions in the world.

They encountered temperatures as low as -67°F (-55°C) and powdery snow 2ft (60cm) deep. They also crossed a 10,000-ft (3,048-m) plateau where the altitude reduced the engine power by more than 40 percent. For some of the journey the tractors were roped together in case one of them fell into a deep crevasse.

The Fergusons supplied to the Antarctic were standard gasoline-engined models, and the modifications included electric wiring with special cold-tolerant insulation, batteries designed for low temperatures, and waterproofed brakes to exclude powdered snow. Specially designed tracks and half-tracks were fitted. The weather protection cabs were fitted after the tractors arrived in Antarctica.

JOHN DEERE
✕ 1947 Dubuque, Iowa

JOHN DEERE MODEL M

John Deere's first all-new model after the war was the Model M, introduced in 1947 as a small tractor to replace the L, LA, and H models, and also the first tractor to be built at the new Deere factory in Dubuque, Iowa.

Right: *This Model M has the regular wheel layout; crawler, industrial, and rowcrop versions were also available.*

Above: *This is one of a batch of Model M industrial tractors given a special paint finish at the John Deere factory to meet a customer's special requirements.*

Specifications

Manufacturer: Deere & Co.	
Location: Dubuque, Iowa	
Model: M	
Type: General purpose	
Power unit: Two-cylinder vertical engine	
Power output: 18.2hp (13.5kw)	
Transmission: Four-speed gearbox	
Weight: 2,695lb (1,223kg)	
Production started: 1947	

The M continued the John Deere tradition of twin-cylinder engines, but this time the cylinders were upright, as in the L and LA models, instead of the usual horizontal layout. The cylinder measurements were 4-in (10.1-cm) bore and 4-in (10.1-cm) stroke, making the Model M one of a very few John Deere tractors powered by a so-called "square" two-cylinder engine. The power output was 18.2hp (13.5kw) with a 1,650rpm rated speed.

Equipment

For a small mid-1940s tractor the Model M was well equipped. The specification included a power takeoff and an electric starter, and the gearbox provided four forward speeds. The M was also the tractor that introduced John Deere's new Touch-O-Matic hydraulic system, a new arrangement for controlling mounted implements. A later version, known as Dual Touch-O-Matic, also included an additional control for leveling mounted equipment.

M tractors were available in a wide choice of versions, including the MI industrial model and the MT with a choice of single, twin, or adjustable front wheels. There was also an MC crawler model, which was assembled at the former Lindeman factory and offered with the choice of track widths 10, 12, or 14 inches (25.4, 30.4, or 35.5cm).

FORD

⚒ 1947 Dearborn, Michigan

FORD 8N

Henry Ford continued to control the fortunes of the huge company he had built until 1945 when, at the age of 82, he handed over the reins to his grandson, Henry Ford II. As Henry Ford senior's influence in the company declined, his partnership with Harry Ferguson also entered its final phase.

In 1945 the Ford organization was losing money, and harsh decisions were necessary to halt the rapidly mounting losses. One of the decisions was to end the "handshake agreement" between Henry Ford senior and Harry Ferguson. The agreement had produced the 9N and 2N tractors, built by Ford and incorporating Ferguson System hydraulics, but marketed by a company controlled by Ferguson.

Legal Action

Ford's American tractor operation was one of the problem areas identified in the 1945–46

financial review, and at the end of 1946 Henry Ford II announced that Ford would stop supplying tractors to the Ferguson marketing company after a six-month notice period, and that the 9N/2N tractors would be replaced by a new model.

This later prompted legal action by Harry Ferguson, who sued the Ford company for patent infringements and damages in an action involving 200 lawyers and more than a million documents. The outcome favored Ferguson, but he was awarded less than $10 million, instead of the $340 million he had claimed.

Above, top: The new 8N tractor bore a superficial resemblance to the old 9N model, and it also included the full Ferguson System linkage and hydraulics.

Above: The Ford 8N's launch brought the Ford–Ferguson partnership to an acrimonious end in what was an extremely bitter and expensive legal action.

Another result of the legal action was an agreement to make design changes to the new Ford tractor in order to stop infringement of Ferguson's patents. The new tractor was the Ford 8N, launched in July 1947 to replace the 9N/2N and offering a list of more than 20 design improvements.

The 8N started its commercial life with the full Ferguson System rear linkage and hydraulics—later modified following the court decision—but the Ferguson-approved gray paint finish was replaced by a pale gray and red, and the three-speed gearbox specified by Harry Ferguson for the previous model was replaced by a four-speed version in the new tractor.

Success

In spite of the legal action and the modifications, the 8N was one of the biggest success stories

the tractor industry has seen, with production peaking at more than 100,000 tractors per year in 1948 and 1949. The only other tractor that has broken the 100,000 per year barrier was Henry Ford's Fordson Model F. However, Harry Ferguson was able to achieve the same distinction by combining the production totals for his British-built TE series tractors and their American TO equivalent.

Ford 8N production continued until 1953 when the new NAA tractor arrived as part of the Ford company's Golden Jubilee celebrations.

Specifications

Manufacturer: Ford Motor Co.	**Transmission:** Four-speed gearbox
Location: Dearborn, Michigan	**Weight:** 2,710lb (1,230kg)
Model: 8N	**Production started:** 1947
Type: General purpose	
Power unit: Four-cylinder engine	
Power output: 21hp (15.5kw) (maximum)	

Left: *This publicity photograph from the Ford archives shows Ford 8N tractors at the end of the 8N production lines at the Ford factory in Dearborn, Michigan.*

MARSHALL
✕ 1947 Gainsborough, Lincolnshire, England

FIELD MARSHALL SERIES II

Fifty years ago the distinctive exhaust note of a single-cylinder Field Marshall tractor engine was a familiar sound on many British farms, and the tractors became a success story for the Marshall company.

Specifications

Manufacturer: Marshall Sons & Co.
Location: Gainsborough, Lincolnshire, England
Model: Field Marshall Series II
Type: General purpose
Power unit: Single-cylinder two-stroke diesel engine
Power output: 40hp (30kw)
Transmission: Three-speed gearbox
Weight: 7,500lb (5,550kg)
Production started: 1947

The first version of the Marshall tractor with its single-cylinder engine was one of a group of diesel tractors that took part in the World Tractor Trials held near Oxford, in England, in 1930. Five tractors took part in the diesel section of the trials, but the Marshall was the only one that was still in production during the 1930s and available after the war.

Series I and II
Interest in diesel-powered tractors increased rapidly during the war, and this probably helped to boost demand for the Marshall tractor, now known as the Field Marshall. The new Series I model announced in 1945 retained the same two-stroke horizontal diesel engine as the prewar Model M, and it also featured a heavy external flywheel to regulate the operation of the single-cylinder engine. The power output was 40hp (30kw) at the 750rpm-rated engine speed, up from 700rpm for the Model M.

Series II Field Marshals were available starting in 1947, and the principle improvements over previous models were a beefed-up transmission, improved brakes, and a bigger clutch. The new version was also equipped with bigger rear tires and a more comfortable driver's seat. There was also a higher specification contractor's model offering a faster road speed and with lights included in the standard specification.

Above: The single-cylinder engine of the Field Marshall tractors played a significant part in boosting diesel power's popularity on UK farms.

MASSEY-HARRIS
1948   Manchester, England

MASSEY-HARRIS 744D

The American-built 44K tractor was the model chosen by Massey-Harris when it decided to start building tractors in Britain, where it was known at first as the 744PD. All British-built Massey-Harris products at that time were identified by a 7 added to the front of the model number, and the PD added to the end of the number stood for Perkins diesel.

Right: *Massey-Harris chose a Perkins diesel engine for the British-built version of its 44 model, known initially as the 744PD.*

Above: *This front-end view of the Massey-Harris 744PD shows the distinctive Perkins badge to indicate the P6 diesel engine.*

Specifications

Manufacturer: Massey-Harris
Location: Manchester, England
Model: 744PD
Type: General purpose
Power unit: Six-cylinder diesel engine
Power output: 46hp (34kw)
Transmission: Five-speed gearbox
Weight: 5,152lb (2,339kg)
Production started: 1948

Massey-Harris decided to standardize on diesel power for its British-built tractor, and as its own diesel engine was not yet available when production started at the company's Manchester factory in 1948, it chose the six-cylinder Perkins P6 with 46-hp (34-kw) rated output.

Disappointing Sales

The combination of the MH 44 tractor with its superior five-speed gearbox plus the excellent P6 engine should have been a big success, but the sales performance was disappointing. After the first pilot batch of 16 tractors had been assembled at the Manchester factory, Massey-Harris switched production to its new tractor and machinery plant in Kilmarnock, Scotland, and at this stage, it seems, the model number was simplified to 744D.

In 1954, the year after Massey-Harris bought Harry Ferguson's tractor business, production of the 744D ended after 17,000 tractors had been built in six years. It was replaced by the new 745 model, which was powered by a Perkins L4 engine that was claimed to offer more power while using less fuel than the P6.

URSUS

1947 **Ursus, Warsaw, Poland**

URSUS C45

Ursus tractors first appeared in the early 1920s, and the first model was a copy of the International Harvester Titan 10-20 tractor built under a license agreement. Tractor production was one of the priorities in the postwar reconstruction of Polish industry, and the Ursus factory started building tractors again in 1947.

Above: *A fully cushioned seat mounted on a coil spring was part of the package of driver comfort features on the Polish-built Ursus C45.*

Above, left: *This picture of the Ursus C45 semidiesel-powered tractor shows how closely the design resembles a Lanz tractor.*

The 1947 tractor was the C45 and, as the photographs show, it was a Lanz Bulldog lookalike—in fact the two tractors are so similar that Bulldog replacement parts fit the Ursus.

Hot-Bulb Engine

The C45 was the result of another license agreement, and the aging Bulldog design became a familiar sight and sound on Polish farms. It featured the familiar Lanz hot-bulb or semidiesel engine, and the standard version featured the usual blowlamp to heat the cylinder head, while the wood-rimmed steering wheel doubled as a starting handle to turn the tractor's engine over.

Customers who were reluctant to spend 20 minutes or so to start the engine from cold could specify an optional electric starter. This system used a trembler coil to provide the spark to ignite gasoline, and the engine continued to run on gasoline until the cylinder head was sufficiently hot to continue running on diesel or paraffin.

The gasoline/electric system speeded up the starting process, but it did not overcome the quite strong possibility that the engine would run backward. This is a characteristic of semidiesels, and in the case of the C45 it would mean that the four forward speeds and one reverse are converted into four reverse speeds and one forward.

Driver Comfort

There are just a few indications on the C45 that driver comfort and convenience were beginning to emerge as significant design features. The seat on the C45 tractor is on a coil spring to allow vertical movement, and it is cushioned—although the cushions in the photograph at left are not the originals. The driving position is also offset, which allows better forward visibility, but also leaves more space for climbing aboard, and the most surprising comfort feature is the leaf spring suspension under the front axle to give the driver a smoother ride.

Production of the Ursus C45 was to continue well into the 1950s, when more modern designs took over; however, the policy of relying on imported technology that had started with the Titan and the Bulldog remained in place. There were close links between Ursus and the Zetor tractor company in Czechoslovakia, and during the 1980s Massey Ferguson provided the know-how to build a new Ursus factory where some MF models and Perkins engines were built under license.

Below: A massive transversely mounted leaf spring under the front axle of the Ursus C45 provided one contribution to driver comfort.

Specifications

Manufacturer: Ursus	**Transmission:** Four-speed gearbox
Location: Ursus, Warsaw, Poland	**Weight:** N/A
Model: C45	**Production started:** 1947
Type: General purpose	
Power unit: Semidiesel engine	
Power output: 45hp (33.3kw)	

COUNTY

1948 **Fleet, Hampshire, England**

COUNTY FULL TRACK

The close links between County Commercial Cars and the Ford Motor Company started in 1929 when County produced its first truck conversion. It was a six-wheeler version of the Ford AA series chassis.

Specifications

Manufacturer: County Commercial Cars
Location: Fleet, Hampshire, England
Model: County Full Track
Type: Tracklayer
Power unit: Four-cylinder engine
Power output: 45hp (33.3kw) (diesel version)
Transmission: Three-speed gearbox
Weight: N/A
Production started: 1948

Above: *County was best known for its four-wheel drive conversions of Ford tractors, but the CFT tracklayer provided its first commercial success.*

County's first venture into the tractor market came in 1948 when it used a Fordson Major tractor as the basis for the County Full Track, later shortened to CFT. It offered the extra pulling power and the reduced ground pressure of a tracklayer, plus the reliability and international parts availability of the Fordson. The combination was so successful that the CFT was the start of County's future development as a specialist tractor company.

Design Features

Standard track width for the CFT was 12in (30.48cm), giving a claimed ground pressure of 4.5psi, but alternative widths were offered later. A special feature of the County track design was a high front wheel and driving sprocket. This improved the performance over rough ground, the makers claimed, and it also reduced the angle of movement for the track plates to minimize wear and stress.

The design also raised the height of the top track, giving the CFT and subsequent County tracklayers a distinctive appearance, but it also made it more difficult for the operator to climb on to the driving seat.

CFT production started with the standard Fordson engine, but this was later replaced by the Perkins-powered diesel Major, boosting the engine power to 5hp (33.3kw).

TURNER
🔧 1949 Wolverhampton, Staffordshire, England

TURNER "YEOMAN OF ENGLAND"

When the Turner Manufacturing Company decided to diversify into tractor production it produced a medium-power model and gave it an upmarket price. Production started in 1949, and the tractor was one of the star attractions when it was launched at the Royal Show, held by the Royal Agricultural Society of England.

Right: *Turner's Yeoman of England was an ambitious attempt to market a mid-range diesel tractor at an upmarket price.*

Above: *Freeman Sanders designed the diesel engine for the Turner tractor using a vee-four layout that bulged out of the engine compartment's sides.*

Specifications

Manufacturer: Turner Manufacturing Co.
Location: Wolverhampton, Staffordshire, England
Model: Yeoman of England
Type: General purpose
Power unit: Vee-four diesel engine
Power output: 34hp (25kw)
Transmission: Four-speed gearbox
Weight: N/A
Production started: 1949

At that stage it was simply known as the Turner tractor, and the "Yeoman of England" name was added later, displayed on a distinctive brass plate. One of the features of the tractor was the diesel power unit. Instead of going to one of the established diesel engine manufacturers, Turner decided to make its own engine. It was designed by Freeman Sanders, an engineer who was previously the engine designer for Fowler tractors, where he introduced a new combustion chamber that improved fuel efficiency and produced a smoother performance.

His design for the Turner engine was unusual, with four cylinders arranged in pairs in a vee formation with a 68° angle. The engine capacity was 1,962.6ci (3,271cc) and the rated output was 34hp (23.5kw). Because of the engine's size and shape it bulged out of the engine compartment to give an impression of power.

Poor Sales
In spite of what was probably a good engine, the Turner tractor failed to achieve the required sales volumes and production of the model ended after eight years. Demand was affected by mechanical problems in the early stages of production, and the tractor was also overpriced, with the power takeoff, hydraulics, rubber tires, and belt pulley all listed as extras.

JOHN DEERE

⚒ **1949 Waterloo, Iowa**

JOHN DEERE MODEL R

When the first of the new Model R tractors arrived in dealers' showrooms in 1949 it was a major milestone in John Deere tractor history. One of the reasons why the R was significant was because it was the last new John Deere model to be identified by a letter of the alphabet. Since then numbers have been used.

Above: *Most of the Model R tractors were equipped with rubber tires, but the rear wheels on this steel-wheel version were fitted with special lugs for rice cultivation.*

Left: *This cutaway picture of the Model R shows the twin-cylinder diesel engine and the five-speed gearbox—both firsts from John Deere.*

The Model R was also the first John Deere tractor to include a steel cab in the list of options and the first to be equipped with a five-speed gearbox. The most important new feature on the Model R was the first diesel engine on a John Deere production tractor. John Deere had been experimenting with diesel power since the early war years, and when it arrived on the market it proved to be one of the best diesels available. The R engine set a new record for fuel efficiency when tested in Nebraska, and it also set a new record as the most powerful engine in a John Deere production tractor.

Engine

The new engine retained the familiar horizontal two-cylinder design, with bore and stroke dimensions of 5.75in and 8in (14.6cm and 20.3cm), and the maximum power output was 51hp (38kw). For starting the diesel engine, the John Deere development team chose a small gasoline engine, a two-cylinder design but with horizontally opposed cylinders. The gasoline engine shared the same cooling system as the big diesel, meaning that heat produced by the starter engine helped to warm up the diesel engine and make it easier to start.

A small electric motor started the gasoline engine, powered by the tractor's batteries. Manually operated starting was also provided as a backup in case the battery was flat. In spite of the complicated starting procedure, the Model R's engine performance showed that John Deere was among the leaders in developing diesel power for farm tractors. The options list included an independent power takeoff with a separate clutch for operating powered equipment.

Production peaked in 1953, and in the following year the last of the Model R tractors rolled off the production line.

Specifications

Manufacturer: Deere & Co.
Location: Waterloo, Iowa
Model: R
Type: General purpose
Power unit: Twin-cylinder diesel engine
Power output: 51hp (38kw)
Transmission: Five-speed gearbox
Weight: 7,603lb (3,452kg)
Production started: 1949

INTERNATIONAL HARVESTER
1949   Doncaster, Yorkshire, England

I.H. FARMALL BM

International Harvester built its first factory in Britain in 1938, but during the war the buildings were requisitioned for use as a munitions works, and International Harvester had to wait until 1946 before it could regain control and begin building machinery for the British market and for export.

Right: *Tractor production at the International Harvester factory in Britain started with the BM, the British version of the highly successful American-built Farmall M.*

Specifications

Manufacturer: International Harvester Co.

Location: Doncaster, Yorkshire, England

Model: BM

Type: General purpose

Power unit: Four-cylinder engine

Power output: 36.7hp (27kw)

Transmission: Five-speed gearbox

Weight: 5,588lb (2,540kg)

Production started: 1949

An important development at the factory came when the production facilities were extended to include tractors for the first time. The first tractor driven off the line in 1949 by Tom Williams, Britain's Minister of Agriculture at the time, was a Farmall M.

The new model was basically a British-built version of the familiar M that had been available in the United States since 1939, but it was subsequently referred to as the BM to identify it as a British product.

The Farmall M was powered by an American-built four-cylinder engine with overhead valves and 242.8 cubic inches (4.0 liters) of capacity. Power output on the belt was 36.7hp (27kw).

Diesel Version

A diesel version called the BMD was added to the Doncaster product line in 1952, and in 1953 the BM and BMD provided the base for the new BT6 and BTD6 models, the first tracklayers to be built at Doncaster. The final stage in the BM and BMD story came in 1953 when both models were updated and relabeled as the Super BM and the Super BMD, both with increased power.

BROCKHOUSE

✄ **1950   Southport, Lancashire, England**

BMB PRESIDENT

As the tractor market expanded in Britain after the end of the war, there was a big increase in the number of companies moving into the market with small tractors. Many of the new mini tractors launched during the late 1940s and early 1950s were poorly designed and made little impact on the market, but the BMB President was one of the exceptions.

Specifications

Manufacturer: Brockhouse Engineering Co.
Location: Southport, Lancashire, England
Model: BMB President
Type: Mini tractor
Power unit: Morris four-cylinder engine
Power output: 14hp (10.4kw)
Transmission: Three-speed gearbox
Weight: 1,800lb (817kg)
Production started: 1950

It was made by the Brockhouse Engineering Co., a well established manufacturer of a range of pedestrian-controlled cultivators. The President was its first tractor, and it was designed for small farms and market gardens.

Design Features

The power unit for the BMB President was a Morris car engine with a paraffin-burning conversion. The capacity was 551.4ci (919cc), and the power output at the rated speed of 2,500rpm was 16hp (11.9kw) on gasoline and 14hp (10.4kw) when running on paraffin. The specification included a three-speed gearbox,

but the power takeoff and three-point linkage were optional extras.

Although one of the best of the new generation of mini tractors, the President's sales figures were disappointing. Introducing an orchard model failed to make much impact on sales, and in 1957 the President was taken over by the London-based H. J. Stockton company.

A new version of the President was launched at the 1957 Smithfield Show in London with different styling and with a twin-cylinder Petter diesel engine. This venture was not a success, however, and appears to have lasted little more than 12 months.

Above: *Brockhouse Engineering chose a 14-hp (10.4-kw) Morris car engine for its President tractor, which was to remain in production for seven years.*

JOHN DEERE

⚒ 1952 Dubuque, Iowa

JOHN DEERE 40

When the old range of John Deere tractors identified by letters was phased out and replaced by the first of the new numbered models, the changeover took two years to complete, and at that stage it was the company's biggest new model launch.

Right: *The 40 was the smallest model in the new range of John Deere tractors identified by numbers.*

Above: *The Model M engine with two vertical cylinders reappeared in the new 40 tractor, but with a faster operating speed to boost the tractor's power output.*

Specifications

Manufacturer: Deere and Co.

Location: Dubuque, Iowa

Model: 40

Type: General purpose

Power unit: Two-cylinder engine

Power output: 22.7hp (16.8kw)

Transmission: Four-speed gearbox

Weight: 3,219lb (1,461kg)

Production started: 1952

The first batch of new models arrived in 1952, and they included the 40, the smallest tractor in the new range. It replaced the Model M and, like its predecessor, it was built at John Deere's Dubuque factory.

Inheritance

The new model also inherited the Model M engine with its twin upright cylinders and its "square" bore and stroke; however, on the new tractor the rated engine speed was increased by 200rpm to 1,850rpm to boost the machine's power output by 4.5hp (3.3kw).

Like the other new numbered models, the 40 styling was based on the late 1930s Dreyfuss appearance, but updated to follow the new look introduced on the Model R. The new 40 tractor also shared some of the driver comfort and convenience features that arrived on the new numbered series, including an improved seat design and an improved steering mechanism that was lighter to operate.

A tracklaying version known as the 40C was available from the former Lindeman plant, and the John Deere 40 was also offered in an S version for rowcrop work.

chapter 6

The Horsepower Race

Although there were plenty of new companies moving into the tractor industry during the 1950s, it was also a time when some of the established manufacturers disappeared through mergers and takeovers, and the biggest takeover was the sale of Harry Ferguson's tractor business to the Massey-Harris company.

Above: *Fordson Dexta tractors built for the UK market were all equipped with diesel power, but a spark-ignition engine was available for export markets.*

Left: *The Perkins diesel badge appeared on more and more different tractors, and in this case it is seen on a Howard Platypus tracklayer.*

Harry Ferguson's decision to sell the business was surprising. He was almost certainly very wealthy, and he was selling one of the most successful tractor companies in the world, yet he was still full of ideas and enthusiasm. In spite of this he appears to have been eager to sell, and the result was the Massey-Ferguson tractor range.

Immediate repercussions of the Ferguson sale included new and updated models as the company tried to maintain both the Massey-Harris and the Ferguson ranges; some of these tractors appear in this chapter. There is also further evidence of the spread of diesel power in the United Kingdom and the United States, and the Doe tractor based on a farmer's ideas provided an early example of a tractor with four-wheel drive and 100hp-plus, a formula that would soon become much more important.

What was missing in 1950s tractor development was significant progress in driver comfort and, more importantly, driver safety. There was increasing data, particularly from Scandinavia, showing that the lack of cabs and other safety structures was causing unacceptable levels of death and serious injury when tractors overturned, but the tractor industry and its customers failed to take serious action over safety cabs until forced to do so by legislation.

FORDSON

1951 Dagenham, Essex, England

NEW FORDSON MAJOR

In spite of its sales success the Fordson E27N had been introduced as a makeshift model to maintain sales while the Ford engineers were working on the New Fordson Major.

As well as the new tractor, they were also developing a completely new engine. The new engine was a diesel, and work had started on the project at the Ford factory at Dagenham in 1944 in spite of considerable opposition from some of the company's senior management. The opponents pointed out, quite correctly, that previous efforts to develop diesel-powered wheeled tractors had achieved little success, and there was no evidence that farmers would be willing to switch to the new fuel.

In spite of the doubts the development program continued, and the new tractor was launched at the 1951 Smithfield Show in London, with deliveries starting the following year. Customers were offered three engine options using gasoline, gasoline/paraffin, and diesel fuel. The diesel version had a 218.5-cubic -inch (3.6-liter) capacity with a 16:1 compression ratio, the paraffin burner was also 218.5 cubic inches but with 4.35:1 compression ratio, and the gasoline engine capacity was

Above: *The new Fordson Major was launched in 1951, with deliveries starting the following year. It was followed by the Super Major and Power Major versions.*

197.8 cubic inches (3.26 liters) with a 5.5:1 ratio. Power output was initially rated at 40hp (29.6kw) at 1,700rpm, but this was increased on later versions of the tractor.

Diesel Success

The diesel engine became a big success. It was one of small group of British engines that helped to introduce a new generation of diesel power with high-speed, multicylinder units that were smoother than previous diesels and easier to start. By the end of the production run of the New Major and its Super Major and Power Major derivatives more than 90 percent of UK customers were specifying the diesel version.

It was not just the engines that pushed the New Major up the UK sales charts and won export success as well. This was the first complete break from the original Fordson Model F design of 1917, and it was more advanced technically and more capable than previous models in every respect. It combined up-to-date styling with a technical specification that included a smooth, dual-ratio gearbox with six forward speeds. It was also well built, and the New Major soon earned a reputation for reliability and durability.

The New Major was also popular as the engine and transmission for the growing number of four-wheel drive and crawler specialists, and the Fordson provided the power for tractors from County, Doe, and Roadless.

Above: *The Fordson Power Major was available from 1958 and based on the New Major, but with a number of detailed improvements.*

Specifications

Manufacturer: Ford Motor Co.
Location: Dagenham, Essex, England
Model: New Fordson Major
Type: General purpose
Power unit: Ford four-cylinder diesel engine
Power output: 40hp (29.6kw)

Transmission: Six-speed gearbox
Weight: 5,308lb (2,409kg)
Production started: 1951

Below: *Toward the end of the Fordson Major production run more than 90 percent of UK customers were specifying the diesel version.*

PLATYPUS
⚒ 1952   Basildon, Essex, England

HOWARD PLATYPUS 30

Arthur "Cliff" Howard was born in Australia, and in the late 1930s he moved to the UK to set up the Howard Rotavator company to build the tractor-powered rotary cultivator he had designed. The company was highly successful, at one stage claiming to be the world's biggest farm machinery manufacturer.

Above: *Various versions of the Platypus tractor were available during the six-year production run, all powered by Perkins diesel engines.*

Specifications

Manufacturer:	Platypus Tractor Co.
Location:	Basildon, Essex, England
Model:	Howard Platypus 30
Type:	Tracklayer
Power unit:	Perkins P4 diesel engine
Power output:	34hp (25.2kw)
Transmission:	Six-speed dual-range gearbox
Weight:	5,684lb (2,578kg)
Production started:	1952

The first Platypus crawler tractors arrived in about 1950, powered by a Standard gasoline engine, and their success encouraged the Howard company to open a new factory at Basildon, Essex, in England, specifically for tractor production, starting in 1952.

Most of the Basildon-built tractors were equipped with Perkins engines, and the most popular model was the Platypus 30 with a P4 engine developing 34hp (25.2kw). There was also a 71-hp (52.9-kw) version powered by a Perkins R6 engine.

Presumably it was the Howard family's Australian connections that prompted the Platypus name for the tractors. A platypus is an Australian marsupial, and according to the Howard sales leaflet for the tractor, it is small but powerful, hard working, and as much at home on the water as on dry land.

Disappointing Sales

In spite of the Platypus name and development of a Bogmaster version with extra-wide tracks designed for working in extremely soft ground conditions, sales volumes for the tractor were disappointing, and production of the Platypus ended in 1958 when the decision was taken to close the loss-making Basildon factory.

Above, left: *Platypus Tractor Co. was a subsidiary of the Howard machinery company, and its crawler tractors were built at a factory in Basildon, Essex, in England.*

MAN
1952 Nürnberg, Germany

MAN AS 440A

Not surprisingly the Maschinenfabrik Augsburg-Nürnberg company abbreviated its name to MAN, and this became a familiar brand name in the German tractor market during the 1950s and 1960s.

Right: *In a less safety-conscious age many European tractor manufacturers added a passenger seat to one of the fenders, or mudguards, of their tractors.*

Specifications

Manufacturer: MAN Ag
Location: Nürnberg, Germany
Model: AS 440A
Type: General purpose
Power unit: MAN four-cylinder diesel engine
Power output: 40hp (29.6kw)
Transmission: Six-speed gearbox
Weight: 4,675lb (2,120kg)
Production started: 1952

Germany has a long tradition of diesel-engine development, and MAN is one of the leading manufacturers. When the AS 440A tractor was introduced in 1952 it was powered by a D9214 series four-cylinder diesel engine built at the MAN factory in Nürnberg. Most of the German-built tractors during the 1950s were relatively low horsepower models designed for small-acreage family farms, many of them run on a part-time basis, but the AS440A was one of the exceptions.

It was a big tractor by contemporary standards, with the engine delivering a maximum output of 40hp (29.6kw) at 2,000rpm, and the tractor in working trim with a full fuel tank weighed just over two tons.

Versions

Two- and four-wheel drive versions were available, and the specification included a six-speed gearbox with almost 17mph (27km/h) available in top gear. MAN tractors are popular with German vintage-tractor enthusiasts, and the well restored model in the photograph includes the optional cab and road lights. The passenger seat on the left-hand fender, or mudguard, was a popular feature on many tractors used in Europe during the 1950s.

SINGER
⚒ **1953 Birmingham, England**

SINGER MONARCH

Singer Motors was one of the smaller companies in the UK car industry during the early 1950s and, in financial terms, it was certainly not the strongest, but its 1953 venture into tractor production was presumably an attempt to broaden its product base in order to generate more turnover.

Specifications

Manufacturer: Singer Motors	
Location: Birmingham, England	
Model: Monarch	
Type: General purpose	
Power unit: Ford four-cylinder industrial engine	
Power output: 17hp (12.6kw)	
Transmission: Six-speed dual-range gearbox	
Weight: 1,430lb (649kg)	
Production started: 1953	

It was a surprising move. The tractor the company chose was the Monarch four-wheeler made by the Coventry-based Oak Tree Appliances company, or OTA.

The Monarch was announced in 1949 and was powered by a Ford industrial engine developing 17hp (12.6kw) at the 2,000rpm rated speed and available in gasoline and gasoline/ paraffin versions. The standard specification for the Monarch included a dual-ratio gearbox with six forward speeds and two in reverse, and there was 42 to 60in (106 to 152cm) of wheel track adjustment for row-crop work.

Although the OTA Monarch was reasonably successful, the Singer Motors decision to buy the production rights was probably not the wisest move in the circumstances. The Monarch had never achieved big sales volumes, and the fact that it was designed to use an engine that was supplied by one of Singer's strongest competitors in the car industry may not have been an ideal arrangement.

Failure
The Monarch did little to improve the Singer company's fortunes. When the Rootes Group, one of the leading car manufacturers, made a successful bid to buy Singer in 1956, one of the first actions the Rootes Group took was to close down the fledgling tractor operation.

Above: Britain's Singer car company made a brief appearance in the tractor market with the Monarch, which was powered by a 17-hp (12.6-kw) Ford industrial engine.

FORD
1953   Dearborn, Michigan

FORD NAA "GOLDEN JUBILEE" MODEL

To mark the Ford Motor Company's 50th anniversary in 1953 the tractor division in America produced a special Golden Jubilee tractor. It was called the Ford NAA, and as it was available for one year only it has become a popular model with Ford tractor enthusiasts.

Above: The hydraulic system on the Ford 8N tractor was improved when it was used on the NAA Golden Jubilee tractor.

Right: Power for the Golden Jubilee tractor was provided by the Ford Red Tiger engine, with a 10 percent increase in capacity to boost the output to 30hp (22kw).

Specifications

Manufacturer: Ford Motor Co.
Location: Dearborn, Michigan
Model: NAA "Golden Jubilee"
Type: General purpose
Power unit: Ford four-cylinder I-head gasoline engine
Power output: 30hp (22kw)
Transmission: Four-speed gearbox
Weight: 2,841lb (1,290kg)
Production started: 1953

The NAA tractor retained the eye-catching pale gray and red colors of the 8N, but introduced new-look styling that was retained for later models. It also displayed a large, circular Golden Jubilee badge; however, a batch of engineering improvements proved that the NAA was more than just a new-look 8N.

Design Features

Maximum power from the NAA engine was 30hp (22kw) compared with 25.5hp (19kw) for the 8N, due mainly to an increase in engine capacity to 133.5 cubic inches (2.2 liters) instead of the previous 121.4 cubic inches (2.0 liters). Both engines were made by Ford, but the 8N was an L-head design, while the Red Tiger engine in the Golden Jubilee tractor was an I-head. The NAA hydraulic system also included a number of design improvements. A series of seals had been added to reduce the risk of metal particles from the gearbox reaching the hydraulic system, and the hydraulic system was also more responsive than the 8N version. There was also a new flow control on the pump, allowing the operator to slow down the drop rate when lowering an implement.

NUFFIELD

1954 Birmingham, England

NUFFIELD 4DM

When the Nuffield tractor business became part of the British Motor Corporation (BMC) in 1952 it was inevitable that some of the tractor engines would be sourced from the new owners. The engine change was soon arranged, and in 1954 the 48-hp (35.8-kw) Perkins P4 power unit that powered the Universal DM4 model was replaced by a brand-new diesel engine designed and built by the BMC.

Below: *The badge on the radiator grille shows that this is one of the later Nuffields built after the Perkins diesel engine was replaced by a BMC power unit.*

The capacity of the new engine was 206.3 cubic inches (3.4 liters) and it developed its 45-hp (33.3-kw) rated output at 2,000rpm. To identify the new version the DM4 model number was changed to 4DM, and another name change followed in 1957 when the same tractor became known as the Universal Four.

This brought it into line with the newly launched Universal Three, a smaller version of the Universal designed to cover a wider sector of the market and compete with the Fordson Dexta and the Massey Ferguson 35.

Other Updates

As well as the engine and name changes, there were also some specification updates, and in 1956 the options list for the 4DM included an independent power takeoff and hydraulic system. The power takeoff was controlled separately by operating a hand-operated clutch.

The new version continued to use the five-speed gearbox that had been part of the standard specification since the first Universal was introduced in 1948.The five-speed box remained until 1964, when the ratios were doubled to ten.

Specifications

Manufacturer: British Motor Corporation
Location: Birmingham, England
Model: Universal 4DM
Type: General purpose
Power unit: BMC four-cylinder diesel engine
Power output: 45hp (33.3kw)
Transmission: Five-speed gearbox
Weight: 5,898lb (2,678kg)
Production started: 1954

FIAT
✗ 1954 Turin, Italy

FIAT 25R

The 25R was the diesel-powered version of Fiat's top-selling tractor model in the mid-1950s. It was announced in 1954 and was available until Fiat announced a full range of new models in 1959 and 1960.

Right: *Fiat's publicity department provided this artistic shot of the 25R powering a water pump for irrigation with the spray jets framing the tractor.*

Above: *The power options for the 25R tractor included a four-cylinder diesel engine complete with electric starting and a glow plug backup.*

Specifications

Manufacturer: Fiat

Location: Turin, Italy

Model: 25R

Type: General purpose

Power unit: Fiat four-cylinder diesel engine

Power output: 24hp (17.9kw)

Transmission: Four-speed gearbox

Weight: 3,108lb (1,410kg)

Production started: 1954

Power for the 25R was provided by a Fiat-built four-cylinder engine with 24-hp (17.9-kw) rated output at 2,000rpm. The capacity of the engine was 3,168ci (1,901cc) and the fact that it was equipped with electric starting plus glow plug assistance for cold-weather starts was promoted in the sales leaflet as one of the most important attractions. The standard specification included a four-speed gearbox, although later versions of the 25R were available with an optional five-speed gearbox.

A three-point linkage and power takeoff were included in the options list for the 25R, and

customers could also specify a belt pulley and a jack. One of the more unusual items in the list of optional equipment was a steel lever for removing punctured tires.

Other Options

As well as the wheeled tractor, Fiat also offered a 25C tracklayer model, and this could be supplied in vineyard, forestry, and industrial versions. On the 25C tractor options list there was also a protective cowling that could be fitted onto the standard crawler tractor to give it a smoother outline for working in orchards.

MASSEY-HARRIS
1955 Detroit, Michigan

MASSEY-HARRIS MH 50

Some of the problems that followed the sale of Harry Ferguson's tractor business to the Massey-Harris company in 1953 were the result of the decision to support both the Massey-Harris and the Ferguson dealer networks with two separate tractor ranges.

Specifications

Manufacturer: Massey-Harris-Ferguson
Location: Detroit, Michigan
Model: Massey-Harris MH 50
Type: General purpose
Power unit: Continental four-cylinder gasoline engine
Power output: 31hp (23kw)
Transmission: Six-speed gearbox
Weight: 3,432lb (1,558kg)
Production started: 1955

Above: *This 1950s publicity photograph was taken at a demonstration to show how easily linkage-mounted implements could cultivate an entire small fenced area.*

The result was a flurry of tractor launches in the mid-1950s as the company—which was briefly called Massey-Harris-Ferguson before the name was abbreviated to Massey Ferguson—tried to be even-handed with both the Massey-Harris and the Ferguson networks in the United States.

New Features

The Massey-Harris MH 50 tractor was one of the consequences of this policy. In January 1955 the Ferguson dealers had started to sell the TO-35 tractor, an updated version of the old TO-30 model. Although the new tractor kept the familiar Ferguson styling, the mechanical improvements included a "live" power takeoff and a new, improved gearbox with six speeds instead of the previous model's four, and there was also a bigger version of the Continental engine to boost the power output.

Massey-Harris dealers were the next in line for a new model, and it arrived at the end of 1955. This was the MH 50, carrying the Massey-Harris name and badge, but underneath the red-painted exterior it featured many of the mechanical features from the Ferguson TO-35. These included the same Continental Z134 engine producing 31hp (23kw), a six-speed gearbox and full Ferguson System hydraulics, and three-point linkage with draft control.

FERGUSON
1955   Detroit, Michigan

FERGUSON F40

The Ferguson F40 tractor was another of the models produced as a result of the Massey-Harris-Ferguson policy of keeping separate tractor ranges in order to keep both of its dealer networks happy.

Right: *The Ferguson F40 was introduced to provide the American Ferguson dealer network with its own type of rowcrop tractor.*

Specifications

Manufacturer: Massey-Harris-Ferguson

Location: Detroit, Michigan

Model: Ferguson F40

Type: General purpose

Power unit: Continental four-cylinder gasoline engine

Power output: 31hp (23kw)

Transmission: Six-speed gearbox

Weight: 3,820lb (1,734kg)

Production started: 1955

When the M-H 50 tractor arrived at the end of 1955 under the Massey-Harris brand name, it provided the former Massey-Harris dealers with a type of rowcrop model that they could sell on an exclusive basis.

The Ferguson dealers complained that they did not have a tractor of this type, and the F40 was added to the line to provide them with a model that was the equivalent of the popular MH-50.

Similarities

Although the Ferguson F40 and Massey-Harris MH 50 did not look similar, most of the differences were superficial, and both models shared the same Continental 132.9-cubic-inch (2.19-liter) engine with a 2,000rpm speed rating, and both used the same six-speed transmission and other mechanical features.

Optional Extras

The 40 model also demonstrated the fact that Harry Ferguson's influence in Massey-Ferguson was waning. He always insisted on gray paint for his tractors and would not have agreed to the creamy white of the Ferguson 40.

The 40 was also the first tractor bearing the Ferguson name to be offered with the option of a tricycle-style wheel layout, another of Harry Ferguson's dislikes.

Ferguson 40 production lasted just over one year, and 10,000 were built during that time.

DAVID BROWN

⚒ 1955 Meltham, Yorkshire, England

DAVID BROWN 2D

When the 1955 Smithfield Show opened its doors in London the star attractions included the new 2D tool-carrier exhibited on the David Brown stand. The unconventional design included a two-cylinder diesel engine, and the main frame contained the air supply for the pneumatic implement lift.

Above: *The lift system for mid-mounted implements was powered by an air supply carried in the steel tubes forming the 2D's main frame.*

Specifications

Manufacturer: David Brown Tractors
Location: Meltham, Yorkshire, England
Model: 2D
Type: Tool carrier
Power unit: David Brown two-cylinder diesel engine
Power output: 12hp (9kw)
Transmission: Four-speed gearbox
Weight: N/A
Production started: 1955

Tool carriers are designed for accurate inter-row work, and the design features include an unobstructed view of the crop ahead of the tractor, light weight to avoid soil damage, and enough underside clearance for carrying mid-mounted implements. The 2D met all of these requirements, and it included additional features that attracted the Smithfield Show visitors.

Options

A mid-mounted toolbar for carrying implements was standard equipment on the 2D, and the model's options list included a second toolbar for the rear of the tractor, improving efficiency by allowing two jobs to be done in a single pass. The lift cylinders that raised the toolbars out of

work were operated by compressed air, using a pressurized air supply provided by a small pump. The steel tubes that formed the main frame of the 2D were also designed to provide the storage capacity for the air supply.

Two-Cylinder Diesel

At a time when diesel engines were increasingly popular when it came to larger tractors, David Brown designed a small two-cylinder diesel developing 12hp (9kw) for the 2D; however, this was later increased to 14hp (10.4kw). The engine was rear-mounted, and it was linked to a four-speed gearbox.

Production ended in 1961, and by that time just 2008 of the 2Ds had been built.

Above, left: *The frame of the 2D tool carrier was designed to carry mid-mounted implements while offering good visibility from the driver's seat.*

INTERNATIONAL HARVESTER

1955 Bradford, Yorkshire, England

INTERNATIONAL HARVESTER B250

As well as the newly equipped factory in Doncaster, International Harvester's UK-based manufacturing operations also included the factory in Bradford, Yorkshire, where the Jowett company had previously built its cars and light vans, and this is where the I.H. McCormick B250 tractor was built.

Right: *International Harvester soon outgrew its new factory in Doncaster, and production of the B250 tractor was based in Bradford, Yorkshire.*

Above: *In 1955 when the B250 tractor was introduced, International Harvester was still promoting the McCormick brand name.*

Specifications

Manufacturer: International Harvester (GB)
Location: Bradford, Yorkshire, England
Model: McCormick B250
Type: General purpose
Power unit: I.H. direct-injection diesel engine
Power output: 30hp (22.2kw)
Transmission: Five-speed gearbox
Weight: N/A
Production started: 1955

The B250 was announced at the 1955 Smithfield Show in London, and production continued until 1961. International Harvester had decided to offer the B250 with diesel power only and no optional paraffin engine, and this is an indication of the rapid progress that had been made in the acceptance of diesel power in the farming industry.

Specification

I.H. used a four-cylinder diesel engine with indirect injection for the B250. The power output was 30hp (22.2kw), putting the B250 into what I.H. described as the medium-power category. It featured a high level of equipment, including live dual-category hydraulics and an automatic pickup hitch, and it was one of the first tractors in its power range to be equipped with a differential lock (to improve traction in difficult conditions) and with disk brakes.

The specification also included a five-speed gearbox, but this was replaced by an eight-speed dual-ratio box with two reverse gears for the 35-hp (26-kw) B275 model available starting in 1958. The B275, which sold alongside the B250 for three years, was produced in both standard and high-clearance versions, but the B250 was built as a standard model only.

JOHN DEERE

🔧 1956 Waterloo, Iowa

JOHN DEERE 820

The most immediate difference between John Deere's new 20 series tractors and the models they replaced was the distinctive two-tone green-and-yellow paint finish; however, there were also some significant performance and driver-comfort improvements.

The first two 20 series tractors, the 320 and 420 models from the John Deere factory in Dubuque, were announced in 1955, with the remaining models following in 1956. There were basically six models in the series, starting with the little one-plow 320 and including the 820 diesel at the top of the range.

Performance

A vertical gasoline engine with cylinders of 4in by 4in (10.1cm by 10.1cm) powered the 320,

which was built in both standard and utility versions. The 420, with 27-hp (20.1-kw) output in its Nebraska tests, was the most versatile 20 series model, available in standard, utility, rowcrop, high-clearance, tricycle, and low-profile wheeled versions, plus a tracklayer with the choice of two different track options.

There were single-wheel, twin-wheel, and wide-axle versions of the 520, the 620 was built as a sleek-looking orchard model and could also be equipped for burning liquefied petroleum

Above: *The top model in John Deere's new 20 series tractors was the diesel-powered 820, with the power output boosted to 64hp (47.7kw) during the two-year production run.*

gas, and there were hi-crop, twin-wheel, single-wheel, and wide-axle options for the 720.

The diesel-powered 820, available as a standard model only, started its production life with the same twin-cylinder engine that had powered the previous 80 model, and the small gasoline-fueled starter motor was also carried over from the 80. Engine updates during the two-year production run boosted the 820's power rated output to 64hp (47.7kw).

Driver Comfort

Evidence that driver comfort was moving up the priority list included the new Float-Ride seat featuring a rubber torsion-spring suspension with an adjustment to suit different driver weights.

There was also a hydraulic shock absorber under the seat, the cushion and backrest were of foam rubber, and cushioned armrests were an option. Foot space on the driver's platform was increased, and the instruments and controls were reorganized to make them easier to use.

Design improvements to the hydraulics to make the three-point linkage system more accurate and give some degree of weight transfer were called the Custom Powr-Trol system, and the technical developments on the engines included modifications to the cylinder head and piston design to increase combustion chamber turbulence and boost power output and fuel efficiency.

Above: The big twin-cylinder diesel engine on the 820 tractor was started by a small gasoline engine, which meant carrying a second fuel supply.

Specifications

Manufacturer: Deere & Co.

Location: Waterloo, Iowa

Model: John Deere 820

Type: General purpose

Power Unit: Deere two-cylinder horizontal diesel engine

Power output: 72.8hp (59kw) (maximum)

Transmission: Six-speed gearbox

Weight: 8,729lb (3,963kw)

Production started: 1956

Below: Smallest of the 20 series tractors with its new two-tone paint finish was the Dubuque-built 320 model introduced in 1955.

MARSHALL

1956 **Gainsborough, Lincs, England**

MARSHALL MP6

The MP6 tractor was designed to take the Marshall company into what was then the top end of the wheeled-tractor market. It was an ambitious program, but it started badly when the preproduction version was displayed at the 1954 Smithfield Show in London. This probably stimulated interest in the tractor, but it was also premature because it took another two years to complete the development work and start production.

Above: *A six-cylinder Leyland diesel engine was the surprise choice for the power unit of the new MP6 tractor from Marshall.*

Above, left: *Marshall's bid for a place in the high-horsepower end of the market was based on the heavyweight MP6 tractor, but sales of the model were disappointing.*

Specifications

Manufacturer: Marshall Sons & Co.
Location: Gainsborough, Lincs, England
Model: MP4
Type: General purpose
Power unit: Leyland six-cylinder diesel engine
Power output: 69hp (51kw)
Transmission: Six-speed dual-range gearbox
Weight: 12,600lb (5,720kg)
Production started: 1956

Some of the initial development work was carried out with a four-cylinder Meadows diesel engine and at that stage the tractor was known as the MP4, but this engine was replaced by a six-cylinder Leyland U/E350 and the tractor was called the MP6.

When a production version was tested at Silsoe by the National Institute of Agricultural Engineering the weight was 12,600lb (5,720kg), the maximum drawbar pull was almost 7,000lb (3,175kg), and the power output was 69hp (51kw) at 1,700rpm.

Top Performer

By 1950s standards these were impressive figures, but few UK farmers were ready for such a big, expensive tractor and, as Marshall expected, most of the orders were for export. Some MP6 tractors were shipped to sugar cane estates in the West Indies for haulage work, and Australia and Spain were also on the list of export markets, but the total sales were disappointing. Adding a long wheelbase version for forestry work brought few orders, and production ended in 1960.

MASSEY-HARRIS-FERGUSON
1956   Racine, Wisconsin

MASSEY-HARRIS MH 333

A flurry of new tractor launches in the period following the purchase of the Ferguson tractor business provided Massey-Ferguson with a strong product range in the low- to medium-power sector, but customers wanting a bigger tractor were offered only updated versions of the old MH 33, 44, and 55 models.

Right: *Massey-Harris relied on updated 33, 44, and 55 models to compete in the medium- to high-horsepower sector of the American tractor market while new models were being developed.*

Specifications

Manufacturer: Massey-Harris-Ferguson

Location: Racine, Wisconsin

Model: Massey-Harris MH333

Type: General purpose and rowcrop

Power unit: Massey-Harris four-cylinder diesel and gasoline engines

Power output: 37hp (27.4kw) (diesel)

Transmission: 10-speed dual-range gearbox

Weight: 6,005lb (2,726kg) (diesel)

Production started: 1956

The new Massey-Harris MH 333, 444, and 555 models were launched in 1956. Like the tractors they replaced, they were built at Massey-Harris's Racine factory in Wisconsin. They retained the original styling, and they also continued to use the old Depth-O-Matic hydraulic system. Power steering was offered as an extra-cost option.

Performance
One of the important changes was the addition of a transfer box to the five-speed gearbox, doubling the number of gears to 10 on all three models. The other significant improvement was the addition of a diesel engine to the options list for the MH 333 and 444 models.

Performance figures for the MH four-cylinder diesel engine powering the MH 333 were a maximum output of 37.15hp (27.7kw) and a top speed of 14mph (22.5km/h) in 10th gear. Fuel economy at the rated engine speed 1,500rpm was 14.8-hp hours per gallon (11-kw hours per 3.8 liters). The equivalent figures for the gasoline engine were 39.84-hp (29.7-kw) maximum output and 12.37-hp hours per gallon (9.2-kw hours per 3.8 liters), providing another example of the extra fuel economy offered by diesel-powered tractors.

LANZ
1956 Mannheim, Germany

LANZ ALLDOG A1806

The first version of the Alldog tool carrier tractor from Heinrich Lanz was the A1205, available in 1951 and powered by an 12-hp (8.9-kw) gasoline engine. When the output proved to be inadequate, Lanz introduced a new A1305 version in 1952 equipped with a single-cylinder diesel engine, and this boosted the power output to just 13hp (9.7kw).

Providing one extra horsepower was not exactly extravagant, and it probably made very little difference to the performance in the field, but at least it was an unusual engine. It was air-cooled and was made by Lanz with a single cylinder and a 2,800rpm operating speed, and, although it was designed to run on diesel, the cylinder head was equipped with a spark plug for starting on gasoline.

Final Version

For the final version of the Alldog, known as the A1806 model, Lanz finally got to grips with the power problem, and they chose an MWM diesel engine with liquid cooling and an 18-hp (13.3-kw) output. The first of the A1806 Alldogs were built in 1956, and production continued until the Lanz company was taken over by John Deere. The link with John Deere

Above: *In spite of being under-powered for most of its production life, the Lanz Alldog was easily the most versatile tool carrier available.*

explains why some of the last Alldogs to leave the factory were painted green, although they still bore the Lanz name.

The Alldog is one of the most unusual and versatile designs the tractor industry has produced, and it might have achieved even more success if it had not been seriously underpowered for much of its production life. The tractor was built on a rectangular framework made of steel tubes, with the driver and the engine at one end, and this left most of the framework free to carry a range of implements and attachments.

Equipment

Lanz provided or approved an extraordinary range of equipment to be mounted on, under, in front of, or behind the Alldog. There were more than 50 items covering most of the activities on arable and livestock farms, and the aim was to make the Alldog the universal power unit for virtually every job on the farm. The range included a mid-mounted plow, a manure spreader, a single-row sugar beet harvester, and even a portable milking machine.

All-round visibility from the driver's seat was excellent because of the open frame, but the lack of engine power was not the Alldog's only design fault. Placing the seat so close to the engine must have produced a noise problem for the driver, particularly when working with the air-cooled diesel model.

Above: *With its air-cooled engine within easy reach of the operator's seat, the Lanz Alldog must have been a noisy tractor to drive.*

Specifications

Manufacturer: Heinrich Lanz	**Transmission:** Five-speed gearbox
Location: Mannheim, Germany	**Weight:** N/A
Model: Alldog A1806	**Production started:** 1956
Type: Tool carrier	
Power unit: MWM diesel engine	
Power output: 18hp (13.3kw)	

Below: *This diagram shows the steel rectangle that formed the main frame of the Alldog tool carrier, with space for equipment mounted above and below the frame.*

MASSEY-HARRIS-FERGUSON

1956 Coventry, England

FERGUSON FE-35

The first new model to leave the Banner Lane tractor plant near Coventry following the Massey-Harris takeover of the Ferguson tractor business in 1953 was the Ferguson FE-35. It was available from 1956 and it was painted in Harry Ferguson's chosen shade of gray paint for the sheet-metal work, but the engine, transmission housing, and other major items were finished in a distinctive and unusual coppery shade.

More than 500,000 of Harry Ferguson's TE series tractors had been produced at the Banner Lane factory, making it one of the most successful tractors ever built, and it was a tough act for the new FE-35 to follow. As well as a new paint finish—usually referred to as gray and gold—there was also new styling with rounded lines, and a hinged panel allowed easy access for checking the battery and the radiator and fuel-tank filler caps.

Design Details

Underneath the new look there were plenty of similarities between the FE-35 and the American-built Ferguson TO-35. Both models shared the same dual-range six-speed transmission, and they also shared an improved hydraulic system with increased pump pressure to boost the flow rate and the lift capacity on the rear linkage. The main difference was that the TO-35's Continental gasoline engine was

Above, top: *Neat lines and an unusual gray-and-copper paint finish helped make the FE-35 a popular replacement for the TE Series tractor.*

Above: *The FE-35 was built in the Banner Lane factory and powered by gasoline and diesel engines supplied by the Standard Motor Co.*

replaced on the Banner Lane tractors by Standard power units. The diesel version developed 37hp (27.4kw) from 3,763ci (2,258cc), and there was also a 3,643-ci (2,186-cc) spark-ignition engine producing 37hp (27.4kw) from the gasoline version, and about 30hp (22kw) burning paraffin or vaporizing oil.

Commercial Life

The FE-35 enjoyed only a brief commercial life. The policy of supporting two product ranges under two brand names was complicated and expensive, and in 1957 it was abandoned.

All future tractors would be painted red and gray, and would carry the Massey-Ferguson brand name—or "Massey Ferguson" from the point when the hyphen was officially eliminated from the company name more than 30 years later.

By the end of the 1957 the gray-and-gold Ferguson FE-35 had been replaced by the new red-and-gray Massey-Ferguson MF 35, although the specification remained the same. A further important development came at the beginning of 1959 when Massey-Ferguson purchased the Perkins engine business, and by the end of that year diesel versions of the MF 35 were powered by a Perkins P3 instead of the Standard engine, although Standard continued to supply spark ignition engines for the 35.

Specifications

Manufacturer: Massey-Harris-Ferguson

Location: Coventry, England

Model: Ferguson FE-35

Type: General purpose

Power unit: Standard four-cylinder diesel engine

Power output: 37hp (27.4kw)

Transmission: Six-speed dual-range gearbox

Weight: N/A

Production started: 1956

Below: *The FE-35 was the result of the official policy of maintaining both Ferguson and Massey-Harris ranges following the Ferguson company acquisition.*

FIAT
✗ 1957 Turin, Italy

FIAT 18 LA PICCOLA

As its name suggests, the Piccola was a small tractor, but it was important because it was the model that turned the Fiat company for the first time from a medium-volume manufacturer into one of the big league companies competing on level terms with other leading European tractor makers such as Renault.

Specifications

Manufacturer: Fiat	
Location: Turin, Italy	
Model: 18 La Piccola	
Type: General purpose	
Power unit: Fiat twin-cylinder diesel engine	
Power output: 16.5hp (12.2kw)	
Transmission: Six-speed gearbox	
Weight: N/A	
Production started: 1957	

Production started in 1957, reaching a total of 20,000 within three years, and these tractors offered a number of high-specification design features not usually found in this power range. The power unit was a Fiat twin-cylinder diesel engine which developed 16.5hp (12.2kw) on the belt pulley and a claimed 14hp (10.4kw) on the drawbar at the 2,200rpm rated engine speed. The engine was designed with a precombustion chamber and the capacity was 1,892ci (1,135cc).

The power was delivered through a transmission, with a dual-range gearbox giving six forward speeds and two in reverse, and

12.7mph (20.4km/h) available in top gear. Four-wheel drive was an unusual option at a time when most manufacturers specified two-wheel drive only, and the Fiat 18 was also available in vineyard and orchard versions, as well as a high-clearance conversion.

Options

A belt pulley was still an important feature on tractors in the 1950s, and on the small Fiat it was positioned just above the power takeoff shaft where it could be fitted on the right-hand side for counterclockwise operation or switched to the left side to give a clockwise drive.

Above: *This publicity picture shows the Fiat 18 with, presumably, someone pretending to be a typical peasant farmer posing at the controls.*

ALLIS-CHALMERS

1958 Essendine, Stamford, Lincolnshire, England

ALLIS-CHALMERS D272

Many of the big North American tractor companies started building tractors in Britain after the war ended in 1945, and one of them was Allis-Chalmers. Its first assembly plant was near Southampton, in Hampshire, but by the mid-1950s it had outgrown the factory and moved to larger premises near Stamford, in Lincolnshire, which is where the Model B replacement was built.

Below: *This studio picture from the Allis-Chalmers publicity department shows strong similarities between the D272 and the Model B it replaced.*

Specifications

Manufacturer: Allis-Chalmers (GB)
Location: Essendine, Stamford, Lincolnshire, England
Model: D272
Type: Rowcrop tractor
Power unit: (diesel version) Perkins P3 engine
Power output: 31hp (22.9kw)
Transmission: Four-speed gearbox
Weight: N/A
Production started: 1958

It was called the D270, and it was available from 1955 until the D272 arrived in 1958. Replacing a big success such as the Model B was not easy, but under the new-look styling of the D270 the designers managed to retain the best features of the old model while introducing a number of improvements. These included a "live" power takeoff, allowing the drive to the wheels to be disengaged without stopping the power takeoff. The D270 specifications also included a four-speed gearbox instead of the Model B's three speeds.

The Model B's three engine options were retained on the new tractor, including a Perkins P3 diesel engine developing, in a later version, 31hp (22.9kw) at 1,900rpm. For the D272 model Allis-Chalmers kept the same styling and retained the Model B's rowcrop design features. The D272 model also offered the same engine choice, but with an extra 4hp (2.9kw) available from the gasoline/paraffin version, and the hydraulic system was improved. A replacement for the D272 arrived in 1960, the year after production had first started.

FORDSON

1958 **Dagenham, Essex, England**

FORDSON DEXTA

With the new Fordson Major dominating what was then the medium to large sector of the United Kingdom's tractor market and a number of export markets as well, the next target for Ford was the small to medium end of the market.

It announced the new Fordson Dexta in 1957, and production started the following year. The styling of the Dexta bore a strong family likeness to the highly successful new Major and, like the Major, the emphasis was on diesel power. The Dexta engine was a special version of the Perkins P3 with 32-hp (23.7-kw) output, and a spark-ignition engine was not available until 1960, and then only for export.

Specification

An up-to-date specification included a dual-range transmission with six forward gears and two in reverse, and the Dexta was also the first Fordson tractor with full draft-control hydraulics. There was also a double-clutch version providing a "live" power takeoff and hydraulics. The options also included a specially equipped Highway Dexta for local authority

Above: *With no suitable engine of its own available, Ford chose a special version of the three-cylinder Perkins P3 diesel engine to power the Fordson Dexta.*

customers, a basic industrial model, and a special grassland version designed for golf courses and other amenity users.

A narrow Dexta for vineyards and orchards arrived in 1960, and 1960 also brought the first major design changes with improvements to the gearbox and hydraulics, plus styling changes that imitated the new Major with the headlights mounted in the radiator grille.

Design Changes

More design changes arrived in 1961 when a new Super Dexta was announced to sell alongside the standard model. It was identified by new front-end styling, and a power increase was achieved by enlarging the engine capacity from 3,933ci (2,360cc) for the original version to 4,166ci (2,500cc) for the Super model, boosting the output to 39hp (29kw).

The final chapter in the Dexta story came in 1963 with updated models for the UK market—although they had already been available in the United States during the previous year. It was the New Performance range, identified on the outside by a new blue-and-gray paint finish, and the power output from the Super Dexta engine was increased again, this time to 44.5hp (33.1kw).

End of an Era

Although the New Performance tractor range was available for little more than one year, it was an important stage in Ford tractor history. These were the last tractors to be built at the Dagenham, Essex, plant before production was moved to the new tractor plant in Basildon, also in Essex, and they were also the last production tractors to carry the Fordson name.

Specifications

Manufacturer: Ford Motor Co.
Location: Dagenham, Essex, England
Model: Fordson Dexta
Type: General purpose
Power unit: Perkins three-cylinder diesel engine
Power output: 32hp (23.7kw)
Transmission: Six-speed dual range gearbox
Weight: 3,393lb (1,540kg)
Production started: 1958

Left: *The pair of headlights built into the radiator grille identifies this tractor as one of the later Dextas built after the design changes introduced in 1960.*

Above: *The new Fordson badge designed for the New Major series was also featured above the radiator of the Dexta.*

JOHN DEERE
1958 **Waterloo, Iowa**

JOHN DEERE 730

The biggest difference between the new 30 series tractors announced in 1958 and the 20 series models they replaced was the increasing evidence that driver safety, comfort, and convenience were becoming much more important factors in tractor design.

Above: *The fuel tank for the gasoline-powered starter engine on the 730 and 830 diesel models was beside the left-hand fender, but electric starting was an option.*

Specifications

Manufacturer: Deere & Co.	
Location: Waterloo, Iowa	
Model: 830	
Type: General purpose	
Power unit: Deere two-cylinder horizontal diesel engine	
Power output: 56.66hp (41.9kw)	
Transmission: Six-speed gearbox	
Weight: 7,899lb (3,586kg)	
Production started: 1958	

Above, left: *Compared with the previous range, the new John Deere 30 series tractors offered a number of detailed improvements affecting driver comfort and convenience.*

On the 30 series tractors this meant, for example, conveniently placed steps and grab handles for extra safety while climbing aboard. There were improved road and work lights, the seat and backrest were redesigned to provide increased comfort for the driver, and the new instrument layout was more convenient to use.

Electric Starter

On all but the two small Dubuque-built 30 series models, the fenders, or mudguards, were extended to give extra protection from mud and dust, and the extension also helped to reduce the risk of injury caused by the driver accidentally contacting the rear tires while the tractor was on the move.

Mechanical differences were few, but on the new 730 and 830 models there was a significant development. The diesel engine on both models could be equipped with a push-button electric starter instead of the small gasoline engine used previously, and this was clear evidence that improvements in design were making the diesel engines on tractors easier to start.

The engine output for the 730 was the same as on the previous 720 model at 57hp (42.5kw) on the belt pulley.

COCKSHUTT

⚒ 1958 Brantford, Ontario, Canada

COCKSHUTT 550

Although the Cockshutt factory at Brantford, Ontario, had become Canada's biggest manufacturer of low- and medium-horsepower tractors, by the mid-1950s the tough competition that had developed in this sector—mainly from American-built tractors—was causing problems for the company.

Right: Cockshutt's 550 tractor was one of the last new models the Canadian company launched before it became part of the American-based White Farm Equipment.

Specifications

Manufacturer: Cockshutt Farm Equipment

Location: Brantford, Ontario, Canada

Model: Cockshutt 550

Type: General purpose

Power unit: Four-cylinder Hercules gasoline and diesel engines

Power output: 38hp (28kw) (diesel)

Transmission: Six-speed gearbox

Weight: 5,695lb (2,586kg)

Production started: 1958

Their response in 1958 was an ambitious program to develop an improved range of tractors with new features and styling, using engines supplied by both Perkins and Hercules. They offered the mid-range 550 model with the choice of gasoline and diesel engines, both supplied by Hercules. Although the power output was just 38hp (28kw) for the diesel model, the Cockshutt sales literature described the 550, with perhaps a degree of optimism, as a three-plow tractor.

Equipment

Cockshutt offered customers a comprehensive standard specification for the 550 model. The equipment list included an electric starter for the engine, a power takeoff, and what the makers described as the strongest transmission in any Cockshutt tractor. The 550 was available until 1962, and during this four-year period the production total reached the fairly modest total of just 2,930 tractors, which must have been a disappointing response to a new model in a popular horsepower range.

By 1962 Cockshutt's financial problems had increased, and the company was taken over by the American-based White Farm Equipment company. White was also the owner of the Oliver company, and it later also acquired Minneapolis-Moline.

DOE

1958 **Ulting, Essex, England**

DOE TRIPLE-D

In the mid-1950s, when a big tractor was 60hp (44.7kw), there were few options available for UK farmers who wanted more horsepower. The obvious choice was a big tracklayer, but in the days of steel tracks there were many farmers who had a strong preference for rubber tires.

This was the problem facing Essex farmer George Pryor. He wanted plenty of power to plow and cultivate his heavy clay soil; the answer, he decided, was to build his own tractor. He bought two Fordson Major tractors and joined them end-to-end, removing the front wheels and axles from both and linking the front of one tractor to the back of the other by an immensely strong turntable that provided the steering action powered by hydraulic rams.

Two Engines

Mr. Pryor's tractor had two engines producing more than 80hp (59kw), two transmissions with four-wheel drive through equal-diameter wheels, and one driver who sat on the seat of the rear tractor operating one set of controls for both power units. Although it looked complicated and awkward, the two-in-one tractor worked well, easily outperforming any of the wheeled tractors available at that time,

Above, top: *The hydraulically operated articulation, or hinge point, between the two tractor units provided the steering action for the Triple-D.*

Above: *This beautifully restored 130hp Doe 130, consisting of two Ford 5000 tractors, is in the Doe company collection.*

and the bend-in-the-middle steering provided reasonable maneuverability.

Ernest Doe & Sons, the local Fordson tractor dealer, took an interest in Mr. Pryor's tractor, and it signed an agreement to build an improved version. The first of the Doe tractors was completed in 1958, and it was called the Doe Dual Power, later changed to Doe Dual Drive, then abbreviated to Triple-D.

Implements

The Triple-D attracted considerable interest from farmers and contractors, but a lack of implements suitable for such a powerful tractor meant that Doe & Sons had to design and build plows and cultivators to sell with the tractors. Using Fordson Power Major skid units produced more than 100hp (74kw) from the Triple-D, and switching to Ford 5000 tractor units in 1964 pushed the output to 130hp (96.9kw), and at that stage the tractors' name

was changed to Doe 130. Similarly the Doe 150 produced 150hp (111.8kw) and was based on two Ford 7000s.

By the mid-1960s there was increasing competition from the 100hp (74kw) plus tractors built by the leading tractor companies and by four-wheel drive specialists such as County and Muir Hill. Their big advantage, compared to the Doe tractor, was having just one engine and one transmission to operate and service. This was a significant attraction, and it helped to put the Doe tractor out of production after well over 300 had been built.

Specifications

Manufacturer: Ernest Doe & Sons
Location: Ulting, Essex, England
Model: Doe Triple-D
Type: General purpose
Power unit: Two Ford four-cylinder diesel engines
Power output: 103hp (76.2kw) (Power Major version)

Transmission: Two six-speed gearboxes
Weight: 11,385lb (5,169kg)
Production started: 1958

Below: *A Doe Triple-D tractor is seen here plowing on a field at Ulting, Essex, close to the Doe company headquarters.*

FORD

✖ 1958   Dearborn, Michigan

FORD POWERMASTER 801

A major reorganization of Ford's American tractor line was announced in 1957 with a new range of models ready for production in 1958, plus revised marketing arrangements and a new two-tone paint finish to help sell them.

Specifications

Manufacturer: Ford Motor Co.

Location: Dearborn, Michigan

Model: Powermaster 801

Type: General purpose

Power unit: Ford four-cylinder gasoline engine

Power output: 44hp (32.6kw)

Transmission: Four-speed gearbox

Weight: 2,981lb (1,353kg)

Production started: 1958

Under the new marketing arrangements the tractor range was divided into two different series. Those powered by the Ford 133.5-cubic-inch (2.2-liter) engine were known as the Workmaster series, while the tractors in the Powermaster range were equipped with the more powerful 169.9-cubic-inch (2.8-liter) Ford engine. As well as splitting the range into two new series, the beefed-up marketing program included an eye-catching new two-tone paint finish to give all the tractors a more up-to-date image.

Design Changes

The Powermasters were based on the previous 800 series introduced in 1955 when the engine

output was 40hp (29.8kw), but Ford updated the 169.9-cubic-inch (2.8-liter) engine to boost the power to 44hp (32.6kw) for the new models. Apart from the engine modifications, the list of design changes introduced with the Powermaster range included a bigger fuel tank capacity to allow longer intervals between refills, and a redesigned instrument display to make it easier to read.

Also included in the standard Powermaster specification was a five-speed gearbox; however, power steering, powered track adjustment and a high/low ratio gearbox were on the options list. Diesel power was added to the list in 1959 using a 169.9-cubic-inch (2.8-liter) Ford engine developing 56hp (41.7kw).

Above: A Ford Powermaster 801 in showroom condition showing the new paint finish and the optional front radiator guard.

COUNTY
✖ 1958   Fleet, Hampshire, England

COUNTY HI-DRIVE

County's international reputation in the tractor market was based on its tracklayer and four-wheel drive conversions it built based on Fordson and Ford skid units, and it is easy to forget that it also produced a much smaller number of special two-wheel drive models.

Right: *The high-clearance County Hi-Drive tractors were based on Fordson Major tractor units.*

Above: *This rear view of the Hi-Drive shows how the rear axle and final drive were modified to provide extra ground clearance.*

Specifications

Manufacturer: County Commercial Cars
Location: Fleet, Hampshire, England
Model: Hi-Drive
Type: High-clearance tractor
Power unit: Ford four-cylinder diesel engine
Power output: 51hp (37.7kw) (Power Major version)
Transmission: Six-speed gearbox
Weight: 5,727lb (2,600kg)
Production started: 1958

The County Hi-Drive is an example. It was built on a Fordson New Major engine and transmission, and it was developed in response to a request from sugar cane producers in the West Indies. Because the sales volumes involved were not sufficient to persuade Ford to produce a special high-clearance tractor, it was County that designed and built the new tractor and called it the Hi-Drive.

Other Markets

Although the sugar estates provided the biggest market for the Hi-Drive, there was also a demand from specialist vegetable producers in the United Kingdom and elsewhere who welcomed the opportunity to buy a relatively big high-clearance tractor.

The design changes introduced by County raised the axle height to 30in (76.2cm), and this was achieved at the rear of the tractor by mounting the wheels on stub axles and providing a gear drive to bridge the gap that this created.

County offered the Hi-Drive as a complete tractor, but it also offered a conversion kit allowing customers to turn an existing Fordson into a high-clearance model. Production of the model ended in 1964.

DAVID BROWN
1958 Meltham, Yorkshire, England

DAVID BROWN 950

Production of the 950 tractor started in 1958, just two years after the launch of the 900 model it replaced. Both tractors were basically similar, and the 950 was introduced as an updated version of the 900.

Specifications

Manufacturer: David Brown Tractors
Location: Meltham, Yorkshire, England
Model: 950
Type: General purpose
Power unit: David Brown four-cylinder diesel-, gasoline-, and paraffin-engine versions
Power output: 42.5hp (31.45kw) (diesel)
Transmission: Six-speed gearbox
Weight: 4,617lb (2,096kg) (diesel)
Production started: 1958

Above: *Production of the various versions of the David Brown 950 tractors was approaching 24,000 in less than five years of production.*

The improved David Brown 950 included an increase in engine power, with a modified injection system raising the output from the diesel engine to 42.5hp (31.45kw), just 2.5hp (1.8kw) more than the equivalent 900 model. There was a slightly smaller power increase for the standard gasoline engine, with a rise from 40hp to 42hp (29.8kw to 31.3kw). David Brown also introduced design improvements for the steering mechanism and the design of the drawbar on the 950 tractor.

New Version

Just one year after the launch of the 950 tractor, David Brown introduced the new 950 Implematic model with major improvements to the rear linkage and the hydraulic system. The big sales feature was the ability to use mounted implements with either depth or draft control using automatic weight transfer.

A further batch of improvements was announced in 1961 when the V and W series 950 tractors arrived on the scene. These provided an increase in the front axle clearance, and there was also a multispeed power takeoff operating in both of the standard settings of 540 and 1,000rpm.

Production of the various versions of the 950 tractor lasted from 1958 to 1961, with the total reaching 23,699 tractors.

FORD
✂ 1959 Dearborn, Michigan

FORD WORKMASTER 541

The Workmaster 600 series tractors arrived in 1958 as part of Ford's American relaunch program that also included the Powermaster models. The Workmasters were the smaller of the two series, using the 133.5-cubic-inch (2.2-liter) engine that had previously provided the power for the Ford NAA "Golden Jubilee" model.

Right: *This is a rare version of the Ford Workmaster, featuring as it does the unusual offset engine position*

Above: *The front view of the Workmaster 541 shows the offset engine position to improve the driver's forward view.*

Specifications

Manufacturer:	Ford Motor Co.
Location:	Dearborn, Michigan
Model:	Workmaster 541
Type:	Rowcrop
Power unit:	Ford 139.6-cubic-inch (2.3-liter) diesel engine
Power output:	43hp (31.8kw)
Transmission:	Four-speed gearbox
Weight:	N/A
Production started:	1959

The power output of the Workmaster version of the engine was given a modest boost to 32hp (23.8kw) instead of the previous 30hp (22.3kw), and the new tractors also benefited from other improvements including the revised instrument layout, a bigger-capacity fuel tank, and the new two-tone paint colors.

Further Developments

In 1959 Ford announced further developments for the Workmaster range. These included new 500 series versions plus, for the first time, a diesel engine option. The 500 series tractors were the rowcrop models, available for the first time in the Ford range with an offset engine position, as shown on the 541 model in the photographs.

This Workmaster 541 is particularly unusual because in addition to having the offset driving position it also features the new Ford diesel engine. This was based on the Ford spark ignition Red Tiger power unit, but was equipped with direct injection and with electric heaters for cold starting.

Ford increased the capacity of the diesel engine that powered the Workmaster to 139.6 cubic inches (2.3 liters), and this boosted the power rating to 43hp (31.8kw).

chapter 7

Innovations in the 1960s

The 1960s were a period of innovation and experiment. Some ideas had little or no commercial impact; this category includes experiments with fuel cells and gas-turbine power, plus the extraordinary Sea Horse amphibious tractor. Other developments, however, had a major long-term impact on tractor design.

Above: *Diesel power in the John Deere range moved down to the smaller models with the launch of the 435 tractor powered by a General Motors engine.*

Left: *David Brown was the first British tractor company to have officially approved cabs available to meet the new safety regulations.*

Four-wheel drive was one of the most important innovations to become commercially established in the 1960s. It was not a completely new development, but pressure to improve farming efficiency was increasing and four-wheel drive offered better traction in difficult conditions.

The need to improve efficiency also brought the first powershift transmissions, allowing gear shifting without breaking the power flow from the engine, and there was an increasing demand for more horsepower to cover a bigger acreage in a shorter time. The obvious way to boost power is fitting a bigger engine, but turbo-charging an existing engine can increase output by about 25 percent, and turbos on tractor engines date from the 1960s.

Another development was the front-mounted cab on the County Forward Control tractor, arguably an early form of the systems tractors that arrived during the next 20 years. Moving the cab forward left space at the rear for carrying equipment such as a spray tank or fertilizer hopper.

Cabs were also an important development, although in this case a belated one. Cabs had appeared previously from time to time, but for the first 80 years or so of tractor history more than 95 percent of drivers were exposed to the weather and to the risk of death or injury if the tractor overturned.

PORSCHE-DIESEL

✴ 1957 Friedrichshafen, Germany

PORSCHE-DIESEL JUNIOR L-108

Some of the men who build glamorous and expensive sports cars are also responsible for producing farm tractors. Examples include the Lamborghini car and tractor brands in Italy, David Brown, who owned both the UK tractor company that bore his name, and Aston Martin, and in Germany Dr. Ferdinand Porsche also designed both cars and tractors.

Specifications

Manufacturer: Porsche-Diesel
Location: Friedrichshafen, Germany
Model: Junior L-108
Type: General purpose
Power unit: Single-cylinder diesel engine
Power output: 16hp (11.8kw)
Transmission: Six-speed gearbox
Weight: 2,575lb (1,169kg)
Production started: 1957

Dr. Porsche had close links with the Allgaier range of tractors for about 10 years after World War II, and in 1955 the company's name was changed to Porsche. The name change was accompanied by a color change from Allgaier's orange to bright red for Porsche, but the styling remained unaltered.

Smallest Tractor

The smallest tractor in the Allgaier range was the A111 powered by a single-cylinder air-cooled diesel engine, and this model became the Porsche-Diesel Junior L-108 under the Porsche brand name. It had also gained an extra 4hp (2.9kw), apparently achieved by increasing the rated engine speed to 2,250rpm. The single cylinder had a 3.74-in (9.4-cm) bore and 4.56-in (11.5-cm) stroke, and the transmission provided six forward speeds.

The adoption of the Porsche name was followed by an export sales drive with the United States and the United Kingdom as two of the principle targets. Surprisingly it was the Junior model rather than some of the more powerful Porsche tractors that featured strongly in the campaign; however, the lack of power may have deterred some customers, and few Porsche tractors were sold in either country.

Above: *In Germany, as in the United Kingdom, farmers were quick to appreciate the benefits of diesel power, and the Porsche-Diesel Junior featured a single-cylinder diesel engine.*

ALLIS-CHALMERS
1957 Milwaukee, Wisconsin

ALLIS-CHALMERS D-14

Below: *The Allis-Chalmers D-14 offered tractor drivers a new type of seat with its own suspension system and adjustability to suit the height and weight of the driver.*

When the new D-14 model was announced in 1957 it brought more evidence of the increasing importance tractor manufacturers were attaching to driver comfort. One of the features designed to make life easier for the man—or woman—on the tractor seat was the cigarette lighter on the dashboard, but much more significant was the design of the seat.

Specifications

Manufacturer: Allis-Chalmers Manufacturing Co.	
Location: Milwaukee, Wisconsin	
Model: D-14	
Type: General purpose	
Power unit: Four-cylinder engine	
Power output: 35.6hp (26.3kw)	
Transmission: Eight-speed gearbox	
Weight: 4,170lb (1,893kg)	
Production started: 1957	

For some reason it was called the "Center-Ride" seat, and according to the sales leaflet it promised to provide "...the finest ride you've ever had!" What made the seat special was the suspension system, which was fully adjustable for the height and weight of the driver, and it also included a shock absorber, described as follows: "Soaks up jolts. Provides smooth, level ride over rough ground."

Design Features

Allis-Chalmers described the D-14 as a three-plow tractor, meaning it was capable of pulling three furrows in most conditions. The power unit was a four-cylinder Allis-Chalmers "Power-Crater" gasoline engine with a rated speed of 1,650rp, and the output measured on the belt pulley was 35.6hp (26.3kw). Power steering was in the standard specification, and the D-14 was also equipped with a "live" power takeoff and an eight-speed transmission.

Also on the features list was the Allis-Chalmers Power Shift rear-wheel adjustment, using engine power to adjust the track settings for rowcrop work. The tractor's high underside clearance allowed mid-mounted implements to be used—a feature the D-14 inherited from the Model B tractor.

ALLIS-CHALMERS

⚒ 1959   Milwaukee, Wisconsin

ALLIS-CHALMERS FUEL CELL TRACTOR

Recent concerns about the cost and future availability of oil have attracted renewed interest in fuel cells, and research carried out in the late 1950s by Allis-Chalmers into their use for powering farm tractors could well become relevant in the future.

The principle of the fuel cell was originally described by a British scientist in 1839, but at that time it was regarded as a curiosity. Interest revived again in the 1950s, and Allis-Chalmers was one of the companies carrying out fuel cell research.

Fuel Cells

A fuel cell works in much the same way as a battery, converting chemical energy into electric power. Chemicals are supplied to the cell in the form of fuel, which is usually a mixture of gases such as propane or methane, but can also be in solid or liquid form, and the fuel produces the chemical reaction that generates electrical energy. Unlike a conventional battery, a fuel cell is not able to store the electricity it produces, and the power must be used to drive an electric motor, for example, as soon as it is produced.

Above: *This publicity photo from Allis-Chalmers shows one of its experimental fuel-cell tractors in action, but the project was abandoned due to financial pressures.*

Potential benefits of fuel cells include the ability to use a wide range of different fuels, including some from renewable sources, and the fact that the process that produces the electricity is highly efficient. Energy losses when fuel is burned in a gasoline or diesel engine amount to well over 50 percent, but this is reduced to 10 percent or less in a fuel cell, although there are additional losses when the electricity is converted to mechanical energy through an electric motor. The fuel cells and their electric motor produce virtually no noise but, at least at the stage of development reached by the 1950s, the cells and their fuel supply were heavy and occupied a large amount of space.

Experimental Tractors

Allis-Chalmers built several fuel-cell tractors for experimental purposes, including one based on a D-12 tractor, and in 1959 it built a special tractor for the research program. The space normally occupied by the engine was filled with 1,008 fuel cells arranged in four main banks, and these were fueled by propane and other gases supplied from high-pressure cylinders carried on the tractor.

Electricity produced by the chemical reaction in the fuel cells, helped by a catalyst, powered a 20-hp (15-kw) direct-current electric motor, and this was used to drive the wheels of the tractor. A press release issued by Allis-Chalmers when the tractor was demonstrated stressed the potential benefits of fuel-cell power. These included the absence of a gearbox, as the forward speed was controlled by varying the amount of electric current fed to the motor, and forward and reverse were selected by changing the polarity of the current.

Specifications

Manufacturer: Allis-Chalmers Manufacturing Co.
Location: Milwaukee, Wisconsin
Model: Fuel-cell tractor
Type: Experimental
Power unit: Electric motor
Power output: 20hp (15kw)
Transmission: Direct drive
Weight: N/A
Produced: 1959

Below: A bank of 1,008 fuel cells produced sufficient electricity to drive a 20-hp (15-kw) motor. Fuel cells are still regarded as a potential power source for the future.

JOHN DEERE
⚒ 1959 Waterloo, Iowa

JOHN DEERE 435

Some John Deere tractor enthusiasts are inclined to dismiss the 435 tractor because it was one of a very small number of pre-1961 John Deere models that did not feature the famous two-cylinder horizontal engine.

Above: *The 435 was the last new model in the John Deere range before the launch of a completely new tractor range in 1960.*

Specifications

Manufacturer: Deere & Co.

Location: Waterloo, Iowa

Model: 435

Type: General purpose

Power unit: Two-cylinder two-stroke diesel engine

Power output: 32.9hp (24.3kw)

Transmission: Five-speed gearbox

Weight: 4,101lb (1,862kg)

Production started: 1959

In spite of using the "wrong" type of engine, the 435 was an important model. It was the first John Deere diesel model aimed at the small- to medium-horsepower sector instead of the top end of the market like previous John Deere diesels, and it was also the company's first tractor with dual-speed power-takeoff settings of 540 and 1,000rpm.

Power Takeoff

The 435 model number was presumably chosen to distinguish the tractor from the 430 model on which it was based. The feature that set it apart from the rest of the 30 series was the 435's General Motors diesel engine with two vertical

cylinders and a 32.9-hp (24.3-kw) output. The 435 had the distinction of being the first tractor to have its power output measured at Nebraska on the power takeoff instead of on the belt pulley. This change of test procedure recognized the fact that fewer farmers were using their tractors with belt-driven equipment, and the power takeoff had taken over as the relevant power standard.

With production ending after just two years, the 435 was the last new model to be introduced by John Deere before the traditional two-cylinder models were swept away by a new range of tractors with the emphasis on four- and six-cylinder engines.

Above, left: *With its 32.9-hp (24.3-kw) General Motors two-stroke diesel engine, the 435 was not a typical 1960s John Deere tractor. Production lasted only two years.*

JOHN DEERE

1960 Waterloo, Iowa

JOHN DEERE 3010

The first batch of John Deere's "New Generation of Power" tractors, the all-new range that swept away the old two-cylinder models, arrived in 1960 when four of the new models were announced.

Right: *John Deere 3010 and 4010 tractors introduced in 1960 featured new hydraulic systems including, for the first time, hydraulic-brake operation.*

Specifications

Manufacturer: Deere & Co.	
Location: Waterloo, Iowa	
Model: 3010 Diesel	
Type: General purpose	
Power unit: Four-cylinder diesel engine	
Power output: 59.5hp (44kw)	
Transmission: Eight-speed gearbox	
Weight: 6,542lb (2,970kg)	
Production started: 1960	

They featured new styling, four-cylinder engines, and—a significant indication of the way tractor power was changing—there was a diesel engine option for each model, but no distillate or paraffin version.

With 59.5hp (44kw) available at the power takeoff, the 3010 was described as a four-plow tractor, and one of the most important selling features was the new hydraulic system it shared with the 4010 model at the top of the new range. The brakes were operated hydraulically, said to be the first time this feature had been used on a farm tractor, and the hydraulic system also included up to three independent "live" hydraulic circuits for operating ancillary equipment.

Other Versions

As well as the diesel engine with its power rating of 2,200rpm, gasoline and liquid petroleum gas (LPG) engines were also offered on the 3010; these produced 51 and 55.4hp (38 and 41.3kw), respectively. The compression ratios for burning the three different fuel options were 16.4 to 1 for diesel and 7.5 and 9.0 to 1, respectively, for gasoline and LPG. The 3010 also included an eight-speed gearbox, and regular and rowcrop front-axle options.

ALLIS-CHALMERS
✖ 1960 Essendine, Lincolnshire, England

ALLIS-CHALMERS ED-40

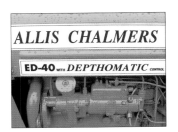

It was the success of the Model B tractor that encouraged Allis-Chalmers to open its UK factory, and when the Model B had reached the end of its commercial life it was followed by the D270 and D272 models.

The sales volumes for the D270 and 272 models were disappointing, and the company needed another success to fill its Lincolnshire factory. The tractor it chose was the ED-40 with styling to give a family likeness to the D-14 and other recent models from the company's factory in the United States.

Diesel power was the natural choice for the new British-built tractor, with no gasoline or gasoline/paraffin alternative, and the obvious choice would have been to buy an engine from Perkins, the company that had supplied diesel engines for previous British-built Allis-Chalmers tractors. Perkins, however, did not get the contract, and this may have been because Massey-Ferguson had bought the Perkins company the previous year to secure its own engine supply, and Allis-Chalmers may have decided not to buy an engine from a company belonging to its biggest competitor.

Above, top: The Depthomatic feature on the ED-40 tractor provided draft sensing through the top link of the implement hitch, giving improved depth control.

Above: Allis-Chalmers powered the new ED-40 tractor of 1960 with a Standard diesel engine instead of the Perkins engines used previously.

Instead it bought an improved version of the 23C diesel engine developed by the Standard Motor Co. for the Ferguson 35 tractor. The improvements had been carried out to provide a power unit for a tractor the Standard company was planning to build at that time.

Although this tractor never went into production, the engine, with its new cylinder head to boost the torque performance and a heater plug in each cylinder to overcome a previous cold-weather starting problem, was available for the ED-40. The power output from the Standard diesel engine was 37hp (27.4kw) when ED-40 production started in 1960; however, this was raised to 41hp (30.5kw) when an improved version of the tractor was introduced after three years.

Another design improvement included on the 1963 version of the ED-40 was the addition of the Depthomatic draft-control feature which used the top link of the three-point hitch to give more accurate depth control for jobs such as plowing.

Later Improvements

One of the features the ED-40 inherited from its illustrious Model B ancestor was sufficient underside clearance to accommodate mid-mounted implements. This was part of the standard design, as it had been on the B, and not restricted to a special high-clearance version as on some other makes.

ED-40 production at the Allis-Chalmers factory at Essendine in Lincolnshire continued until about 1968. It was the last Allis-Chalmers tractor to be built in the United Kingdom, although some machinery production continued at the factory for a few more years.

Specifications

Manufacturer: Allis-Chalmers Manufacturing Co.

Location: Essendine, Lincolnshire, England

Model: ED-40

Type: General purpose

Power unit: Standard four-cylinder diesel engine

Power output: 37hp (27.4kw)

Transmission: Eight-speed gearbox

Weight: 3,584lb (1,626kg) (shipping weight)

Production started: 1960

Left: *The ED-40 rear linkage included the Depthomatic system providing automatic control of the working depth of rear-mounted implements.*

INTERNATIONAL HARVESTER
1961   Chicago, Illinois

I.H. GAS TURBINE TRACTOR

Gas turbines were generating a great deal of interest in the late 1950s when most of the leading car manufacturers were experimenting with gas turbine power and it was widely assumed that turbines would replace piston engines for road transportation.

Specifications

Manufacturer: International Harvester

Location: Chicago, Illinois

Model: HT-340

Type: Experimental

Power unit: Gas turbine

Power output: Derated to 40hp (29.8kw)

Transmission: Hydrostatic

Weight: N/A

Produced: 1961

Air entering the front of a gas turbine is heated by burning fuel, and as it expands it is forced out of the back of the engine at high speed, driving the blades of a turbine in the process. Advantages include compact size and light weight—not particularly useful in a farm tractor—but gas turbines are smoother than a piston engine and more reliable, which would both be welcome. Disadvantages for vehicles include high noise levels, high fuel consumption, and the absence of engine braking.

Hydrostatic Transmission

International Harvester was surprisingly open about these problems in 1961 when it demonstrated its HT-340 experimental tractor.

A subsidiary company of International Harvester was developing gas turbines to power helicopters, and one of these was used in the tractor, designed to develop 80hp (59.6kw) but derated to 40hp (29.8kw) for the tractor. The turbine was linked to a hydrostatic transmission, powering a pump to force oil around a circuit to drive motors in the tractor wheels.

The hydrostatic drive was more relevant to future tractor design than the gas turbine. It eliminates the need for a gearbox and provides an infinitely variable range of speeds up to the maximum without altering the engine rpm; hydrostatic drives are also reliable and easy to use. International Harvester later became the leading manufacturer of hydrostatic-drive tractors.

Above: *International Harvester's experimental HT-340 tractor was powered by a gas-turbine engine and featured a hydrostatic transmission with infinitely variable travel speed.*

FORD
⚒ 1962 Birmingham, Michigan

FORD 4000 SELECT-O-SPEED

It was in 1962 that Ford replaced the eye-catching paint finish of the Workmaster and Powermaster tractor series with the company's new internationally standardized blue-and-gray color scheme.

Right: Ford's American-built 4000 series tractors replaced the previous Powermaster series and included three- and four-cylinder power units.

Specifications

Manufacturer: Ford Motor Co.

Location: Birmingham, Michigan

Model: 4000 Select-O-Speed

Type: General purpose

Power unit: Four-cylinder gasoline engine

Power output: 45.4hp (33.6kw)

Transmission: 10-speed gearbox

Weight: 4,885lb (2,218kg)

Production started: 1962

As well as altering the appearance of the tractors, the model change was also aimed at simplifying the rather complicated American-built small-tractor range. The various Workmaster models, both agricultural and industrial, joined the new 2000 series, and there was also a new 4000 series consisting of the former Powermaster models.

Versions

In spite of the attempted simplification, the two ranges still remained quite complicated. The 4000 series offered a choice of three- and four-cylinder engines, including a three-cylinder diesel version, and there was also a choice of much more advanced transmissions. Customers could choose either an eight-speed gearbox or the recently introduced Ford Select-O-Speed version with 10 forward speeds and a powershifting facility allowing the driver to change gear without using the clutch pedal.

Maximum power output when the four-cylinder gasoline version was tested at Nebraska was 45.4hp (33.6kw) at the power takeoff. The 192-ci (320-cc) engine had 4.4-in and 4.2-in (11.1-cm and 10.6-cm) bore and stroke measurements, and the drawbar horsepower peaked at 39hp (29kw).

There was also a three-cylinder gasoline version with 46.3hp (34.5kw) available at the power takeoff, and output figures for the 4000 with a four-cylinder diesel engine were 46.7hp (34.8kw) at the rated engine speed and 39.4hp (29.3kw) at the drawbar.

MASSEY-FERGUSON

1962 **Detroit, Michigan**

MASSEY-FERGUSON SUPER 90

The acquisition of Harry Ferguson's tractor business by Massey-Harris resulted in a new Massey-Ferguson range offering an attractive choice of models in the small to medium sector, but much less for customers wanting more power.

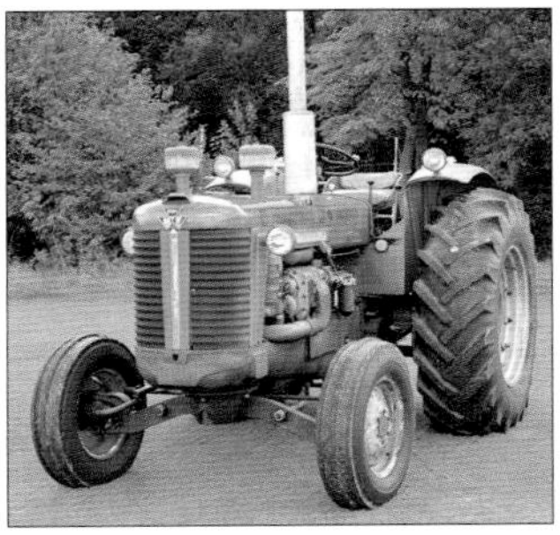

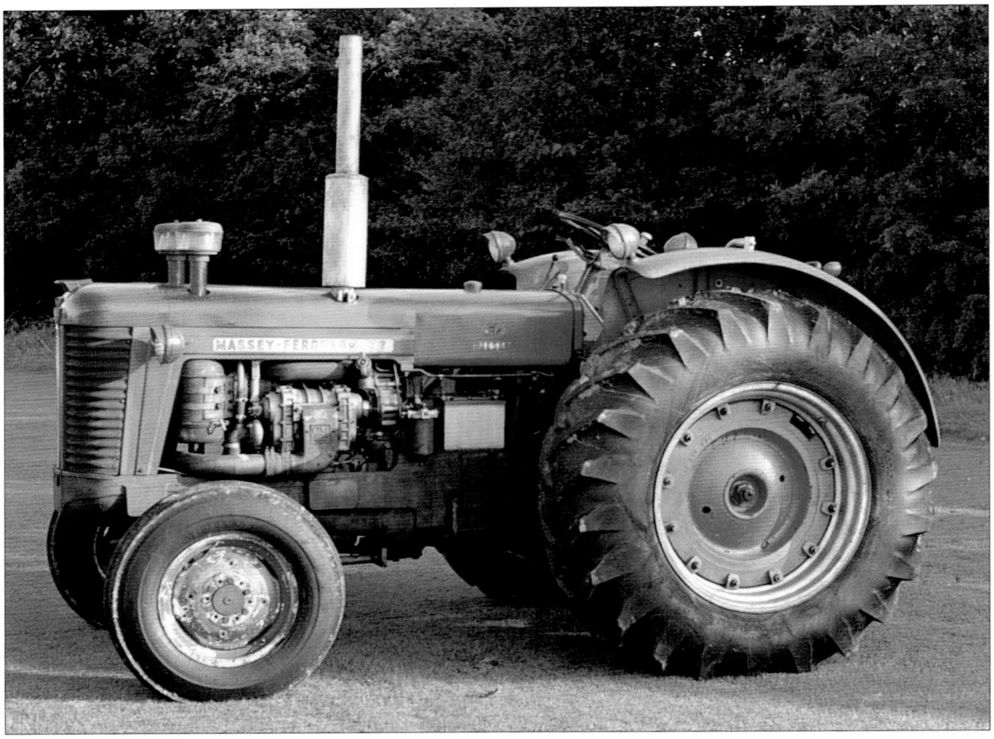

Above: *The Super 90 tractor was one of the big 90 series models hurried onto the market to strengthen the Massey-Ferguson range in the fast-growing high-horsepower sector.*

Specifications

Manufacturer: Massey-Ferguson
Location: Detroit, Michigan
Model: Super 90 Diesel
Type: General purpose
Power unit: Four-cylinder diesel engine
Power output: 68.5hp (50.7kw) (at the power takeoff)
Transmission: Eight-speed gearbox
Weight: 7,245lb (3,289kg)
Production started: 1962

Above, left: *Massey-Ferguson's Super 90 tractor with its 68.5-hp (50.7-kw) Perkins diesel engine was said to be the most powerful Ferguson System tractor available.*

Unfortunately it was the bigger tractors that were providing the fastest sales growth, particularly in the North American market, and Massey-Ferguson dealers risked losing business because they only had the aging Massey-Harris models to offer their big-acreage customers. To fill the gap Massey-Ferguson introduced the new 90 series tractors, but in order to speed up the process it bought in some of the new models from rival companies, creating complications.

Bought-in Tractors

Minneapolis-Moline G-507 tractors were sold under the Massey-Ferguson badge and colors as the MF-97 in the United States and as the MF-95 in Canada, and the Oliver company supplied 500 diesel-powered tractors to be sold as the MF-98. As bought-in tractors, these two models did not have the Ferguson System linkage and hydraulics.

The Super 90 was a Massey-Ferguson development, although the engine for the diesel version was bought in from Perkins. Super 90 production started in 1962, and the power output from the diesel version was 68.5hp (50.7kw) at the power takeoff, making it, the makers claimed, the most powerful Ferguson System tractor available. The four-cylinder engine had a rated speed of 2,000rpm, and the transmission provided eight forward speeds.

MASSEY-FERGUSON
1964   Coventry, Warwickshire, England, and Detroit, Michigan

MASSEY-FERGUSON MF-135

Project DX was an ambitious program to develop a new range of Massey-Ferguson tractors to be built in the company's American, British, and French factories, and one indication of the size of the project is the fact that the Engineering Division allocated one million man-hours for design work and building and testing the prototypes.

Right: MF-135 models were easily Massey-Ferguson's top-selling tractors in the mid-1960s, with production based in Detroit and Coventry.

Above: The Project DX development program produced a new range of Massey-Ferguson tractors, including the popular MF-135 model.

Specifications

Manufacturer: Massey-Ferguson

Locations: Coventry, Warwickshire, England, and Detroit, Michigan

Model: MF-135

Type: General purpose

Power unit: Three-cylinder diesel engine

Power output: 37.8hp (28kw)

Transmission: 12-speed gearbox

Weight: 3,645lb (1,655kg)

Production started: 1964

The aim of the project was to provide Massey-Ferguson with an all-new range of tractors that were technically advanced and could be marketed on a global scale, and the MF-135 was among the first of the new models. Production started in 1964 at the Detroit factory and in the following year at the Coventry plant. The diesel version was powered by a Perkins engine—Perkins had been taken over by Massey-Ferguson in 1959.

Maximum power output from the three-cylinder diesel engine, recorded in Nebraska in the power-takeoff tests, was 37.8hp (28kw), and the specification included a transmission with 12 forward speeds. American customers were also offered a gasoline-fueled version equipped with a Continental engine.

Top Seller

The MF-135 was the top seller of the MF tractor range in the mid-1960s. Production totaled almost 13,000 tractors at the Detroit factory in 1965, more than one-third of Massey-Ferguson's total U.S. production in that year; the 44,246 MF-135s built in 1966 was well over half of the company's UK output for the year.

COUNTY

1964 Fleet, Hampshire, England

COUNTY SEA HORSE

There is not much demand for a tractor that floats. Nonetheless, County Commercial Cars developed one in 1964, called the Sea Horse. Although it certainly earned plenty of publicity, there is no record of any sales.

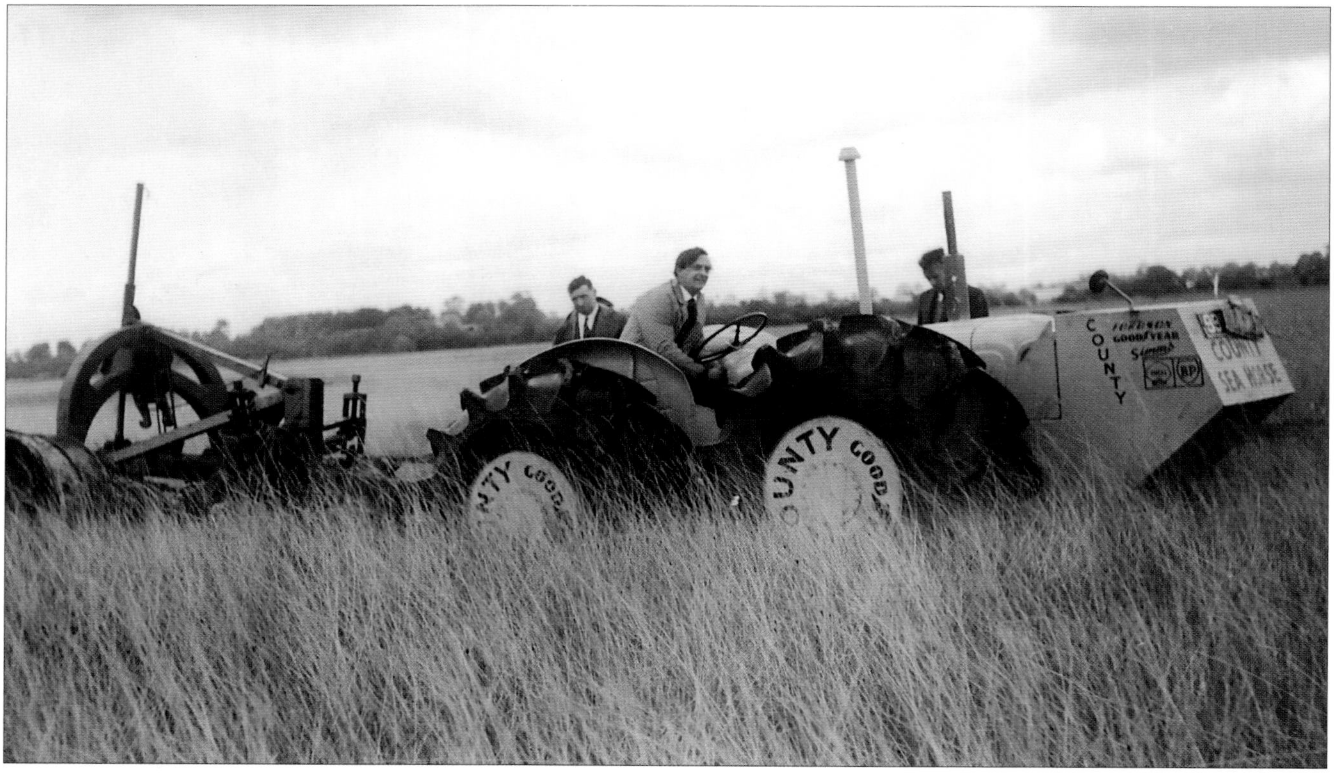

Above: *County's Sea Horse tractor photographed during a demonstration as a four-wheel drive tractor working on dry land.*

The County Sea Horse was based on the 52-hp (38.5-kw) engine and transmission of a Fordson Super Major tractor equipped with a County four-wheel drive conversion. Exactly what is was that prompted the company to produce a floating version of the tractor is not clear, but the development work appears to have been reasonably easy.

Flotation System

Most of the flotation was provided by the large volume of air in the four oversize Goodyear tires, but sealed compartments were also fitted on each wheel to provide additional air volume. County also built large flotation tanks made of sheet steel, and these were mounted on the front and rear of the tractor to provide extra stability in stormy conditions or when passing through the wash of a big ship. The tanks could also be used as ballast containers when the tractor was working on dry land, the company explained.

Apart from the air tanks, the modifications needed to turn the Sea Horse into a marine

tractor were surprisingly few. There was no elaborate waterproofing, but the clutch housing was fully sealed, the standard dipsticks were replaced by a screw-in type, and all the transmission housings were equipped with breathers opening above the waterline.

The propulsion system of the Sea Horse was even more straightforward. When the wheels were turning, the tread patterns on the four giant tires acted like paddle wheels, forcing the tractor either forward or backward. The steering mechanism worked in the same way as it would on land, although the turning circle was very much wider.

There were, it seems, just two problems. The propulsion provided by the wheels was much less efficient in the water than on land, and this reduced the forward speed to about 3kts (5.5km/h) in top gear, and the second problem was that the driver of the Sea Horse was soaked by the splashing caused by the wheels.

Channel Crossing

County publicized its latest tractor by taking it for a trip across the English Channel from France to England, completing the 28 nautical miles (51.8km) in 7 hours and 50 minutes. It also took it to Florida and attracted more publicity when it took the Sea Horse for a trip among the pleasure boats at Fort Lauderdale. If County expected the Sea Horse to sell in large numbers, it was doomed to disappointment, but if, as seems likely, the aim was publicity it was probably delighted.

Specifications

Manufacturer: County Commercial Cars
Location: Fleet, Hampshire, England
Model: Sea Horse
Type: Amphibious
Power unit: Four-cylinder engine
Power output: 52hp (38.5kw)
Transmission: Six-speed gearbox
Weight: 7,830lb (5,794kg)
Production: 1964

Left: *An original publicity photograph of the Sea Horse mingling with pleasure boats off the Florida coast.*

Left: *Another publicity photograph, this time showing the Sea Horse on its way across the English Channel from France to England.*

241

JOHN DEERE
✕ 1964 Waterloo, Iowa

JOHN DEERE 4020

Another instalment of John Deere's "New Generation of Power" arrived in 1963 when the new top-of-the-range 5010 model was announced, and there were further developments the following year when the 3010 and 4010 models were updated to become the 3020 and 4020.

Specifications

Manufacturer: Deere & Co.	
Location: Waterloo, Iowa	
Model: 4020	
Type: General purpose	
Power unit: Six-cylinder diesel	
Power out: 91hp (67.3kw)	
Transmission: Powershift	
Weight: 8,945lb (4,061kg)	
Production started: 1964	

The biggest difference between the new 3020 and 4020 and their predecessors was the addition of a powershift transmission. This was to prove a significant development because powershifts gradually took over as the preferred transmission for big tractors, but in 1964 they were still an unusual feature.

Advantages of Powershift
Advantages of a powershift include enabling the driver to shift to a different gear ratio smoothly without using the clutch pedal and without interrupting the power flow from the engine to the tractor wheels. This is important in situations where the tractor is working hard, such as pulling a heavy load up a gradient or plowing in difficult conditions, as the tractor loses momentum while the drive is disengaged for a conventional gear change. As well as improving productivity, powershifts also make life easier for the driver, as less physical effort is needed compared with a conventional gear shift.

Other developments featured on the new 4020 model included a hydraulically operated differential lock, using a foot pedal to deliver power equally to both driving wheels in order to reduce the risk of wheelslip, and there was also a power boost to 91hp (63.7kw).

Above: The most significant development on the new John Deere 4020 tractor was the powershift transmission, providing easier gear shifting without interrupting the power flow from the engine.

COUNTY
✖ 1965   Fleet, Hampshire, England

COUNTY FORWARD CONTROL FC1004

When tractor manufacturers County introduced its first Forward Control model in 1965 it was aimed partly at the agricultural market and partly at industrial and forestry users.

Right: Sales of the County Forward Control models were disappointing, perhaps because the design concept was too far ahead of its time.

Specifications

Manufacturer: County Commercial Cars

Location: Fleet, Hampshire, England

Model: FC1004

Type: General purpose

Power unit: Six-cylinder diesel engine

Power output: 102hp (75.5kw)

Transmission: Eight-speed gearbox

Weight: 9,394lb (4,265kg)

Production started: 1965

The design was highly unconventional. Like other County models, it was based on a Ford engine and transmission with the addition of the County four-wheel drive system through equal-diameter front and rear wheels. The most unusual feature, however, was the driving position, with the cab moved right to the front of the tractor, ahead of the front wheels, leaving a large area behind the cab that could be used for carrying equipment such as a mounted spray tank.

Power Unit

Production started with the FC654, and this was followed by the FC754, but it was the FC1004 version introduced in 1967 that achieved most of the sales. The power unit for the 1004 was a Ford 2703C industrial engine. This was a six-cylinder unit with overhead valves, 358.1 cubic inches (5.9 liters) of capacity and a 102-hp (75.5-kw) output. It was linked to an eight-speed Ford gearbox giving a top speed of just over 18mph (28km/h).

Tractors with a rear load-carrying platform have become increasingly popular during the past 20 years or so, but in the late 1960s the FC1004 was ahead of its time and sales were disappointing. FC1004 production continued on a small scale until 1977, when it was deleted from the County tractor range.

DAVID BROWN
✕ **1967   Meltham, Yorkshire, England**

DAVID BROWN 1200 SELECTAMATIC

The Selectamatic hydraulic system introduced by David Brown in 1965 was designed to make the three-point linkage easier to operate in order to simplify the driver's job and also to speed up work rates. It was restricted to the 770 model initially, but it was so successful that the system was added to all the company's models by the end of the year.

It was also included in the standard specification for the new 1200 model when it was announced in 1967, two years after David Brown had adopted its new "orchid white and chocolate brown" color scheme.

The 1200 also arrived just a few years before the British government introduced legislation to enforce the use of approved safety cabs or frames for driver protection. David Brown was the first British tractor manufacturer to have suitable cabs available almost two years before the 1970 deadline, and the first three approval certificates issued by the government went to David Brown.

As the 1200 tractor was available both before and after the new legislation, the company's

Above: David Brown introduced the 67-hp (50-kw) 1200 model in 1967 with the Selectamatic hydraulic system designed to simplify the operation of the rear linkage.

publicity photographs show the 1200 with and without the cab, which was an optional extra on UK-specification tractors during the period before the cab regulations came into effect.

Another indication of the increasing importance of driver safety and comfort was the addition of what the company called "a new luxury suspension seat," and this was included in the standard specification for the 1200.

Four-Wheel Drive

The 1200 was equipped with a David Brown four-cylinder diesel engine. The power output was initially 67hp (50kw), but this was boosted to 72hp (53.6kw) during the second year of production. Special design features on the new tractor included a separate hand-operated clutch to give independent control of the

power takeoff, the first time this had been available on a David Brown tractor. There was also a direct drive from the front of the engine to the hydraulic pump.

One of the important trends in UK tractor design in the late 1960s was the increasing demand for four-wheel drive. Putting the engine power through both the rear and the front wheels can significantly increase traction and pulling performance on wet or loose soil, and the number of farmers who were willing to pay a premium price for four-wheel drive was growing rapidly.

David Brown introduced a four-wheel drive version of the 1200 tractor in 1970, and in 1971 the specification was improved to allow the drive to the front wheels to be engaged while the tractor was on the move.

Specifications

Manufacturer: David Brown Tractors
Location: Meltham, Yorkshire, England
Model: 1200 Selectamatic
Type: General purpose
Power unit: Four-cylinder diesel engine
Power output: 67hp (50kw)
Transmission: Six-speed gearbox
Weight: 6,040lb (2,742kg)
Production started: 1967

Below: *As the demand for four-wheel drive tractors increased, David Brown introduced a 4WD version of the 1200 model in 1970.*

NUFFIELD

1967 **Bathgate, Scotland**

NUFFIELD 4/65

Profit margins at the British Motor Corporation were hit by industrial unrest and other problems at some of the group's car factories, and one result of this was a shortage of money to finance urgently needed development work on the company's Nuffield tractor range.

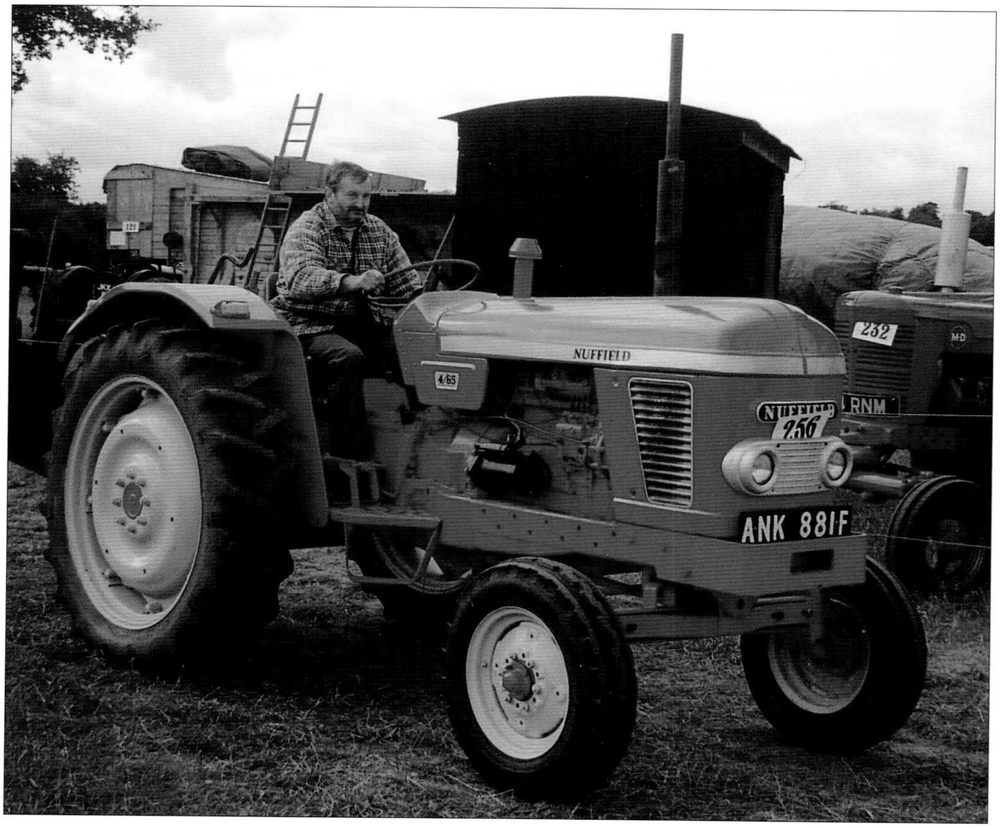

Specifications

Manufacturer: British Motor Corporation

Location: Bathgate, Scotland

Model: 4/65

Type: General purpose

Power unit: Four-cylinder diesel

Power output: 65hp (48.4kw)

Transmission: Ten-speed gearbox

Weight: N/A

Production started: 1967

Above: *The 4/65 was one of the new-look Nuffield tractors introduced in 1967 from the Leyland factory in Bathgate, Scotland.*

The Nuffield range had become one of the success stories of the UK tractor industry, with a particularly strong performance in export markets, but by the mid-1960s the basic design of the tractors was almost 20 years old, and a new tractor range was urgently needed.

New Models

When the new models arrived in 1967, the completely new styling made them look quite different to the previous Universal series, but the mechanical differences were much more modest. The new models were the 3/45 to replace the previous 10/42 model, and the 10/60 with its 60-hp (44.7-kw) engine, originally described as Britain's most powerful production tractor, became the new 4/65. In both cases the previous engine and transmission were retained, but the power output of the 10/60 was given a 5-hp (3.7-kw) boost to provide 65hp (48.4kw) for the new model. The list of improvements on the new models also included a second hydraulic pump to operate the draft control system, alteration to the design of the steering linkage and improvement to the 4/65 rear linkage through the addition of a double-acting top link.

LEYLAND
🔧 1968 Bathgate, Scotland

LEYLAND 154

When the British Motor Corporation was absorbed into British Leyland as part of the 1960s rationalization of the British car and commercial vehicle industry, the Nuffield tractor operation in Scotland was included in the deal.

Right: When Leyland took over the Nuffield tractor operation it relaunched the 4/25 model in its new two-tone blue color scheme and called it the Leyland 25.

Specifications

Manufacturer:	British Leyland
Location:	Bathgate, Scotland
Model:	Leyland 154
Type:	General purpose
Power unit:	Four-cylinder engine
Power output:	25hp (18.5kw)
Transmission:	Nine-speed gearbox
Weight:	N/A
Production started:	1968

The smallest tractor in the Nuffield range was the 4/25 Mini-Tractor, originally launched in 1965 with an 15-hp (11.1-kw) engine. It was designed, the makers claimed, as a low-priced tractor for small farms while also being suitable for use as a backup tractor on larger acreages. It was equipped with a four-cylinder engine, and the transmission was based on a three-speed gearbox with a second high-, medium-, and low-ratio box to provide nine forward speeds.

Relaunch

In 1968 the original Mini-Tractor was relaunched as the Nuffield 4/25. Market research had shown that customers considered that an 15-hp (11.1-kw) tractor did not offer enough power, and the output on the new version was increased to 25hp (18.5kw) with the choice of gasoline or diesel engines. This was the version that became a British Leyland product in 1968 and appeared in the following year in the two-tone blue color scheme chosen for the Leyland tractor range. At the same time the model number was changed to 154.

Under British Leyland management the little 154 was to remain in the product line for another 10 years; however, sales continued to be disappointing and it faced increasing competition from imported Japanese compact tractors. Production ended in 1979.

KUBOTA

1969 Osaka, Japan

KUBOTA TALENT 25

The principle reason for Kubota building the Talent 25 tractor was probably to generate some publicity, but the tractor also featured some interesting ideas that the company may have been considering for some of its future production tractors.

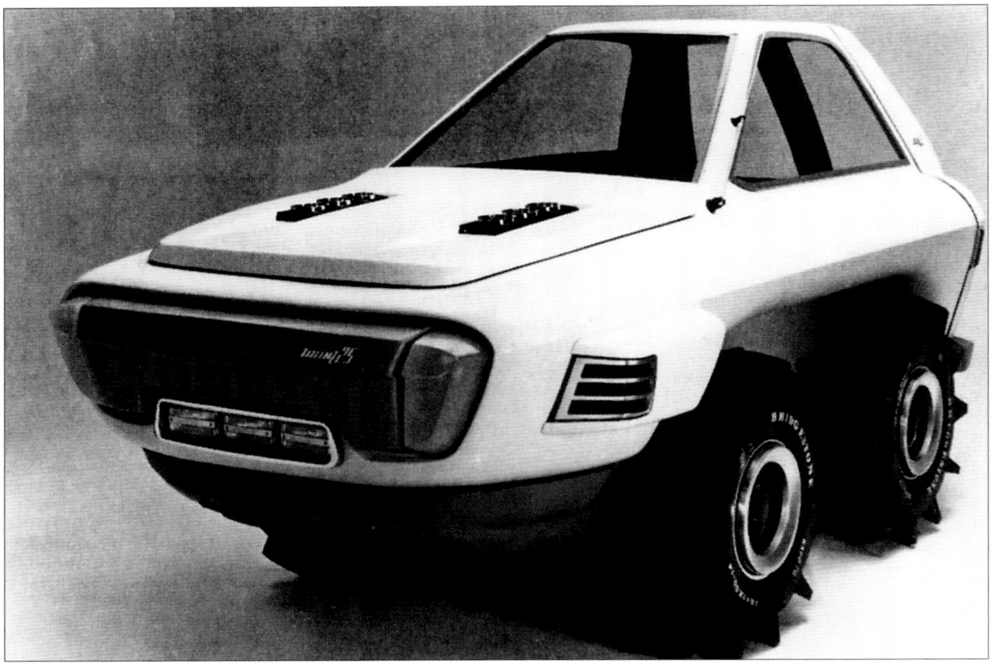

Above: *Kubota built the futuristic Talent 25 tractor to exhibit on a show stand in 1969 and to try out new ideas such as the externally mounted CCTV cameras.*

Specifications

Manufacturer: Kubota Iron & Machinery Works	
Location: Osaka, Japan	
Model: Talent 25	
Type: Experimental	
Power unit: Diesel engine	
Power output: 25hp (18.5kw)	
Transmission: N/A	
Weight: N/A	
Produced: 1969	

Kubota completed this unique tractor in 1969 and displayed it on its stand at the following year's World Fair in Japan. It featured a number of novel ideas, some of them possibilities for the future, while others were quite obviously impractical.

Closed-Circuit TV

One of the more interesting ideas was using closed-circuit TV cameras to enable the driver to overcome blind spots in his view outside the tractor. The Talent 25 had three cameras linked to a screen inside the cab, and the driver could select which camera he wanted to show images on the screen.

This probably seemed highly futuristic in 1969, but since then some production tractors and self-propelled machines have been fitted with such cameras, usually for safety reasons when the driver is reversing.

Less practical was the shape of the Talent's side panels curving over the tires, which would soon suffer from stone damage and mud splashes. Probably the least practical design feature was the cab with its pair of rear doors for the driver to enter or leave the cab.

Even the most nimble of drivers would find it difficult to climb aboard or make a dignified exit with a large and spiky machine attached to the rear of the tractor. Leading car manufacturers often produce models with futuristic styling only once for their show stands, and these often have more to do with attracting publicity than with assessing reaction to new ideas. Kubota's Talent 25 model is probably also in the same category.

LELY
✗ 1970 Maasland, Holland

LELY HYDRO 90

Lely is best known as one of Europe's leading farm machinery manufacturers, but the company has also experimented with several different tractor projects, although none of them has achieved a lasting commercial impact.

Right: *Lely was one of several companies attracted by the advantages of hydrostatic transmissions.*

Above: *The Hydro 90 model was powered by a six-cylinder MWM engine, and both two and four-wheel drive versions were planned.*

Specifications

Manufacturer: C Van Der Lely NV

Location: Maasland, Holland

Model: Hydro 90

Type: Experimental

Power unit: MWM six-cylinder diesel engine

Power output: 87hp (64kw)

Transmission: Hydrostatic

Weight: 7,062lb (3,210kg) (with four-wheel drive)

Produced: 1970

One of the ideas that attracted the engineers at the Lely company's headquarters in Holland was the idea of using a hydrostatic drive system. This does away with the usual gearbox and clutch, and power is transmitted to the wheels by using a flow of oil driven by a pump and circulating through motors attached to the wheels. The result is a smooth power flow and an infinitely variable travel speed at constant engine rpm.

Engine

Lely's Hydro 90 tractor with hydrostatic drive was demonstrated in 1970. The power unit was a six-cylinder MWM diesel engine with 271.3 cubic inches (4.47 liters) of capacity and an 87-hp (64-kw) output at the rated speed of 2,600rpm. The drive system allowed forward speed to be selected up to a maximum of 12.5mph (20.1km/h), and the top speed in reverse was 7.5mph (12km/h). The tractor was also available in a four-wheel drive version.

As well as the benefits, there is also the major disadvantage with hydrostatic transmissions that they are less efficient than a mechanical gear drive, and this may have been the reason why Lely abandoned the project after building several experimental tractors.

MASSEY-FERGUSON
1970 Detroit, Michigan

MASSEY-FERGUSON MF-1200

Articulated or bend-in-the-middle steering was the answer favored by most of the North American tractor manufacturers for achieving a reasonably small turning radius from a big tractor with equal-diameter front and rear wheels.

Below: *With four-wheel drive, bend-in-the-middle articulated steering, and a 105-hp (78-kw) output, the MF-1200 was impressive.*

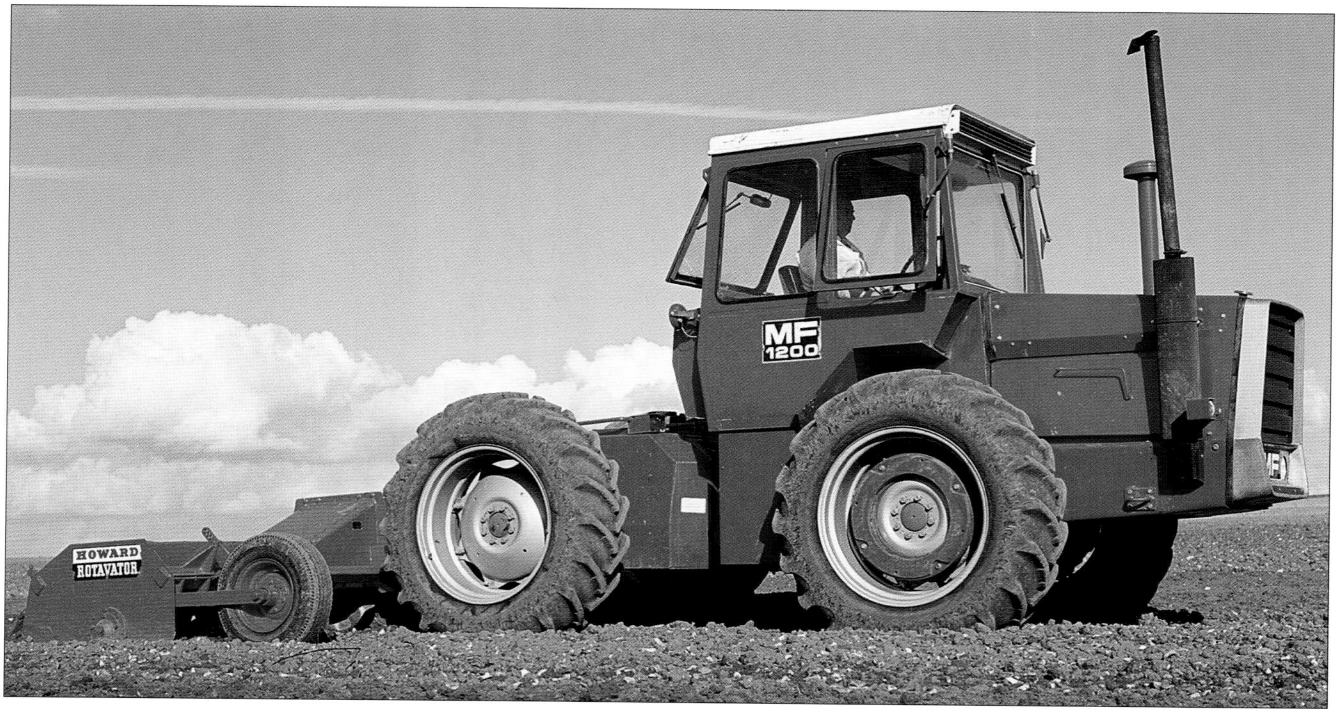

With conventional front-wheel steering the large-diameter wheels and tires contact the frame of the tractor before they achieve a wide-enough steering angle, but steering from a hinge point in the middle of the tractor was an effective alternative.

It was the steering system chosen by Massey-Ferguson engineers when they designed the MF-1200 tractor. This was a big tractor, introduced as part of the DX program that produced a complete new range of Massey-Ferguson tractors, including the MF-35.

Engine Power

The power output from the MF-1200's six-cylinder diesel engine was 105hp (78.2kw), but when it first appeared in the United Kingdom as the flagship of the MF range, many people assumed that such a big tractor would have an even bigger engine. The engine power was delivered through a Multi-Power transmission. This was an MF-patented development, which used a hydraulically operated epicyclic gear pack to double each of the gear ratios, and on the MF-1200 it provided 12 forward speeds and four in reverse.

The MF-1200 remained in the Massey tractor range until 1980. There was also an MF-1250 version that provided a modest power boost to 112hp (83.5kw) and also offered more hydraulic power to increase the lift capacity on the rear linkage.

Specifications

Manufacturer: Massey-Ferguson
Location: Detroit, Michigan
Model: MF-1200
Type: General purpose
Power unit: Six-cylinder diesel engine
Power output: 105hp (78.2kw)
Transmission: Multi-Power 12-speed gearbox
Weight: N/A
Production started: 1970

DUTRA

⚒ **1970 Budapest, Hungary**

DUTRA D4K-B

Dutra tractors were built in Hungary—the company name is an abbreviation for dumper and tractors, the two principle products—and they built substantial export sales in countries such as Britain where they offered the opportunity to buy a high-output tractor at an attractive price.

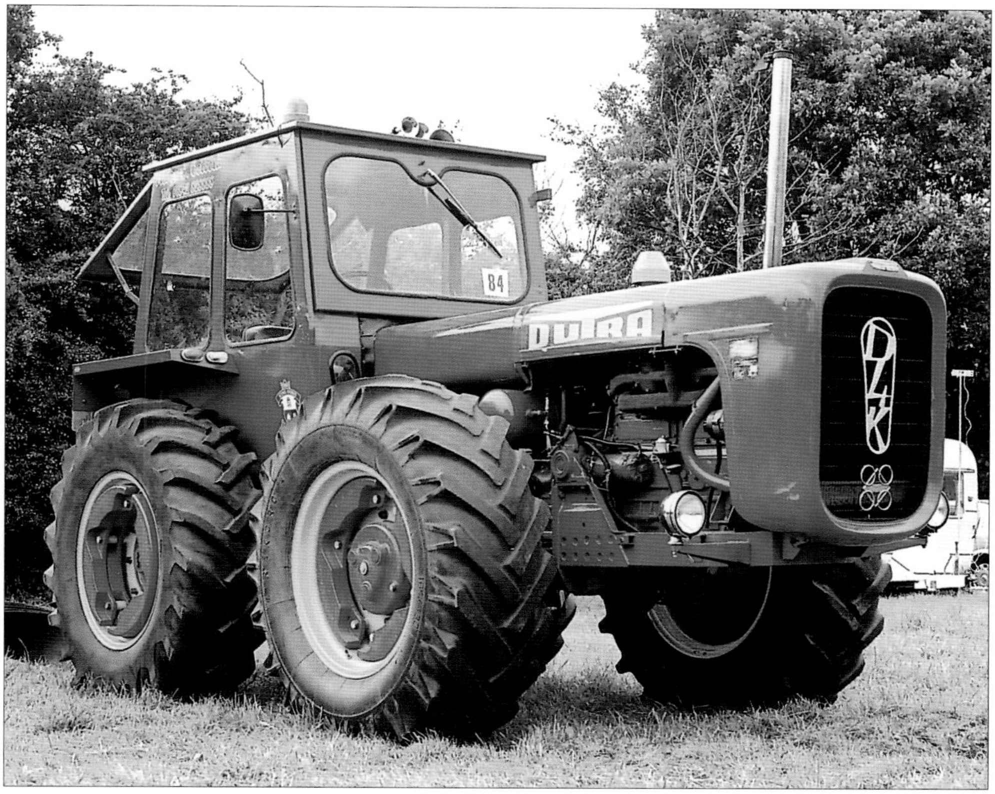

Right: *The Dutra was one of the few tractors in the early 1970s offering four-wheel drive and 100hp (74kw).*

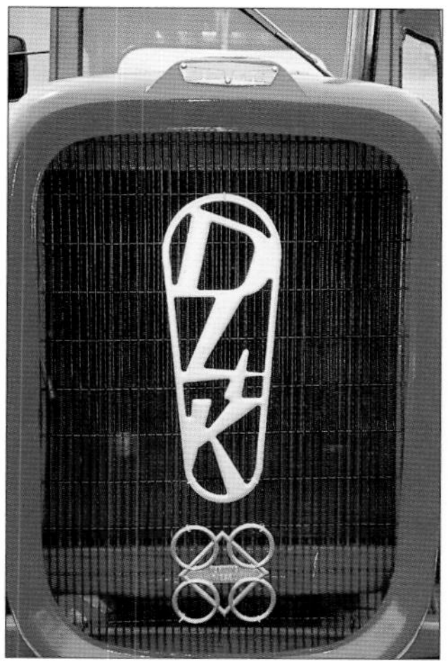

Above: *Most West European buyers preferred the Perkins engine in the D4K-B tractor, and few of the Csepel-powered versions were sold.*

Specifications

Manufacturer:	Dutra Tractor Works
Location:	Budapest, Hungary
Model:	D4K-B
Type:	General purpose
Power units:	Six-cylinder diesel engine
Power output:	100hp (74kw)
Transmission:	Six-speed gearbox
Weight:	11,220lb (5,100kg)
Production started:	1970

The high output came partly from using engines of 100hp (74kw) and above at a time when only a small number of Western manufacturers offered this amount of power. The performance was also helped by providing four-wheel drive through equal-diameter front and rear wheels, the most efficient form of four-wheel drive.

Perkins Engines

Dutra's breakthrough in the West came in the mid-1960s when it began offering familiar Perkins engines as an alternative to the Hungarian-built Csepel power units. In 1971 customers for the 100-hp (74-kw) D4K-B model could choose either a Csepel DT613S Csepel or a Perkins 6.354(TA) engine. Both engines had six cylinders and were four-stroke diesels, but it was the Perkins version that achieved the highest sales volume.

The standard specification for the Dutra included a safety cab and hydraulic braking on all four wheels, and the gearbox provided six forward speeds. The steering was power-assisted, and operated conventionally through the front wheels, and with large-diameter front wheels this must have resulted in a very wide turning circle.

FORD

⚒ 1971   Romeo, Michigan

FORD 7000

Project 6X was the program that rationalized the Ford tractor range and produced the new 1000 series models for world markets. The program brought together the company's three main production facilities in Highland Park in the USA, Antwerp in Belgium, and the brand new tractor plant in Basildon, Essex, in England. Their initial job was to build four new models covering the small to medium sectors of the market.

The first batch of new tractors was announced in 1964. There were four models, starting with the Ford 2000 with a 37-hp (27.5-kw) output, the 3000 powered by a 46-hp (34.3-kw) diesel engine, and, at the top of the range, the 65-hp (48.4-kw) rated Ford 5000. The fourth model was the 4000, the top-selling 1000 series tractor with 55hp (41kw) available from the diesel-powered version.

Options

All the 1000 series tractors, apart from the 2000 model, were equipped with an eight-speed manual gearbox, but the Ford Select-O-Speed transmission with 10 forward speeds was on the options list. Select-O-Speed was one of the first powershift drive systems, allowing clutchless gear shifting. The options also included gasoline engines for some markets, including North

Above, top: The 7000 was one of the new 1000 series tractors developed for world markets under Ford's Project 6X program.

Above: Ford's 4000 series tractor was the best-selling 1000 series model, and the tractor in the photograph is still in regular use.

America, and the 4000 was available in a rowcrop version known as the 4200. Updated versions were introduced in 1968 with minor styling changes and additional power output.

Extra Power

Another major development was the 7000 model announced in 1971, a new addition to the 1000 series that was designed to provide the extra power many farmers were demanding. The engine for the 7000 was based on the 5000 power unit, using a turbocharger to produce the extra power.

Turbocharging is a technique for increasing the power output of an engine. It uses the waste gases from the engine exhaust system to spin a tiny impeller wheel at very high speeds, and the impeller blows extra air into the combustion chamber of the engine.

Turbocharging typically boosts the power output of a diesel engine by about 20 to 25 percent, and this is why it was used on the Ford 5000 engine. Another result of adding a turbo is that the fuel is burned more efficiently, and this produces cleaner exhaust fumes.

Increasingly strict controls over exhaust emissions have recently made turbo engines much more popular, and almost all new tractor engines above about 75hp (55.9kw) now have a turbo fitted.

The turbo engine in the Ford 7000 produced 94hp (69.6kw) compared with 75hp (5.9kw) from the equivalent Ford 5000 nonturbo or naturally aspirated engine.

Specifications

Manufacturer:	Ford Tractor Division
Location:	Romeo, Michigan
Model:	7000
Type:	General purpose
Power unit:	Four-cylinder turbocharged engine
Power output:	94hp (69.6kw)
Transmission:	Eight-speed gearbox
Weight:	N/A
Production started:	1971

Below: *Instead of developing a special engine for the new Ford 7000 model, the design team added a turbocharger to the 5000 series engine to boost the output.*

chapter 8

Piling on the Horsepower

Bigger tractors with more horsepower was one of the principle tractor trends in the 1970s and 1980s, as farmers and contractors demanded faster work rates in order to boost efficiency. Tractor manufacturers responded by using bigger engines, often with turbochargers and intercoolers to produce even more power. The result in North America was a new generation of giant tractors for the biggest farms.

Above: *Some new ideas were quietly forgotten, including the road wheel kit developed by Track Marshall to give extra mobility to its Britannia tracklayer.*

Left: *First produced in 1990, the Fiat Winner 140 was introduced by Italian automobile builder Fiat to increase their share of the European tractor market.*

The high-horsepower tractors featured four-wheel drive, often with dual or even triple wheels all around for improved traction and to help reduce soil compaction. The tractors were usually built in two sections with a hinge point in the middle to provide the articulated steering action. Engines for the 300-hp (220-kw) plus models usually came from specialists such as Cummins and Caterpillar, but John Deere's giant tractors were powered by Deere engines.

Caterpillar produced what was probably the most important advance in crawler tractor design for 50 years when it announced the new Challenger series tracklayers with steel-reinforced rubber tracks. The Challenger tracks or belts could be used on public roads and allowed much faster travel and working speeds than traditional steel tracks, and they halted years of decline in tracklayer sales.

Other developments included new interest in transportation tractors, prompted by the high-speed Trantor and the experimental transportation vehicle developed at Britain's Silsoe research center, and including the highly successful JCB Fastrac. Renault had a cab-suspension system, and there was a foretaste of the huge impact electronic control systems would soon have on tractor operation.

LEYLAND
⚒ 1972 Bathgate, Scotland

LEYLAND 255

The numbers used by some manufacturers to identify their tractor models have no particular significance and appear to be chosen at random; however, there are also some companies with model numbers that give specific information about the tractor.

Specifications

Manufacturer: British Leyland	
Location: Bathgate, Scotland	
Model: 255	
Type: General purpose	
Power unit: Four-cylinder diesel engine	
Power output: 55hp (41kw)	
Transmission: 10-speed gearbox	
Weight: N/A	
Production started: 1972	

Most Nuffield tractors were identified by numbers that carried information, and this approach continued following the merger that put the Leyland name on the tractors instead of Nuffield. For a few years after the 1967 merger Leyland continued to sell what were basically the old Nuffield models with a blue paint finish and some minor design changes. The first of the new Leyland-designed tractors did not arrive until 1972.

New Tractors
The new range included the 255 model, a number that indicated two-wheel drive and an engine with approximately 55-hp (41-kw) output. Later models included the 472 with four-wheel drive and a 72-hp (53.6-kw) engine. When this model was upgraded by turbocharging the engine to deliver more power, the model number was changed to 482.

The 255 was a popular mid-range tractor powered by a four-cylinder engine and with a specification that included an independent power takeoff and a gearbox with 10 forward speeds. Power steering was still an extra-cost option, but it was included as standard equipment when the 255 was replaced by the more powerful 262 model in 1976.

Above: *The Leyland 255 tractor was launched in 1972 with a standard specification that included a 10-speed transmission and an independent power takeoff.*

MERCEDES-BENZ
✗ **1972 Gaggenau, Germany**

MERCEDES-BENZ MB-TRAC 65/70

The Mercedes-Benz MB-trac was one of a group of systems tractors developed in Germany during the early 1970s, and it was launched at the same time as the Deutz Intrac at the 1972 German DLG machinery event.

Right: MB-trac features included four-wheel drive through equal-sized wheels, a top speed of 25mph (40 km/h), and a transmission with 12 speeds forward and in reverse.

Specifications

Manufacturer:	Daimler-Benz
Location:	Gaggenau, Germany
Model:	65/70
Type:	General purpose
Power unit:	Four-cylinder engine
Power output:	65hp (48kw)
Transmission:	12-speed gearbox
Weight:	N/A
Production started:	1972

Other similarities included the provision for front as well as rear linkage and power takeoff, four-wheel drive through equal-size wheels, and a small load space behind the cab.

The first MB-trac was the 65/70 equipped with a 65-hp (48-kw) Mercedes engine. The gearbox provided 12 speeds forward and in reverse; the maximum speed in top gear was 25mph (40km/h). Both axles were equipped with a differential lock to boost the traction in difficult conditions, and a passenger seat in the cab was included in the standard specification.

Later versions offered more power—up to 180hp (134.2kw) on the 1800 model. Most also had a reversible driving position, based on a seat that could be swiveled through 180° with some of the foot and hand controls, allowing the driver to face backward when operating some types of rear-mounted equipment.

Top Seller
The MB-trac became the top-selling systems tractor during the 1970s and 1980s. In spite of its success, Daimler-Benz decided to pull out of the agricultural tractor market, although it continued to build the Unimog all-terrain truck which is often used by farmers and contractors for jobs such as spraying.

DEUTZ
✖ 1972 Cologne, Germany

DEUTZ INTRAC 2005

Most of the development work that produced the first "systems" tractors was carried out by German companies during the early 1970s, with Deutz taking the lead with its Intrac tractors.

There were two Intrac models, the 2002 and 2005, and they were both shown for the first time at the DLG agricultural show in 1972. The design of the Intrac followed a new analysis of the way tractors were used on German farms and the equipment that they powered. The analysis also looked at forecasts of the way farming was likely to develop during the next 20 years or so.

Systems Tractors

It was an ambitious project and the result was the Intrac systems tractor, designed to meet the requirements of farmers through the 1970s and beyond. The conclusion reached by the Deutz research team was that tractors would increasingly be used with different combinations of machinery to do a sequence of jobs in a single operation. To achieve this the Intrac was

Above: When the Intrac models were announced in 1972 they were regarded as the pattern for future systems-tractor development.

designed to carry both front- and rear-mounted equipment, using an implement linkage and power takeoff at each end of the tractor. The driver's cab was moved to the front of the tractor to leave space for mounting equipment such as a hopper for carrying fertilizer or a tank for spray chemicals.

Other design features of the Intrac included a cab with a large glass area to allow good all-round visibility from the driver's seat, and the transmission for the 2005 version was a hydrostatic drive with two speed ranges, a slower range for field work and a faster range with a maximum speed of 25mph (40km/h) for road travel. Hydrostatic drive was chosen for the Intrac 2005 because it provides infinitely variable adjustment of the forward and reverse travel speed without altering the engine speed and power output.

Four-Wheel Drive

Four-wheel drive was standard on the Intrac 2005, using equal-sized front and rear wheels, but only an option on the smaller 2002 version, which also had smaller-diameter front wheels and a mechanical transmission. Power for both models was provided by a Deutz air-cooled engine providing 90hp (66.6kw) for the 2005 and 51hp (38kw) for the 2002.

The Intracs attracted enormous interest, and they were widely regarded as the first stage in a new revolution in tractor design. They and some of the other early examples of systems tractors were certainly influential, and some of the features of the early systems models are still available on some current production tractors. The Intracs did not achieve the sales volumes that were widely predicted, however, and in commercial terms they were not a big success.

Specifications

Manufacturer: Klöckner/Humboldt-Deutz AG

Location: Cologne, Germany

Model: Intrac 2005

Type: Systems tractor

Power unit: Five-cylinder diesel engine

Power output: 90hp (66.6kw)

Transmission: Two-range hydrostatic

Weight: N/A

Production started: 1972

Below: *A mid-mounted cab plus attachment points for front- and rear-mounted equipment gave the Intrac exceptional versatility.*

CASE
1974 Racine, Wisconsin

CASE TRACTION KING 2670

Case moved into the high-horsepower sector of the market with the Traction King range of heavyweight tractors during the mid-1970s. These followed the American fashion for four-wheel drive through large-diameter front and rear wheels, but the Case models were different because they did not use articulated or pivot steering.

Specifications

Manufacturer: J. I. Case

Location: Racine, Wisconsin

Model: Traction King 2670

Type: Pulling tractor

Power unit: Six-cylinder diesel engine

Power output: 220hp (163kw)

Transmission: 12-speed semipowershift

Weight: 20,810lb (9,448kg)

Production started: 1974

The Traction King 2670 model was launched in 1974, equipped with a six-cylinder Case diesel engine producing 220hp (163kw) at the power takeoff when the tractor was tested in Nebraska. The engine had a rated speed of 2,200rpm, and the cylinder bore and stroke measurements were 4.6in and 5.0in (11.6cm and 12.7cm) respectively.

Steering System

The specification included a semipowershift transmission with 12 forward speeds giving a top speed of 14.5mph (23.3km/h) on the road.

Also included in the standard specification was a four-wheel steering system offering the choice of four different modes available at the press of a button. These included a conventional front-wheel-only setting, plus steering by the rear wheels only—useful for maneuvering the tractor's rear end when hitching up to an implement. With the four-wheel steering mode selected, the front and the rear wheels steer in opposite directions to give the smallest turning radius. In the fourth mode all four wheels steer in the same direction to give a crab-steering action, useful for moving close to a fence or building.

Above: *While some European manufacturers were designing for versatility, there was big demand in North America for pulling tractors such as the high-horsepower Case 2670.*

RENAULT

1974 **Le Mans, France**

RENAULT 851-4

The late 1960s were an important period for the Renault tractor company in France. Production was moved to a new factory near Le Mans, where up-to-date equipment helped to boost efficiency and production volumes, and two years later in 1969 the tractor operation became a separate business within the state-owned Renault group.

Right: *Renault had stopped making tractor engines and relied on outside suppliers, and the engine in the Renault 851-4 tractor was built in Germany by MWM.*

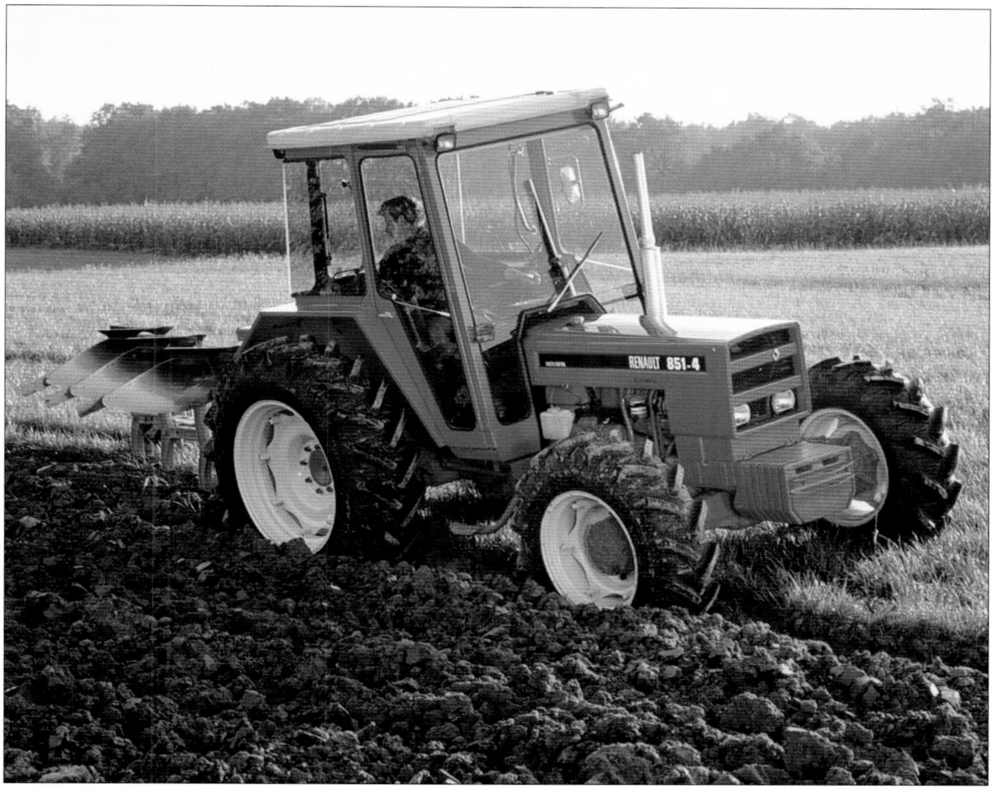

Specifications

Manufacturer: Renault Agriculture
Location: Le Mans, France
Model: 851-4
Type: General purpose
Power unit: MWM four-cylinder diesel engine
Power output: 85hp (63kw)
Transmission: Shuttle gearbox with 12 speeds forward and in reverse
Weight: N/A
Production started: 1974

These developments were followed by a series of new model launches for the company, which included four-wheel drive tractors and the first diesel engines.

At the same time Renault was continuing to phase out its own tractor engines, replacing them with power units that were supplied mainly by MWM, but also by other companies including Perkins.

New Models

Renault's 851-4 tractor arrived as part of a major new model launch spread over several years in the mid-1970s. The new models covered the power range from 30 to 145hp (22.3 to 108.1k) using MWM engines, and each model was identified by a number indicating the power output of the engine plus a "2" for two-wheel drive; the number "4" was used on tractor with four-wheel drive. On this basis the power output of the 851-4 was 85hp (63kw) and it was the four-wheel drive version.

Production of the 851-4 totaled 2,496 tractors between 1974 and 1980, and a further 4,227 of the improved 851-4S version were built during the nine-year period to 1989.

VALMET
✖ 1975 Jyväskylä, Finland

VALMET 1502

There is plenty of evidence that four-wheel drive provides more efficient traction than two-wheel drive when the ground surface is wet and slippery. Similar information about the effectiveness of six-wheel drive, however, is not as widely available.

Specifications

Manufacturer: Valmet Oy
Location: Jyväskylä, Finland
Model: 1502
Type: General purpose
Power unit: Six-cylinder diesel engine
Power output: 136hp (100kw)
Transmission: 16-speed gearbox
Weight: 16,434lb (7,470kg)
Production started: 1975

The Valmet company in Finland presumably decided that the extra cost of six-wheel drive could be justified, and it announced its first—and also its last—six-wheel drive tractor in 1975. The front end of the Valmet 1502 tractor was conventional, with a single axle and two driving wheels; however, the rear end was supported on a bogie unit with a set of four close-coupled powered wheels.

Six-Wheel Drive
Valmet engineers designed the rear bogie unit to allow plenty of vertical movement of both the front and the rear sections, and the company claimed that this ensured efficient traction over rough ground, with a smoother ride for the operator. An extra benefit was reduced soil compaction as the weight of the tractor was spread over six wheels instead of the usual four. One of the options demonstrated by the company was a steel track unit over the two rear wheels on each side, allowing a further improvement in both the traction and the low ground-pressure characteristics of the tractor.

Valmet designed the 1502 tractor to suit the industrial and forestry markets as well as the farming industry, but sales of the model were disappointing, and customers were clearly not convinced that the extra cost of six-wheel drive was justified by the benefits.

Above: In 1975 the Valmet company in Finland, now known as Valtra, introduced the 136-hp (100-kw) 1502 model with six-wheel drive.

STEIGER
✖ 1976 Fargo, North Dakota

STEIGER PANTHER ST-325

In 1957, when the Steiger brothers wanted a more powerful tractor for their farm in Minnesota, they decided to build their own, using a 238-hp (117.4-kw) Detroit Diesel engine. The performance of the home-made tractor soon attracted orders from neighbors, and by 1969 the Steiger company was established in a new factory in North Dakota.

Right: Steiger was one of the North American giant tractor specialists and its late 1970s range included the 325-hp (240-kw) Panther ST-325.

Specifications

Manufacturer: Steiger Tractor Inc.

Location: Fargo, North Dakota

Model: Panther ST-325

Type: Pulling tractor

Power unit: Caterpillar six-cylinder engine

Power output: 325hp (240kw)

Transmission: 10-speed gearbox

Weight: 31,080lb (14,110kg)

Production started: 1976

Sales growth was dramatic, rising from more than $20 million in 1973 to $104 million in 1976, helped by a big increase in exports sales to Australia and Canada as well as in the United States. Some of the growth was due to the success of the Panther models, including the ST-325 version powered by a turbocharged six-cylinder Caterpillar engine. The engine had a 2,100rpm rated speed and the cylinder measurements were 5.4-in (13.7-cm) bore and 6.5-in (16.5-cm) stroke.

Transmission

A 10-speed transmission was included in the standard specification, but Steiger also offered a CM-325 version with 20 forward speeds. As there was no power-takeoff shaft the tests to measure power output at the power takeoff were omitted when the Panther was tested in Nebraska; however, the results of the drawbar-pull tests—the most important measure of performance in a tractor of this type—were certainly impressive.

The maximum pulling power in fifth gear was 16,535lb (7,498.8kg), with wheelslip measured at 4.03 percent.

The Steiger Tractor company was bought by Case I.H. in 1986, and this was followed by a color change from the Steiger lime green to Case I.H. red.

FORD

1976 **Fargo, North Dakota**

FORD FW-60

Ford signed a deal with the specialist manufacturer, Steiger, when it decided to move into the top end of the high-horsepower market in 1976. Under the deal Steiger agreed to supply a four-model range of tractors painted in Ford colors and identified as the FW series.

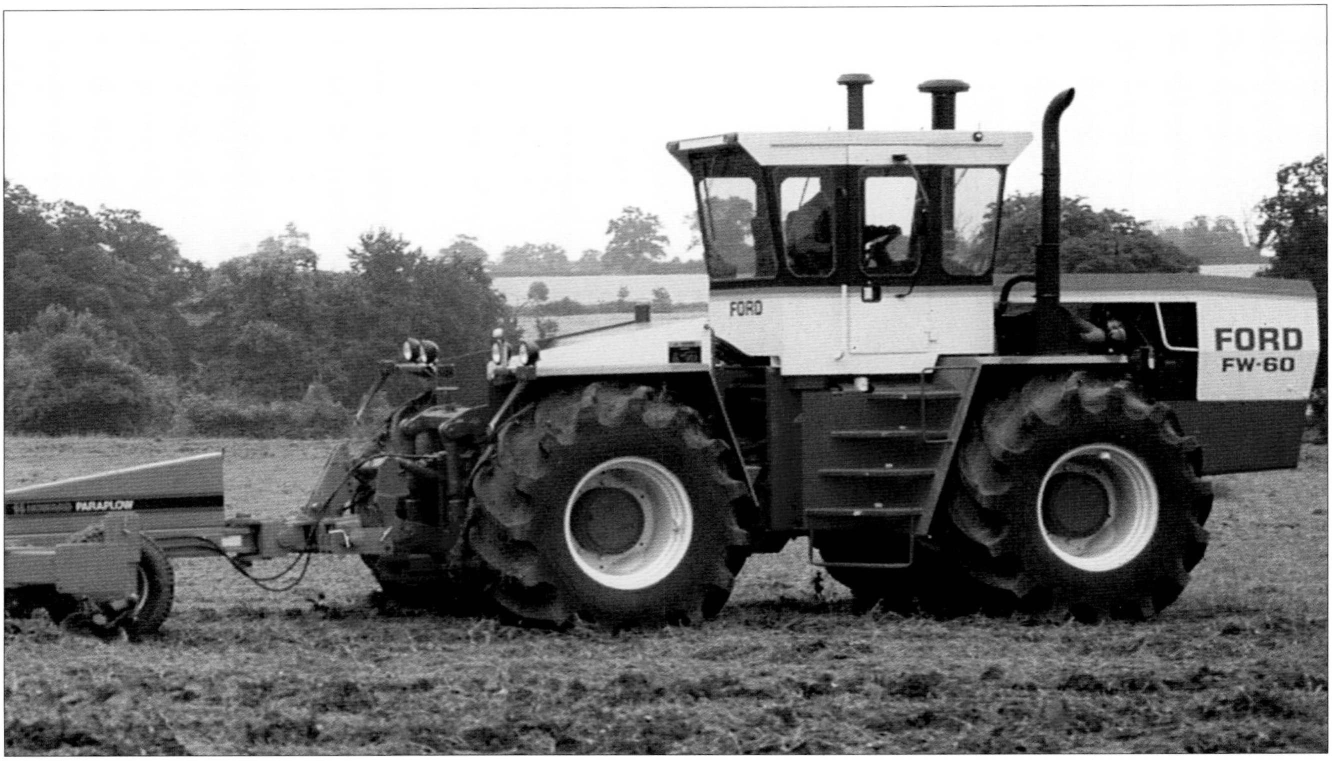

Below: *Ford's FW series high-horsepower tractors were built by Steiger and they included the 335-hp (248-kw) FW-60 model at the top of the range.*

The four tractors were all powered by Cummins V-8 diesel engines producing power outputs ranging from 210hp (156.5kw) for the FW-20 at the bottom of the range to 335hp (248kw) from the turbo engine in the FW-60. The FW-60 specification also included a 20-speed transmission with a top speed of 21.8mph (35km/h) for road travel, but, as the big FWs were designed mainly as heavy-duty pulling tractors, there was no power takeoff.

Driver Comfort

Giant tractors such as the FW models are used mainly on big farms where drivers often spend long hours at the controls, and for this reason driver comfort is particularly important. The FW tractor cab was equipped with tinted glass to reduce glare, air conditioning, sound insulation, and a stereo sound system including a radio and an eight-track tape player.

An updated version of the FW-60 arrived in 1984 with some minor styling and engine changes, and in the following year a further improvement was made, with a 10-speed automatic gearbox was added to the options list.

Case I.H. made a successful takeover bid for the Steiger company in 1986, and Ford bought the Canadian-based Versatile tractor company in 1987 to secure its future supply of high-horsepower tractors.

Specifications

Manufacturer:	Steiger Tractors Inc.
Location:	Fargo, North Dakota
Model:	Ford FW-60
Type:	Pulling tractor
Power unit:	Cummins V-6 diesel engine
Power output:	335hp (248kw)
Transmission:	20-speed gearbox
Weight:	31,100lb (14,119kg)
Production started:	1976

LELY

✖ 1977   Temple, Texas

LELY MULTIPOWER

One of the surprise competitors in the high-horsepower sector of the North American tractor market was the Lely company from Holland, and it also produced one of the most unconventional designs.

Above: *When European machinery specialist Lely decided to break into the American high-horsepower market it built the 420-hp (311-kw) Multipower with two engines.*

Specifications

Manufacturer: C Van Der Lely NV
Location: Temple, Texas
Model: Multipower (later called 420)
Type: General purpose
Power unit: Two Caterpillar V-8 diesel engines
Power output: 420hp (311kw)
Transmission: Two 10-speed gearboxes
Weight: 35,000lb (15,890kg) (shipping weight)
Production started: circa 1977

As one of Europe's leading manufacturers of power takeoff driven machines, Lely wanted to expand the sales of its equipment in the United States and Canada, but one of the problems in the 1970s was the absence of a three-point linkage and power takeoff drive on the biggest tractors.

Twin Engines

The Lely company decided to build its own high-horsepower tractor to work with power takeoff equipment, and it assembled a team of engineers at its American distribution center in Texas to design and build one or more prototype tractors. Presumably it was an expensive project, but it did not run smoothly. The design included articulated steering and two engines producing 210hp (155.5kw) each.

The engine in the front section drove the front wheels and could be used on its own to reduce fuel consumption when full power was not needed, while the rear engine powered the back wheels and also provided power for the power takeoff shaft.

The twin engine idea, which also involved two transmissions and two fuel tanks, was expensive and put the Multipower at a cost and weight disadvantage. When the tractor was launched, Massey-Ferguson threatened legal action because it had already registered the Multipower name, and Lely had to back down and call the tractor the Lely 420 instead.

It is not known if any Multipower or 420 tractors were sold, but we do know that Lely soon abandoned the project to concentrate on its machinery business.

VERSATILE

1977 Winnipeg, Manitoba, Canada

VERSATILE 1080 "BIG ROY"

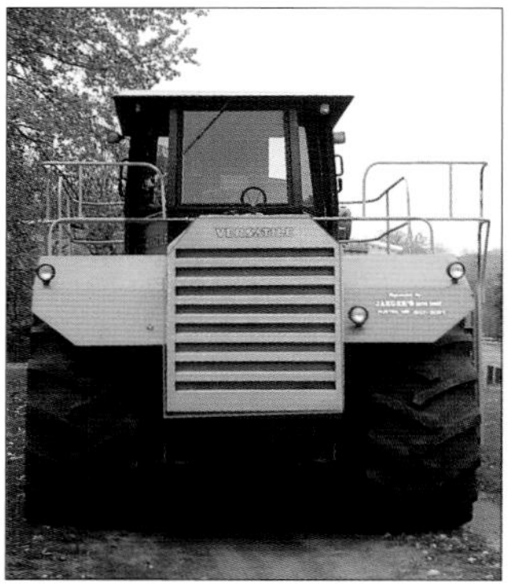

By the mid-1970s competition in the high-horsepower sector of the tractor market was intense, and there was rivalry to offer the most powerful tractor. The Canadian-based Versatile company was one of the leading manufacturers of big four-wheel drive tractors and Roy Robinson, its high-profile managing director, who stood at 6 ft 4 in (1.93 m) tall, decided to put his company ahead in the power race by building the biggest tractor in the world.

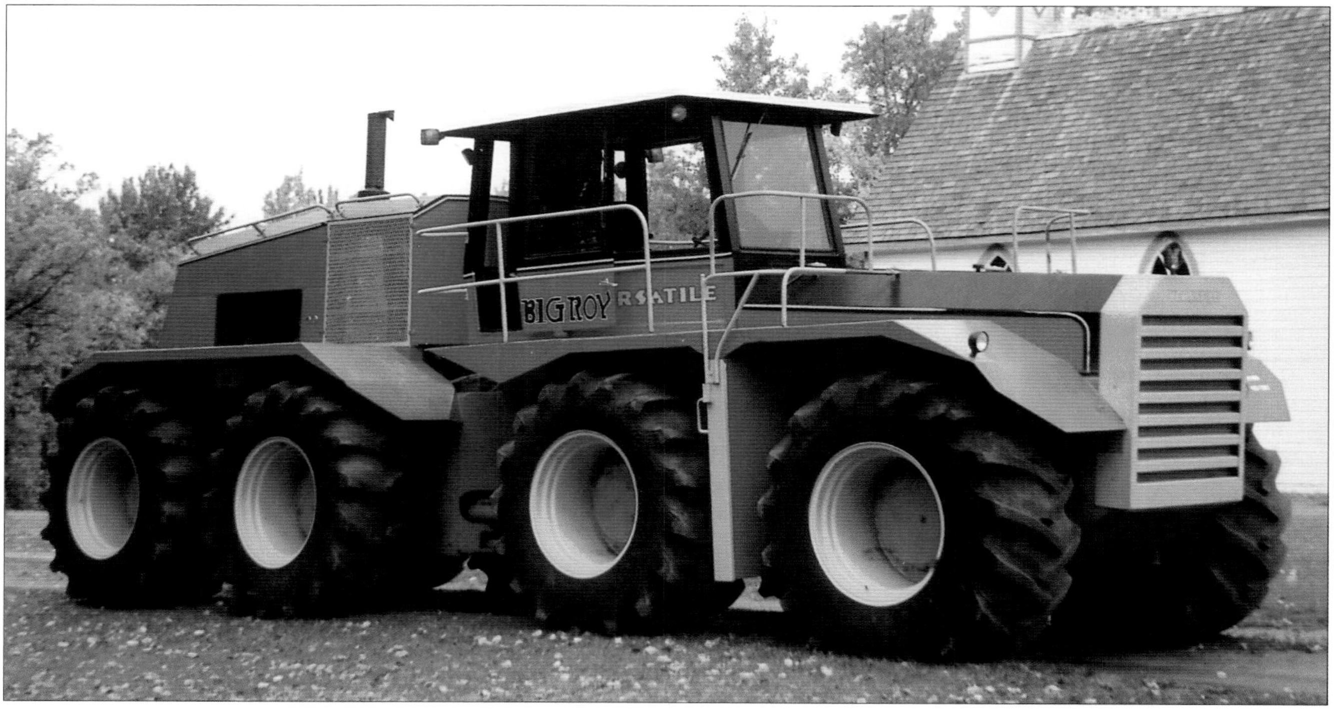

In the mid-1970s the biggest tractors were about 350hp (260kw), but Versatile engineers decided to use a Cummins engine producing 600hp (444kw) from 1153.3-cubic-inches (19-liters) capacity. In terms of tractor design this was venturing into unknown territory, and there were concerns about tire damage when transmitting so much engine power, and also the soil damage that might be caused by so much weight on just four wheels and tires.

Articulated Tractor

To overcome these problems the design team used four axles and an eight-wheel drive layout, and the tractor was in two halves with a pivot point in the middle to provide hydraulically operated articulated steering. The tractor was completed in 1977 and it was called "Big Roy" in honor of Mr. Robinson.

The weight of the finished tractor was 26.4 tons (26.8 tonnes), and the overall length was

Above, top: *The Canadian-based Versatile company named its most powerful tractor Big Roy after Roy Robinson, its managing director.*

Above: *A CCTV camera on the back of Big Roy was used when reversing, as the 600-hp (444-kw) engine was mounted behind the cab where it blocked the rear view.*

33ft (10m). It was—and still is—probably the most impressive-looking tractor ever built.

A ladder on each side provided access to the cab, and inside the cab there was plenty of space for the driver and a passenger. The cab was air-conditioned, a rare luxury when Big Roy was built, and there was also a small screen connected to a closed-circuit TV camera at the rear of the tractor. The rear view from the driver's seat was totally blocked by the engine compartment mounted high up on the rear section of Big Roy, and the TV equipment was essential when reversing and to position the tractor correctly when hitching up to an implement.

When the tractor was completed it was taken to some of the leading American and Canadian agricultural shows, where it attracted considerable publicity, and there were plenty of big-acreage farmers who were interested in buying a 600-hp (444-kw) tractor.

Problems

Big Roy was taken on a demonstration tour, and this is where the problems emerged. There were virtually no implements big enough for a tractor of this size, and excessive damage to the tire lugs and casing was caused by the steering action. Development work on Big Roy was abandoned, and was replaced by a more modest project to build a 470-hp (350.4-kw) tractor that became the Versatile 1150. Big Roy found a new home in the Agricultural Museum in Brandon, Manitoba, where it is one of the main attractions.

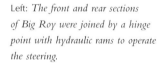

Specifications

Manufacturer: Versatile Manufacturing
Location: Winnipeg, Manitoba, Canada
Model: 1080 Big Roy
Type: Pulling tractor
Power unit: Cummins KTA six-cylinder diesel engine
Power output: 600hp (444kw)
Transmission: Six-speed gearbox
Weight: 57,580lb (26,141kg)
Produced: 1977

Left: *The front and rear sections of Big Roy were joined by a hinge point with hydraulic rams to operate the steering.*

TRANTOR
1978   Stockport, Manchester, England

TRANTOR SERIES 1

Conventional tractors are designed mainly for heavy, slow-speed draft work such as plowing, but a survey of the way tractors were actually used on British farms showed that on many farms up to 75 percent of tractor working hours were spent on haulage work and general jobs such as operating power-takeoff driven equipment.

The survey was carried out in the early 1970s by Stuart Taylor as part of his thesis for an MSc degree, and he decided that the design of conventional tractors was not ideal for much of the work they did. He joined forces with Graham Edwards to develop a new type of tractor that was designed mainly for transportation and power-takeoff work, and the result was the Series 1 Trantor.

Design Features

Because the Trantor was not designed as a plowing tractor, the Series 1 specification did not include four-wheel drive and the driving wheels were smaller than those found on an ordinary tractor. It was equipped with a 78-hp (58-kw) Perkins engine, and the power was delivered through a synchromesh gearbox which provided 10 forward speeds and two in

Above, top: The Trantor development project followed a survey showing that farm tractors spend up to 75 percent of their working time on transportation and power-takeoff jobs.

Above: The Trantor could operate power-takeoff driven equipment and carry out light to medium draft work.

reverse, with a 60mph (96.5km/h) travel speed on the road.

To cope with this fast travel speed the Trantor was equipped with air-over-hydraulic brakes that operated on all four wheels, and air-operated trailer braking was included in the standard specification. The equipment list also included independent suspension on all four wheels, a pickup hitch with its own suspension, a two-speed power-takeoff and a three-point hitch for mounted implements. The design also included a fully integrated cab with a centrally positioned driver's seat, plus passenger seats on each side.

Series II

The production version of the Series 1 Trantor was launched at the 1978 Royal Show, where its unconventional design and top speed of 60mph (96.5km/h) attracted enormous interest. It also attracted orders, particularly from those farmers who could make good use of the fast transportation and travel speed.

When the Series II Trantor was launched in 1983 it featured an 80-hp (59.6-kw) Leyland engine, and the cab position was moved forward to provide additional space at the rear for a load-carrying platform. Four-wheel drive was added in 1985 when the Trantor Hauler was announced at the Royal Show. The power unit was a 126-hp (93.9-kw) Perkins engine and the payload was increased to 18.2 tons (18.5 tonnes).

Although Trantor production ended in the late 1980s, Graham Edwards, one of the original partners in the Trantor project, had continued to carry out research and development work with a view to developing a new version for transportation work in countries such as India, and an agreement was signed in 2004 for Trantors to be built in India.

Specifications

Manufacturer: HST Developments
Location: Stockport, Manchester, England
Model: Trantor Series 1
Type: Transportation tractor
Power unit: Perkins diesel engine
Power output: 78hp (58kw)
Transmission: 10-speed gearbox
Weight: N/A
Production started: 1978

Below: The Trantor was designed for transportation work at speeds up to 60mph (96km/h) on the road and was equipped with truck-type brakes on all four wheels.

MASSEY-FERGUSON

1978 Des Moines, Iowa

MASSEY-FERGUSON 4880

The 4000 series tractors took Massey-Ferguson into the high-horsepower sector of the market, with three models providing outputs ranging from 180 to 273hp (134.2 to 202kw) measured at the power takeoff.

All three models were powered by Cummins V-8 engines, but the engine in the 4880 model at the top of the range included a turbocharger to boost the output. The cylinder dimensions were 5.5-in (13.9-cm) bore and 4.75-in (12-cm) stroke, and the semipowershift transmission provided 18 forward gears and a top speed of 19.2mph (30.8km/h).

With plenty of engine power, four-wheel drive with dual wheels all round plus articulated steering, the 4000 series had all the characteristics of the typical giant North American pulling tractor, but they were equipped with a three-point linkage and a power takeoff to increase their versatility. They were also the first production tractors with an electronic control system for the rear linkage. Electronics were becoming familiar on tractors and combine harvesters by the late 1970s, but mainly for collecting and displaying information from sensors that monitored factors such as the speed of drive shafts or the engine cooling system's temperature.

Electronic Breakthrough

The electronics on the 4000 series tractors represented a breakthrough in technology because they collected data from sensors measuring the pulling force on the linkage arms and the implement depth, and they used the information to adjust the linkage position automatically, providing faster, more accurate control than even an experienced tractor driver.

Above: *Massey-Ferguson's 4000 series high-horsepower models were the first tractors with an electronic control system for the rear linkage.*

Specifications

Manufacturer: Massey-Ferguson
Location: Des Moines, Iowa
Model: 4880
Type: General purpose
Power unit: V-8 turbo diesel engine
Power output: 273hp (202kw)
Transmission: 18-speed semipowershift
Weight: 31,090lb (14,115kg)
Production started: 1978

TRACK MARSHALL
1980 Gainsborough, Lincolnshire, England

TRACK MARSHALL TM135

When Lincolnshire farmer Charles Nickerson bought Aveling Marshall, Britain's only remaining manufacturer of agricultural crawler tractors, as well as reintroducing the earlier Track Marshall name, he also introduced a series of new models.

Right: With new styling and an easy-to-operate single-lever steering system, the TM135 crawler tractor was a popular addition to the Track Marshall range.

Specifications

Manufacturer: Track Marshall
Location: Gainsborough, Lincolnshire, England
Model: TM135
Type: Tracklayer
Power unit: Six-cylinder diesel engine
Power output: 136hp (102kw)
Transmission: Five-speed gearbox
Weight: 22,799lb (10,341kg)
Production started: 1980

The first addition to the range in 1980 was the TM135, and this became Britain's best-selling crawler tractor. Tracklayers have never been noted for stylish good looks, but the design team gave the TM135 a distinctively modern appearance, and this was matched by an up-to-date technical specification that helped the tractor to win a silver medal award at the 1981 Royal Show.

Design Features
Power was provided by a six-cylinder Perkins engine developing 136hp (102kw) to provide more than 9.8 tons (10 tonnes) of pulling power in first gear. The specification included a cab with a large, flat floor area, air conditioning, and a stereo sound system in the standard equipment list. The specification also included a three-point linkage with more than 7.8 tons (8 tonnes) of lift capacity for handling mounted equipment, and there was also a power takeoff for driving big power harrows and other powered cultivators for seedbed preparation.

The TM135 was also equipped with the Track Marshall patented single-lever steering system. This was a small lever that operated the power-assisted steering mechanism using just fingertip pressure; less tiring and much more precise than a traditional two-lever tracklayer steering system.

FORD

1980 **Basildon, Essex, England**

FORD 8401

This is one of the more unusual models in Ford's 1980s tractor range—unless you happen to be in Australia. The 8401 was designed specifically for the Australian market where its purpose was to compete with the locally built Chamberlain tractor.

Specifications

Manufacturer: Ford Tractor Operations

Location: Basildon, Essex, England

Model: 8401

Type: Pulling tractor

Power unit: Six-cylinder engine

Power output: 109hp (80.7kw)

Transmission: 16-speed gearbox

Weight: N/A

Production started: 1980

Above: *The 109-hp (80.7-kw) 8401 was designed and built in Britain to strengthen the Ford tractor range in the important Australian market.*

The design of the 8401 was based on feedback from the Ford sales team in Australia. They had asked for a low-priced pulling tractor with a big engine, two-wheel drive, and a no-frills specification that did not include a rear linkage.

This was the blueprint used by the Basildon design team in England, and the team also provided the distinctive styling and paint finish.

Local Assembly

Although the tractor was a Basildon product, the initial assembly work was contracted out to a local engineering firm. It produced a skid unit ready for shipping, and this consisted of the engine, transmission, and controls, leaving the final assembly work to be completed in Australia using locally produced wheels, tires, sheet-metal work, and the optional cab. The 8401 was based on a Ford 7700 chassis and powered by a derated TW-10 engine producing 109hp (80.7kw), and the power was delivered through a 16-speed transmission.

Production of the Anglo-Australian 8401 started in 1980 and continued until about 1985, and during this time the tractor made a small but important contribution to Ford's Australian tractor sales.

DAVID BROWN/CASE
⚒ 1980   Meltham, Yorkshire, England

DAVID BROWN/ CASE 1290

David Brown Tractors produced one of Britain's most successful tractor ranges, but financial problems in the early 1970s lead to a successful takeover bid by Tenneco, the U.S.-based company that already owned Case and later acquired International Harvester.

Right: *Like other British-built 90 series tractors, the 1290 model was sold under the David Brown name in the United Kingdom and some export markets.*

Above: *All American- and British-built 90 series tractors sold in the United States carried the Case brand name.*

Specifications

Manufacturer: David Brown Tractors

Location: Meltham, Yorkshire, England

Model: 1290

Type: General purpose

Power unit: Four-cylinder diesel engine

Power output: 54hp (40kw) (at the power takeoff)

Transmission: 12-speed gearbox

Weight: 6,570lb (2,983kg)

Production started: 1980

The new owners decided to continue to feature the David Brown name for several years. David Brown had many loyal customers and dealers, and when the new 90 series tractors were launched in 1980 they still carried the David Brown name and badge in most markets including the United Kingdom; the Case name was used for those exported to the United States.

End of the Line
The 90 series was the result of a coordinated development program, with the Case factory at Racine building the high-horsepower models that were introduced in 1978, while the small to medium tractors were built at the David Brown plant. The 1290 was one of the British-built tractors, powered by a four-cylinder engine that delivered 54hp (40kw) at the power takeoff when it was tested under the Case brand name at Nebraska.

Production of the British-built 90 series tractors came to an end when they were replaced by the 94 series, and the bad news for David Brown enthusiasts was that this was also the end of the line for David Brown tractors, as the new 94 models all carried the Case badge.

INTERNATIONAL HARVESTER
⚒ **1981 Doncaster, Yorkshire, England**

I.H. HYDRO 85

Hydrostatic transmissions attracted considerable interest during the 1970s, and several manufacturers built relatively small numbers of tractors with this type of transmission, but International Harvester took the idea more seriously than any of the other leading companies.

Specifications

Manufacturer: International Harvester
Location: Doncaster, Yorkshire, England
Model: Hydro 85
Type: General purpose
Power unit: Four-cylinder engine
Power output: 77hp (57kw)
Transmission: Hydrostatic
Weight: 6,044lb (2,741kg)
Production started: 1981

The first I.H. Hydro tractor was the American-built 656 model available starting in 1967, and it was followed by further models built in the United States and at the Doncaster factory in England. The Doncaster-built 84 series tractors were introduced in 1977 as a complete new range with outputs from 35 to 136hp (26 to 101.4kw), and they included the new 77-hp (57-kw) Hydro 84 model with hydrostatic drive.

Updated Model
The Hydro 84 was updated in 1981 to produce the new Hydro 85, part of the new I.H. Fieldforce 85 series. The four-cylinder engine of the Hydro 84 was not affected by the update, and the power output remained at 77hp (57kw) for the new version, but the big news was the new 85 series XL cab design. It featured a much bigger window area reaching down to floor level on both sides at the front, and this allowed good visibility for precise steering.

The last batch of Hydro 85 tractors was built in 1985, and this was also the end of the road for the I.H. hydrostatic tractor program. Sales of the Hydro 85 had been falling steadily and Tenneco, the company that bought the agricultural division of the International Harvester group in 1985, decided not to continue developing hydrostatic tractors.

Above: International Harvester was easily the biggest manufacturer of tractors with a hydrostatic transmission until production ended in 1985.

TRACK MARSHALL
1982 Gainsborough, Lincolnshire, England

TRACK MARSHALL BRITANNIA

Track Marshall's success with the TM135 tracklayer was not repeated when it launched the Britannia model two years later. With a 71-hp (52.5-kw) engine it was less powerful than the other TM models and offered less output, and many customers decided the more expensive TM135 was better value for money.

Right: *In a bid to improve the mobility of its steel-tracked crawler tractors, Track Marshall developed a transportation wheel kit for its Britannia model.*

Specifications

Manufacturer: Track Marshall	
Location: Gainsborough, Lincolnshire, England	
Model: Britannia	
Type: Crawler tractor	
Power unit: Four-cylinder diesel engine	
Power output: 71hp (52.5kw)	
Transmission: Five-speed gearbox	
Weight: N/A	
Production started: 1982	

Britannia has just two claims to fame. It was named after the Britannia Works where Marshall steam engines, tractors, and other farm equipment had been built for more than 100 years, and it was the model Track Marshall used for a project to design a set of transportation wheels to give crawlers mobility on the road.

Transportation Wheels

Tracks used on crawler tractors in the early 1980s were made of steel and could not be driven on public roads. This was a major problem for many farmers and contractors, and Track Marshall was aware that it was one of the reasons for a decline in sales of crawler tractors in many countries, including the United Kingdom.

The company's engineers developed a set of wheels that would allow the Britannia to drive on the road for short distances. Two wheels were attached to a frame that operated hydraulically, raising the front of the tractor while folding back toward the engine compartment. The rear wheels were mounted on special stub axles attached to each of the drive sprockets at the rear of the tractor, and the back of the tractor had to be jacked up while the rear wheels were attached or removed. However, demonstrations of the transportation kit met a negative reaction, and the idea was quietly abandoned.

INTERNATIONAL HARVESTER
1981 Doncaster, Yorkshire, England

INTERNATIONAL HARVESTER 956XL

International Harvester announced its new Sens-o-draulic hydraulic control system with a fanfare of publicity, claiming improved accuracy and quicker response times.

Specifications

Manufacturer: International Harvester
Location: Doncaster, Yorkshire, England
Model: 956XL
Type: General purpose
Power unit: Six-cylinder engine
Power output: 95hp (70kw)
Transmission: 16-speed gearbox
Weight: N/A
Production started: 1981

Above: *International Harvester claimed important benefits from the Sens-o-draulic control system for the three-point linkage.*

By the early 1980s the revolution started by Harry Ferguson was almost complete, and the hydraulically operated three-point linkage was standard equipment on most new tractors. Much of the field work on farms was now handled by linkage-mounted machines, and this meant that the performance of the linkage control system was an important sales feature for tractor manufacturers.

Hydraulic Controls

I.H. introduced its Sens-o-draulic control system in 1983. It was available initially on three of its 56 series models, the 856XL, 956XL, and the 1056XL. The advantage of the new system, according to I.H., was that it was all-hydraulic, eliminating mechanical components in the operation of the lift control. The result was a faster, more sensitive response to variations in the soil, providing more precise control of the working depth of plows and other linkage-mounted implements.

Unfortunately for I.H. its all-hydraulic control system would soon be overtaken by the electronic system developed by Massey-Ferguson and already available on the high-horsepower MF 4000 series tractors, offering even more speed, accuracy, and a higher level of automation. The 956XL tractor was one of the popular 56 series tractors from the I.H. factories in Britain and Germany. The 56 series were updated versions of the previous 55 models, and the 956Xl model featured a 90-hp (67.1-kw) engine and a 20-speed transmission.

JOHN DEERE 8850

1982 Waterloo, Iowa

JOHN DEERE 8850

Below: *Deere & Co. was one of the leading manufacturers of giant tractors and, unlike most of its rivals, it used its own engines.*

Most of the American and Canadian companies competing in the high-horsepower sector of the market bought in their engines from companies such as Cummins and Caterpillar, but Deere was one of the exceptions.

Specifications

Manufacturer: Deere & Co.	
Location: Waterloo, Iowa	
Model: 8850	
Type: General purpose	
Power unit: V-8 diesel with turbo and intercooler	
Power output: 304hp (225kw)	
Transmission: 16-speed gearbox	
Weight: 37,700lb (17,116kg)	
Production started: 1982	

It built its own engine for the 8850 model at the top of the John Deere range. It was a V-8 diesel and it was equipped with a turbocharger and an intercooler to boost the output to the 304-hp (225-kw) maximum recorded in Nebraska during the power-takeoff test with the engine set at its rated speed.

Intercooling

Intercooling is widely used on today's tractors, but in the 1980s it was still unusual. An intercooler is used, like a turbo, to increase engine output, and it achieves this by cooling the air flowing into the combustion chamber. Colder air is more dense, and this means more air and thus more oxygen is forced into the combustion chamber to burn extra diesel fuel and produce more power.

The standard specification list for the John Deere high-horsepower 8850 series included a transmission with 16 semipowershift speeds, dual wheels, and articulated steering.

Other models in the John Deere 8050 series included the 8650 with 239hp (178.2kw) available from a six-cylinder Deere engine with turbo and intercooler, while a six-cylinder engine in the 8450 produced 187hp (139.4kw) at the power takeoff.

INSTITUTE OF ENGINEERING RESEARCH

1983 Silsoe, Bedfordshire, England

SILSOE EXPERIMENTAL FARM TRANSPORTATION VEHICLE

The importance of transportation operations on many farms prompted a project to design an experimental transportation vehicle for farms. The vehicle, designed at what was then called the Institute of Engineering Research at Silsoe, Bedfordshire but is now known as Silsoe Research Institute, was completed in 1983 and was used in an evaluation program.

The tractor unit designed by the Silsoe team was initially powered by a 80-hp (60-kw) Perkins engine, but the engine was later upgraded to boost the output to 126hp (93.9kw). For research purposes the vehicle was equipped with two transmissions, one based on a 10-speed gearbox and the other using a hydrostatic drive system giving infinitely variable speed control. Both transmissions could be operated with two- or four-wheel drive, and the maximum speed from the mechanical transmission was 40.3mph (65km/h).

Steering Systems

Another design complication added mainly for experimental purposes was two different steering systems. Articulated steering from a hinge point just behind the cab was used for normal transportation and for turning in the field, but this was supplemented by a power-

Above, top: *Silsoe's engineers designed the front-mounted cab with a big window area for good all-round visibility.*

Above: *Various unit loads, including the manure spreader in the picture, could be mounted or demounted using a hydraulic system operated from the cab.*

operated rear-axle steering system for maneuvering where space was restricted.

The driver's cab was over the front axle, leaving plenty of unobstructed space at the rear for a load-carrying platform. The vehicle was designed to carry up to 4.9 tons (5 tonnes), giving a gross weight of 9.8 tons (10 tonnes), and it was used with a set of specially modified equipment that was loaded onto the platform using the vehicle's hydraulic system and a joystick-type control lever inside the cab.

The loading system also included a tipping mechanism that allowed containers to be easily emptied.

Power Takeoff

As well as tipping containers for harvest work, the platform also carried powered equipment such as a modified manure spreader or a fertilizer spreader, using a mid-mounted power takeoff shaft. An attachment system and power takeoff drive for front-mounted equipment was also available, and was demonstrated with a forage harvester blowing the grass into a special container mounted behind the cab. A front-mounted loader allowed the vehicle to provide a self-contained loading and transportation unit.

The evaluation program showed that the vehicle offered some benefits, but there were also problems—and cost was one of them. The vehicle would be expensive to build, and customers also needed some special equipment to carry on the platform.

Also, for commercial use, a more powerful vehicle would be needed, as 4.9 tons (5 tonnes) load capacity would be inadequate for jobs such as hauling grain or potatoes from the harvester. With little commercial interest from farmers or the tractor industry, the transportation vehicle project was eventually abandoned.

Specifications

Manufacturer: Institute of Engineering Research
Location: Silsoe, Bedfordshire, England
Model: Farm Transportation Vehicle
Type: Experimental
Power unit: Perkins diesel engine
Power output: 80hp (60kw)
Transmission: 10-speed gearbox plus hydrostatic transmission
Weight: 11,000lb (5,000kg)
Produced: 1983

Below: *This picture shows the farm transportation vehicle with its specially designed front loader, plus a display of some of the equipment available for the rear load platform.*

FORD
⚒ 1985   Basildon, Essex, England

FORD FORCE II 6610

When the first of the new 10 series models were announced in 1981 they were an important development in the Ford tractor range. They arrived at a time when Ford tractors were enjoying international success, holding second place in the international sales charts.

Specifications

Manufacturer: Ford Tractor Operations
Location: Basildon, Essex, England
Model: Force II 6610
Type: General purpose
Power unit: Four-cylinder engine
Power output: 86hp (63.6kw)
Transmission: Eight-speed gearbox
Weight: N/A
Production started: 1985

Major developments on the 10 series tractors included an average 10 percent increase in engine power compared to the models they replaced. There were also improvements to the hydraulic system and a new eight-speed change-on-the-move gearbox was added to the options list.

Updated Version

The 10 series tractors were given a major update in 1985 when the Force II range was introduced. A new Super Q cab with a lower roof line was the obvious improvement, available on the medium-horsepower and higher horsepower models, and there were also

several mechanical improvements including quieter engines plus a big performance boost for the rear linkage on the Force II versions of the big Belgian-built TW models, raising the lift capacity to almost 6.8 tons (7 tonnes), which was a creditable figure for 1980s tractors in this power range.

The Ford Force II 6610 powered by an 86–hp (63.6-kw) engine was one of two models to be equipped with new saddle-mounted tanks for fuel, and it was one of three models offered in a wide-axle version for rowcrop work. Force II production continued until 1989, when they were replaced by another updated range, the Generation III tractors.

Above: An improved cab with a lower roof line was the obvious difference when the new Force II models arrived from Ford in 1985.

MARSHALL
⚒ **1986   Scunthorpe, Lincolnshire, England**

MARSHALL 132

A company that goes through frequent changes of ownership and moves from factory to factory can lose the confidence of many of its customers and dealers, and this was the misfortune that befell Nuffield tractors.

Right: Following another change of ownership, the new 132 model with a number of Yugoslavian components was added to the Marshall tractor range.

Specifications

Manufacturer: Bentall-Simplex Industries

Location: Scunthorpe, Lincolnshire, England

Model: Marshall 132

Type: General purpose

Power unit: Four-cylinder diesel engine

Power output: 35hp (26kw)

Transmission: Eight-speed gearbox

Weight: N/A

Production started: 1986

Apart from the name changes from Nuffield to Leyland, then to Marshall, there were also mergers, takeovers, and financial problems that brought six changes of ownership plus production relocations from Birmingham to Scotland and to two different locations in Lincolnshire.

New Models

By 1986 the company was owned by Bentall-Simplex Industries, and it transferred the tractor business to a factory at Scunthorpe, Lincolnshire. Its first new model was the Marshall 132, finished in the attractive "Harvest Gold" color that had already replaced the Leyland blue and the original Nuffield orange-red. Although the new model was assembled at Scunthorpe, some of the main components were bought in from Yugoslavia, and these included the eight-speed transmission and the 35-hp (26-kw) engine based on a Perkins design.

The 132 was a dual-purpose design to sell as both a small agricultural tractor and a large compact tractor suitable for mowing grass and other amenity work, and the owners of the new Marshall brand offered a full range of compact models, as well as building up the agricultural range with additional models and improvements to the cab specifications. They achieved some success in a highly competitive market, but by this time the Marshall name had lost some of its original luster and in 1989 there was yet another ownership change.

MASSEY-FERGUSON

1986 Beauvais, France

MASSEY-FERGUSON 3070 AUTOTRONIC

Massey-Ferguson's high-horsepower 4000 series tractors had already demonstrated the benefits of using electronics to control the rear linkage, and in 1986 improved versions of the same system were introduced on the new MF 300 and 3000 series.

Above: *The launch of Massey-Ferguson's new Autotronic and Datatronic information and control systems added electronic speed and precision to tractor operation.*

Two levels of electronic control were available, a standard version on the Autotronic models, while those with the more advanced version were the Datatronic tractors. In both versions much of the operation and control of the rear linkage and of other functions was automated, simplifying the driver's job and, in many cases, operating with more speed and accuracy than even a skilled driver. There was also protection from some of the risks of mechanical faults.

Both systems relied on data collected by sensors at various points on the tractor, and this was transferred electronically to a mini-computer under the floor of the cab. The functions covered by the Autotronic system included managing the differential lock, and there was also a safety cut-out that disconnected

the drive to the power takeoff automatically if the sensor detected either an abnormal load or a blockage in the machinery being powered.

Hydraulic System

There was also a protective cut-out in the hydraulic system. If the warning light for incorrect hydraulic oil pressure showed for more than two seconds the computer automatically shut down the functions that might be damaged by a hydraulic fault. On four-wheel drive models, the computer disconnected the power to the front wheels at speeds above 8.7mph (14km/h) to avoid the extra tire wear that can occur when four-wheel drive is used on the road. Drive to the front wheels was engaged again if the driver activated the rear differential lock to achieve better traction, and it was also engaged for improved stopping power if the driver used the brakes.

Additional features on the Datatronic tractors included high-tech electronic controls to minimize wheelslip, and there was also a comprehensive information display on a small screen inside the cab.

Data available on the screen included the engine rpm, forward speed, fuel consumption rates, actual work rate, fuel reserve in hours, and also the time in hours to the next service. The screen could show the work done in terms of distance or area covered, and also in unit terms—useful for showing the number of bales produced, for example.

Attractive Innovation

Most current medium- and high-horsepower tractors have some form of electronic control and information system, but in the 1980s the Massey-Ferguson systems were a major step forward and attracted a huge amount of interest when they first appeared.

The 3000 series tractors introduced with the new electronic system included the MF-3070 with a 93-hp (69-kw) engine and equipped with a shuttle transmission providing 32 speeds forward and in reverse.

Specifications

Manufacturer: Massey-Ferguson

Location: Beauvais, France

Model: MF 3070

Type: General purpose

Power unit: Four-cylinder diesel engine

Power output: 93hp (69kw)

Transmission: 32-speed shuttle

Weight: 9,039lb (4,100kg) (four-wheel drive version)

Production started: 1986

Below: *The Autotronic electronics package on the new MF 3000 series tractors brought automatic control to a wide range of functions in order to simplify the driver's job.*

CATERPILLAR
1987 Peoria, Illinois

CATERPILLAR CHALLENGER 65

Tracklaying tractors are unbeatable for turning engine power into drawbar pull when the ground conditions are wet and slippery, and they are also unbeatable for spreading the weight of the tractor over a larger surface area to reduce soil compaction. The traditional steel tracks do, however, have some serious disadvantages.

Steel tracks are noisy, they are not suitable for fast travel speeds, and in most countries they are not allowed to drive on public roads because of the damage they cause. Sales of tracklayers remained high while the only alternative was a two-wheel drive tractor, but as more manufacturers offered four-wheel drive models from the 1950s onward sales of crawler tractors fell sharply.

By the early 1980s it seemed increasingly likely that crawler tractors would soon be restricted to niche markets such as farms with very steep land, where the tracks give extra stability, but then, in 1987, the situation changed as the Caterpillar Challenger 65 tractor arrived with its steel-reinforced rubber tracks.

New Tracks

The new tracks—Caterpillar call them the Mobil-trac system—were probably the most important technical development in crawler

Above, top: *Rubber tracks arrived on the Caterpillar Challenger 65, bringing a halt to the steady decline in crawler-tractor sales.*

Above: *Claas took over the marketing of Caterpillar Challenger tractors in the United Kingdom and other European countries.*

tractor design for 50 years or more. The rubber-tracked Challenger 65 and the models that followed retain the traditional tracklayer benefits of efficient pulling power and low ground pressure, but they can also be used on public roads, they can travel at the same speed as an ordinary wheeled tractor, and the driver benefits from much lower noise levels than conventional steel tracks.

Reports from Challenger users showed that the tracks could compete with rubber tires in terms of strength, durability, and replacement cost on tractors of similar horsepower, and Challenger sales increased. The success of the Challenger 65 and subsequent Caterpillar models encouraged more tractor manufacturers to offer their own rubber-tracked models, reversing the previous downward trend in crawler tractor sales.

Engine

The Challenger 65, the tractor that introduced the benefits of rubber tracks, was powered by a Caterpillar engine with turbocharger and intercooler. The engine power was 270hp (200kw), delivered through a powershift transmission with 10 forward speeds. Driver-comfort features included full air conditioning and an air-cleaning system with a dust extractor. There was also a cigarette lighter and an ashtray. Steering was controlled by a steering wheel with a differential control system that speeded up one track and slowed down the other.

Having achieved so much success with its Challenger tractors, Caterpillar caused considerable surprise in the industry when it decided to pull out of the agricultural equipment market in 2002, selling the Challenger tractor business to Agco.

Specifications

Manufacturer:	Caterpillar
Location:	Peoria, Illinois
Model:	Challenger 65
Type:	Pulling tractor
Power unit:	Six-cylinder engine
Power output:	270hp (200kw)
Transmission:	10-speed powershift
Weight:	31,000lb (14,060kg)
Production started:	1987

Below: *The Challenger's rubber tracks offered the pulling efficiency of traditional steel tracks, but without the restrictions on road travel and forward speed.*

SAME
✘ 1988 Treviglio, Italy

SAME DUAL TRAC 90

Tractors equipped with a reversible driving position—sometimes known as bi-directional or two-way—filled an important niche market in the 1980s, and the Italian-based Same company was one of the leading suppliers.

Above: *Changing between the forward and reverse driving positions on the Dual Trac 90 took about 30 seconds for an experienced operator.*

Specifications

Manufacturer: Same Trattori
Location: Treviglio, Italy
Model: Dual Trac 90
Type: General purpose
Power unit: Four-cylinder engine
Power output: 90hp (67kw)
Transmission: 16-speed shuttle gearbox
Weight: 7,370lb (3,350kg)
Production started: 1988

The main advantage of being able to operate the tractor while facing either forward or backward is extra versatility. Some types of rear-mounted equipment including trenching machines and forklift attachments are much easier to operate if the driver is facing backward out of the rear window of the cab. This is more efficient and also less tiring for the driver than facing forward and frequently looking back over his shoulder.

Steering Wheel

On most reverse-drive tractors the seat swivels through 180°, usually taking most of the hand-operated controls with it, and with a duplicated set of foot pedals at the back of the cab. On the Same Dual Trac 90 the steering wheel was disconnected from its place at the front of the cab and transferred to the rear.

Converting the driving position from front to rear, or back again, took less than one minute, according to Same.

It based the Dual Trac reverse-drive tractor on its standard 90-hp (67-kw) Explorer II model which, like all the company's tractors at that time, was equipped with a Same engine with air cooling supplemented by an oil cooling system. The Dual Trac also shared the Explorer's four-wheel braking system, a feature included on most Same tractors.

Above, left: *The Same Dual Trac 90 was just one of the many 1980s tractors with a reversible or bi-directional driving position.*

FIAT
⚒ 1990 Modena, Italy

FIAT WINNER F140

Fiat announced the Winner range of tractors in the year before it bought a controlling interest in the Ford tractor and farm machinery business, and the Winners remained in production for several years after the takeover.

Above: *The F140 was the top model in Fiat's Winner range, producing 140hp (104kw) from a six-cylinder engine linked to a 32-speed transmission.*

Specifications

Manufacturer:	Fiatagri
Location:	Modena, Italy
Model:	Winner F140
Type:	General purpose
Power unit:	Six-cylinder engine
Power output:	140hp (104kw)
Transmission:	32-speed gearbox
Weight:	N/A
Production started:	1990

The Fiat agricultural business, known since the early 1980s as Fiatagri, claimed a 15 percent share of the European tractor market when the Winner series was announced, and the new models were designed to give another boost to the market-share figure. There were four models initially, starting with the F100 and going up to the F140, and an additional F115 model followed two years later. In each case the model number was an approximate indication of the engine power.

Design Features

All the Winners were powered by an updated version of the six-cylinder 8000 series engines from Fiat Iveco, and the high specification also included a three-speed power takeoff with push-button speed selection. Both the rear linkage and the optional front linkage were electronically controlled.

There was also a wide choice of transmission options, starting with the standard 32-speed version with 16 reverse speeds. A shuttle gearbox provided 16 speeds both forward and in reverse, and there was also an Eco speed transmission with 20 forward and 16 reverse speeds. Customers who used low-speed equipment such as hedge trimmers or vegetable transplanters could specify an additional creep-speed gearbox that doubled the number of ratios in the standard transmission to 64 forward and 32 in reverse.

FORD
⚒ 1991 Basildon, Essex, England

FORD 8640

Most of the "new" tractors that are launched each year are not, in fact, totally new, but simply updated versions of previous models. This arrangement can be effective, and a series of updated and improved models kept Ford among the top three tractor makes worldwide throughout most of the 1970s and 1980s.

This is why the Series 40 models were officially described as the first completely new tractors from the Basildon factory for 27 years—although even they were not totally new. They were introduced at the 1991 Smithfield Show, a six-model range covering the big-selling 75- to 120-hp (55.9- to 89.4-kw) sector initially, but an extra model introduced later brought the output up to 125hp (93.2kw).

New Engines

All the Series 40 tractors were equipped with new engines developed in the Genesis project, and in some markets, including the United Kingdom, they were known as the PowerStar engines. The engines were available in four- and six-cylinder versions, but both shared the same 75.8 cubic inches (1.25 liters) per cylinder capacity so that many of the components could

Above: Ford's 40 series tractors launched in 1991 were said to be the first completely new tractor range from the factory in Basildon, Essex, in England, for 27 years.

be shared. The three Series 40 tractors below 100hp (74kw) used the four-cylinder, 303.5-cubic-inch (5-liter) engine, and the 100-hp (74-kw) 7840 was the smallest of three models with the six-cylinder engine.

All the design work for the new cab for the high-spec Series 40 tractors was carried out in the USA. It was called the SuperLux cab and it provided more internal space than its predecessor, and the noise level was reduced to an impressively low 77 decibels.

Transmission Options

Probably the most impressive feature of the new tractor range was the choice of transmission options, and two of them were making their first appearance on the Series 40 models. Electronics were playing an increasingly important part in the operation and control of tractor transmissions, and the new ElectroShift was an example.

It was described as a semipowershift, with manual shifting between two sets of four powershift speeds, but a pair of press-buttons on the main gear-shift lever, operated with fingertip pressure, provided clutchless changing between the gears within each powershift group. This provided eight speeds, all available both forward and in reverse by using a shuttle-control lever, but these were doubled to 16 speeds each way by using the high/low ratio selector, and the addition of optional creep speeds for jobs requiring slower travel speeds increased the number of ratios to 24 each way.

As well as introducing the new Series 40 tractors in 1991, Ford also announced that its tractor and agricultural machinery business had, in effect, been sold to Fiat. This is why the first production Series 40 tractors carry the Ford name and oval badge; during 1994 these were replaced by the New Holland brand name and the new stylized-leaf badge.

Specifications

Manufacturer: Ford Tractor Operations

Location: Basildon, Essex, England

Model: 8640

Type: General purpose

Power unit: Six-cylinder engine

Power output: 100hp (74kw)

Transmission: ElectroShift with up to 24 speeds

Weight: N/A

Production started: 1991

Left: *Most new tractors launched from the late 1970s onward included electronic systems, and on the series 40 Fords they played a major part in operating the semipowershift transmission.*

RENAULT
✖ 1991 Le Mans, France

RENAULT 110.54 HYDROSTABLE

One of the benefits of belonging to a big company with a varied product range is the ability to share technical information, and this played an important part in Renault's development of the first tractor cab with a proper suspension system.

Renault introduced the cab in 1988 on their high-specification TZ and Z tractors. The suspension system consisted of a coil spring at each corner to soak up some of the bounce and vibration coming from the tractor wheels, plus longitudinal and transverse torsion bars arranged to provide extra stability and to reduce any rolling movements as the tractor traveled over uneven ground. Engineers at Renault had been working on cab suspension development for some time, and they were helped by colleagues who were designing suspension systems for Renault truck cabs.

The tractor version, called the Hydrostable cab, was recognized as a major step forward in driver comfort, winning a gold medal at the

Above, top: Engineers at Renault Agriculture were able to use expertise from Renault trucks to help with the Hydrostable cab development.

Above: The Hydrostable cab was a big improvement for driver comfort, but sales were disappointing at first.

SIMA machinery event in Paris and a silver medal at the Royal Show in England.

New Cab

Further confirmation of the cab's benefits came from the DLG research organization in Germany, where vibration levels were measured on two 145-hp (108.1-kw) Renault 155-54 tractors. One of the tractors was equipped with a standard nonsprung cab, while there was a Hydrostable cab on the other tractor.

Both tractors were put through a series of tests in the field and on a track, while the drivers' level of exposure to vibration was measured, and the suspension system reduced vibration levels by between 30 and 35 percent in some tests. As well as giving the driver a smoother, more comfortable ride, suspension systems on farm tractors also offer financial benefits. There is evidence to show that lower levels of vibration encourage drivers to work longer hours when necessary, and they are also more likely to engage a higher gear and increase their output for some types of field work.

Full Suspension

Renault was easily the first tractor manufacturer to fit a cab with a full suspension system, establishing a 10-year lead over many of their competitors. The high-spec versions of most models in the Renault range can be equipped with either the TZ or the Z series Hydrostable cab, including the Tracfor models, which have a medium specification. The Tracfor 110.54 is powered by a six-cylinder MWM engine with 100-hp (74-kw) output, and the standard specification includes a shuttle gearbox with 16 forward and reverse speeds.

Specifications

Manufacturer:	Renault Agriculture
Location:	Le Mans, France
Model:	110.54 Z
Type:	General purpose
Power unit:	Six-cylinder engine
Power output:	100hp (74kw)
Transmission:	16-speed shuttle gearbox
Weight:	N/A
Production started:	1991

Below: *The Hydrostable cab suspension system uses a combination of coil springs and torsion bars to absorb some of the bounce and vibration, and provide a stable ride.*

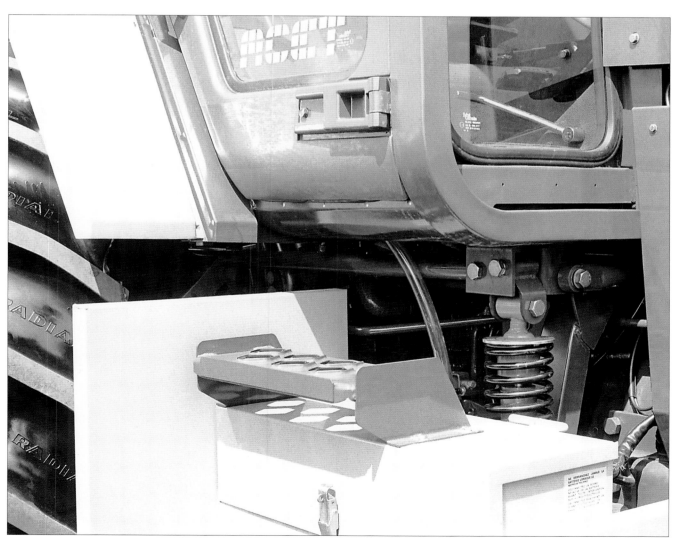

JCB

✖ **1991   Cheadle, Staffordshire, England**

JCB FASTRAC 145

During the 1970s and 1980s a large number of familiar names vanished from the tractor industry in the United States and Europe as a result of mergers, takeovers, and bankruptcies, and this is a continuing trend. It is more unusual for a big company to move into tractor production for the first time, but this happened in 1991 when JCB introduced the Fastrac tractor range.

J CB is a world leader in the production of backhoe loaders and other construction machinery, and it also claims to be the biggest manufacturer of telescopic loaders for the farming industry. Even for a big company such as JCB, trying to challenge the established names in the tractor industry with just another conventional tractor would have been extremely difficult, but instead they chose a highly unconventional design.

High Speed

The Fastrac was described in the original JCB press release as "the world's first genuine high-speed tractor." The first production models were each capable of pulling a 13.7-ton (14-tonne) load at more than 40mph (64km/h) on the road, almost twice the top speed of most conventional tractors, but the Fastrac's four-wheel drive through equal-diameter front and rear wheels was also designed to provide

Above, top: *The move by JCB, a leading manufacturer of construction equipment, into the overcrowded tractor market was a surprise.*

Above: *Although the Fastrac's road performance dominated much of the original publicity, the tractors were also designed for heavy draft work such as plowing.*

efficient slow-speed traction for jobs such as plowing.

The first two Fastrac models were the 125 and the 145, with the model number in each case indicating the horsepower. All Fastracs are equipped with Perkins engines, with a turbocharger added to the engine of the 145 model to boost the power output, and the transmission for both models provided 18 forward speeds and six in reverse.

Fastrac Suspension

Tractors designed for such a high transportation speed must have plenty of braking power, and the Fastracs were equipped with a truck-type braking system with air-operated disks on all four wheels. Another design feature to help cope with the fast travel speeds was a full suspension system on both the front and the rear wheels, helping to smooth out the bumps and provide increased stability to improve the steering control.

A special feature designed into the Fastrac suspension—still used on the latest models—is the self-leveling action at the rear. This is essential for jobs such as plowing where it is important to maintain a constant depth while carrying the weight of a mounted plow on the rear linkage.

Another Fastrac feature is a load space behind the cab with of capacity of 2.4 tons (2.5 tonnes), often used to carry crop-spraying equipment, and the options list on all models includes a factory-fitted front linkage.

The first Fastracs were built at the main JCB plant, but production was transferred to a separate factory operated by JCB Landpower, the agricultural equipment arm of JCB.

Specifications

Manufacturer: JCB Landpower

Location: Cheadle, Staffordshire, England

Model: Fastrac 145

Type: General purpose

Power unit: Six-cylinder turbo diesel engine

Power output: 145hp (107kw)

Transmission: 18-speed gearbox

Weight: 13,831lb (6,274kg)

Production started: 1991

Below: *Design features of the Fastrac include a front and rear suspension system, four-wheel braking, and a load platform behind the cab.*

chapter 9

Ready for the Robots

One result of the rapid advances in electronics, and developments such as the Global Positioning System (GPS), is that it opens up the possibility of using driverless tractors for many of the routine jobs on farms. The necessary technology has been commercially available since the late 1990s. There are several systems that will manage the steering and automatically maintain the optimum choice of engine and transmission settings.

Above: *The Kirov tractor plant in the former Soviet Union is offering the "Peter the Great" model in a bid to attract customers in Western countries.*

Left: *The rubber track revolution that followed the introduction of the Caterpillar Challenger has been followed by crawler models in other ranges, including John Deere.*

So far this type of equipment is being used to make the driver's job easier, allowing him or her to concentrate on other aspects of tractor and implement management. The next step is likely to be the driverless tractor or farm robot, but the commercial application is so far limited.

One of the areas where electronics have made a major contribution is in the development of a new generation of tractor transmissions. The first constantly variable transmission, or CVT, was called the Vario, and it was pioneered in Germany by Fendt; however, most leading tractor manufacturers now have their own versions. CVTs consist of a combination of hydrostatic- and mechanical-drive systems, and they offer infinitely variable speed adjustment with a high degree of automatic control.

The past decade or so has also brought new variations on the systems tractor theme, and there has been a big increase in the number of manufacturers offering crawler tractors with rubber tracks. The average power output of new tractors has increased steadily, and the tractor industry has been experiencing more mergers and takeovers, leaving most of the production capacity in Europe and North America under the control of just five main groups.

MOFFETT

⚒ **1991 Dundalk, County Louth, Ireland**

MOFFETT MULTI-FUNCTION TRACTOR

Ireland's track record as a tractor manufacturer is limited. There were two brief periods when the Fordson was produced at a factory near Cork and, more recently, the Moffett MFT tractor was built at Dundalk during the 1990s.

The 1980s and 1990s were a difficult time for the tractor industry, with shrinking sales causing financial problems and forcing many of the long-established manufacturers into takeovers and mergers. At the same time the industry also attracted some new names, usually companies such as JCB offering a tractor with new features, and this category also includes the MFT, or Multi-Function Tractor, from Moffett Engineering.

Two-Way Operation

MFT tractors were designed with a reversible driving seat and controls for two-way operation, and they were equipped with a heavy-duty industrial loader mounted on the rear of the tractor where the weight was carried over the rear axle—the strongest part of the tractor. With the loader in position and the driving position reversed, the MFT was ready for work as a high-output loader for jobs such as silage handling or

Above: The original Massey-Ferguson-based version of the Moffett Multi-Function Tractor, or MFT, working as a conventional tractor.

loading sugar beet. Removing the loader, a job that took about four minutes, and returning the driver's seat to the normal forward-facing position allowed the MFT to work as a normal four-wheel drive tractor.

Production started at the Moffett family's factory in 1991, with the MFT based on a much-modified Massey-Ferguson tractor powered by a 90-hp (66.6-kw) Perkins engine. An MF transmission with a shuttle control provided 12 speeds forward and in reverse, ideal for a two-way tractor because the choice of gears and travel speeds is the same in both directions. An experienced operator could change the position of the Moffett-designed seat and controls in less than half a minute.

The big advantage of the Moffett tractor was that on some farms it enabled one tractor unit to deal with the materials-handling jobs and the field work, allowing a significant reduction in capital costs, and the MFT was particularly successful on medium-sized dairy farms, particularly in the United Kingdom, which was easily its biggest export market.

Improved Version

In 1994 the original 90-hp (66.6-kw) MFT was replaced by an improved version based on a 120-hp (89.4-kw) Massey-Ferguson tractor unit, and two years later the company switched from MF to New Holland, choosing a 100-hp (74.5-kw) 7840 tractor powered by a six-cylinder engine and equipped with a 24-speed shuttle transmission.

In spite of its versatility, the MFT lacked the lift height and the forward reach of a telescopic loader, particularly for jobs such as bale handling. It was a disadvantage that helped to limit the sales of the Moffett tractor, and production ended in about 1999.

Specifications

Manufacturer:	Moffett Engineering
Location:	Dundalk, County Louth, Ireland
Model:	Multi-Function Tractor
Type:	Tractor with a heavy-duty loader
Power unit:	Perkins four-cylinder engine
Power output:	90hp (66.6kw)
Transmission:	12-speed shuttle
Weight:	N/A
Production started:	1991

Below: *This is the later MFT based on the Ford Series 40, with the driving position in the reversed position to operate the rear-mounted industrial loader.*

ZETOR

1990 Brno, Czech Republic

ZETOR 9540

During the Communist era, some tractor ranges from the factories in Eastern Europe lagged behind their Western rivals in terms of technical features, styling, and finish, but prices were low. However, Zetor tractors from what is now the Czech Republic were different.

Above: *A container inside the engine compartment of the 9540 collects heat from the exhaust manifold to provide a supply of warm water for hand washing.*

Specifications

Manufacturer: Zetor	
Location: Brno, Czech Republic	
Model: 9540	
Type: General purpose	
Power unit: Four-cylinder turbo engine	
Power output: 90hp (66.6kw)	
Transmission: 16-speed gearbox	
Weight: N/A	
Production started: 1990	

Above, left: *Like many models in the Zetor range, the 9540 specification includes a pump to provide an air supply for powering small hand tools or inflating tires.*

Instead of signing a license agreement to build outdated Massey-Ferguson or Fiat models like some of the other East European factories, Zetor produced its own designs, and when the new Forterra series models were introduced in 1990 they were the first part of a new range with up-to-date styling and turbo engines to help meet Western requirements for cleaner exhaust emissions.

Unusual Features

The power output of the Forterra series 9540 with four-wheel drive and the 9520 two-wheel drive version was 90hp (66.6kw) from a four-cylinder engine, and the specification included some unusual features that are also available on some of the other models from Zetor. The standard specification included a compressor to power an air-braking system for trailers, and this was also used to supply high-pressure air to inflate tires and to operate small air-powered tools to allow simple maintenance and repair jobs to be carried out in the field when there is no electrical power available.

Another unusual Zetor convenience feature was a clean-water container in the engine compartment. It was located where it collected waste heat from the exhaust manifold, and after a few hours' work it provided a supply of warm water for hand washing.

SCHLUTER
⚒ 1991 Munich, Germany

SCHLUTER EUROTRAC

Although Claas, the German harvest-machinery specialist, was closely involved in the development of the Eurotrac, it was the Schluter name that appeared on the tractor. The Eurotrac was produced as a prototype in 1991, when it was demonstrated to the farming press and was also a big attraction at the German Agritechnica machinery show.

Right: The Schluter Eurotrac, designed in collaboration with Claas, featured a mid-mounted engine below the floor of the cab, and the cab tilted sideways to allow access to the engine.

Specifications

Manufacturer:	Anton Schluter
Location:	Munich, Germany
Model:	Eurotrac 1600
Type:	Systems tractor
Power unit:	Six-cylinder engine
Power output:	160hp (118kw)
Transmission:	N/A
Weight:	N/A
Production started:	1991

At that stage there were reports that Schluter planned to build a first production batch of 50 Eurotracs, but they never materialized and the Schluter company stopped building tractors a few years later.

Schluter had established a niche in the German market based on big, high-powered tractors that were well engineered and expensive. They enjoyed an enthusiastic and loyal following among agricultural contractors and big-acreage farmers in Germany, but were less popular in export markets.

The Eurotrac was a systems-type tractor, designed with four-wheel drive through equal-diameter front and rear wheels, and the cab was mid-mounted and equipped with a reversible driver's seat and controls. The engine was also mid-mounted, and was located under the cab, which was hinged on one side so that it could be tipped hydraulically to allow access for engine maintenance.

Extra Weight

Another unusual feature was the red object at the front, over what is normally the engine compartment. This was a 1.4-ton (1.5-tonne) ballast weight that could be moved forward hydraulically to maintain the correct weight distribution when carrying heavy equipment on the rear linkage.

CLAYTON

1992 **Stockton on Tees, Durham, England**

CLAYTON C4105 BUGGI

The special feature of the Clayton C4105 Buggi tractor was the load space behind the cab, and this was ideal for carrying fertilizer-spreading equipment or a crop sprayer.

Specifications

Manufacturer: Lucassen Young
Location: Stockton on Tees, Durham, England
Model: C4105 Buggi
Type: Load-carrying tractor
Power unit: John Deere four-cylinder engine
Power output: 110hp (81kw)
Transmission: 10 speeds
Weight: 7,700lb (3,500kg)
Production started: 1992

Above: *Clayton's Buggi, now available under the Multidrive name, is another form of systems tractor with a platform over the rear wheels for carrying demountable equipment.*

Clayton tractors were built by Lucassen Young, and they were designed as light vehicles that would be suitable for spraying and fertilizer spreading, but could also be used for field jobs such as pulling a set of rollers or a light cultivator. The first C4105 model introduced in 1992 was powered by a four-cylinder John Deere engine with 110-hp (81-kw) output.

The transmission was based on a five-speed gearbox with full synchromesh, plus a transfer box providing 10 forward speeds with full synchromesh and four-wheel drive. The maximum travel speed on the road was 27.6mph (44.4km/h), and the Clayton tractor was equipped with a front-and-rear-axle suspension system consisting of coil springs and rubber shock absorbers. Maximum gross weight of a fully loaded C105 was 8.8 tons (9 tonnes), including 3.4 tons (3.5 tonnes) for the tractor and 5.4 tons (5.5 tonnes) for the load.

Later Version

Later versions of the Clayton tractor—the Buggi name was not used after about four years—included an 85-hp (63.3-kw) model plus a bigger version powered by a 120-hp (89.4-kw) engine, and the list of specification improvements included four-wheel steering, a new synchro gearbox with 10 speeds, and the choice of three different wheelbase weights.

The Yorkshire-based Multidrive has taken over the Clayton tractor business, and improved versions of the model are now sold under the Multidrive brand name.

KIROV

⚒ **1992 Kirov, St. Petersburg, Russia**

KIROV TURBO K-734

Russia's oldest tractor factory is at the Kirov tractor plant, where production started in 1924, and since the mid-1950s it has concentrated on building high-horsepower models.

Right: *"Peter the Great," the big tractor from the Kirov factory in the former Soviet Union, was exported in 250- and 350-hp (185- and 261-kw) versions.*

Specifications

Manufacturer: Kirov Tractor Plant
Location: Kirov, St. Petersburg, Russia
Model: Turbo K-734
Type: General purpose
Power unit: Turbo diesel engine
Power output: 250hp (185kw)
Transmission: 16-speed powershift
Weight: 34,012lb (15,460kg)
Production started: circa 1992

It is not clear when the Kirov factory began building its Turbo K-734 model with articulated steering, but it was probably in the early 1990s, and by 1996 it had been chosen to lead a sales campaign to open up the European and North American markets to high-horsepower tractors from the Kirov factory to sell alongside the small- to medium-horsepower Belarus models.

Export Version

Export versions of the tractor were called "Peter the Great," and they displayed a special emblem of a rider on a prancing horse, adding to the Turbo K-734's modern styling and eye-catching red-and-white paint finish. The technical specification was also impressive, with a 250-hp (185-kw) engine providing 216hp (161kw) at the power takeoff and 7.8 tons (8 tonnes) of lift capacity on the rear linkage. Peter the Great was also equipped with a powershift transmission with 16 forward speeds and eight in reverse.

In addition to the Turbo K-734, the Kirov factory was also hoping to sell the Turbo K-744 model powered by a 350-hp (260.9-kw) engine. Although both tractors were the same size, the bigger engine on the 744 provided 294hp (219.2kw) at the power takeoff and boosted the maximum lift on the three-point linkage to 9.8 tons (10 tonnes).

FENDT

⚒ 1994 Marktoberdorf, Germany

FENDT XYLON 520

Fendt had been selling various versions of its tool-carrier systems tractors for years, but when it introduced the Xylon 500 tractor series in 1994 they were based on a completely new design and featured the latest ideas in systems-tractor development.

Above: *Fendt's long experience in the systems-tractor market produced the new 500 series models with a choice of three power outputs.*

Specifications

Manufacturer: Xaver Fendt	
Location: Marktoberdorf, Germany	
Model: Xylon 520	
Type: Systems tractor	
Power unit: Six-cylinder MAN engine	
Power output: 110hp (81.4kw)	
Transmission: N/A	
Weight: N/A	
Production started: 1994	

Three models were available, the 520, 522, and 524, and they were all powered by six-cylinder MAN engines with power outputs of 110, 125, and 140hp (81.4, 93.2, and 104.3kw), respectively. The standard specification included four-wheel drive through large-diameter wheels, and the powershift transmission provided 44 forward speeds, including creep speeds for slow-speed jobs. The maximum forward speed of the Xylon was 31mph (50km/h), above the legal limit on public roads in some countries for tractors that do not have full four-wheel braking. The transmission also included the Turbomatic clutch, a patented feature shared with other models in the Fendt range, providing smoother operation with less vibration, the makers claimed.

Systems Tractor
The systems-tractor design features included front- and rear-implement mounting and power takeoff, and there was a load space for carrying equipment such as a sprayer tank behind the well-equipped two-seater driver's cab. The front axle was equipped with its own suspension system and was also designed with a swivel joint to improve traction when traveling over uneven ground.

Above, left: *The 500 series tractors had all the usual systems-tractor features, including front and rear implement-mounting points, four equal-size driving wheels, and a mid-mounted cab.*

FENDT

✂ 1995   Marktoberdorf, Germany

FENDT VARIO 926

Three German companies were developing constantly variable transmissions or CVTs at the same time. The company that won the race to market a tractor with a CVT was Fendt with its Vario 926 model announced in 1995, narrowly beating Claas and the transmissions specialist ZF.

Right: Fendt became the first company to market a tractor with an electronically controlled constantly variable transmission (CVT) when it announced the Vario 926 in 1995.

Specifications

Manufacturer: Xaver Fendt
Location: Marktoberdorf, Germany
Model: Favorit 926 Vario
Type: General purpose
Power unit: MAN six-cylinder engine
Power output: 260hp (191kw)
Transmission: Constantly variable
Weight: 17,160lb (7,800kg)
Production started: 1995

In the medium- and high-horsepower sector of the market the CVT is probably the most important development in tractor drive systems since the powershift. It is a combination of a mechanical gear drive plus a hydrostatic transmission operating side by side and offering some of the benefits of both types of drive system. The power from the engine is split, with some going through the hydrostatic system and some through the gears; after this section the drive from both sections is reunited.

CVT Benefits

Although the CVT provides most of the benefits of a hydrostatic transmission, such as ease of use and stepless speed adjustment, it also reduces the power loss—the biggest disadvantage of a hydrostatic drive. There is just one control lever that moves forward to increase the travel speed, and moving the same lever backward engages reverse and adjusts the speeds backward. There is also a "cruise control" setting that automatically maintains a constant travel speed, adjusting both the engine rpm and the transmission settings to compensate for gradient and other changes.

The success of the 260-hp (191-kw) Vario 926 encouraged other tractor companies to introduce CVT on some of their models, and Fendt has extended the use of its Vario transmission to include some models below 100hp (74.5kw), proving that it is not just for high-horsepower tractors.

CLAAS

✖ 1997   Harsewinkel, Westphalia, Germany

CLAAS XERION 2500

When its joint project with Schluter to develop the Eurotrac tractor did not result in a production tractor, Claas adopted the do-it-yourself approach and developed its own systems tractor. It was called the Xerion, and it was the most ambitious systems tractor produced so far, requiring substantial financial and technical resources.

Claas is Europe's biggest and most successful manufacturer of harvesting machinery, but it has also had ambitions to move into the tractor market, and the Eurotrac and the Xerion were steps toward achieving this aim.

Systems Tractor

The Xerion followed the usual systems-tractor layout of four-wheel drive through equal-diameter wheels plus attachment points for equipment at the front and the rear of the tractor. Three power-takeoff points were provided at the front, rear, and middle of the tractor, and there was also space to carry equipment on the load area over the rear section. The Xerion's versatility as a power unit went much further than previous systems tractors, however, and it was designed to operate complex wraparound equipment such as root-harvesting machines which, in some cases, almost obscured the tractor unit.

Above: With equipment on the front and rear linkages and on the load platform, the Xerion was the newest addition to the list of systems tractors.

Instead of a reversible driving seat and controls, the complete cab on the Xerion could swivel hydraulically to face forward or to the rear, and there were also two positions for the cab, one at the front and the other near the middle of the tractor, with hydraulic power to switch positions.

Transmission

Less eye-catching, but with much more long-term significance, was the transmission developed by Claas for the new tractor. It was based on a mechanical gearbox with eight ratios, plus a separate hydrostatic transmission. The hydrostatic drive allowed stepless travel-speed adjustment in each of the eight gears without varying the speed of the engine, and transmissions of this type would soon be appearing elsewhere in the tractor industry.

The steering system on the Class Xerion was also unconventional. It was capable of being operated through all four wheels, and the driver was able to select from three different steering modes.

Claas demonstrated a prototype version of the Xerion in 1993; after further development work the first production tractors arrived in 1997. They were available in versions of 200, 250, and 300hp (149.1, 185, and 233.7kw), powered by six-cylinder engines equipped with a turbocharger and intercooler. They were aimed at big-acreage farms and the largest agricultural contractors, who form the exclusive top end of the tractor market in Europe.

Specifications

Manufacturer: Claas

Location: Harsewinkel, Westphalia, Germany

Model: Xerion 2500

Type: Systems tractor

Power unit: Six-cylinder engine

Power output: 250hp (185kw)

Transmission: Constantly variable

Weight: N/A

Production started: 1997

Above: *This Xerion tractor is almost hidden under a specially designed wraparound sugar-beet harvester.*

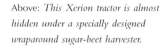

Left: *The Xerion was the first tractor designed with a cab that could be moved hydraulically to the middle or front to suit the job it is undertaking.*

JOHN DEERE
⚒ 1997 Mannheim, Germany

JOHN DEERE 6910

When John Deere introduced its new 6010 series tractors in 1997, one of the sales features was the new Triple Link Suspension, or TLS, available as an option on models from 100hp (74.5kw) upward.

Above: *John Deere 6010 series tractors were among the first to be offered with a suspension system on the front axle.*

Specifications

Manufacturer: Deere & Co.
Location: Mannheim, Germany
Model: 6910
Type: General purpose
Power unit: Six-cylinder engine
Power output: 135hp (100kw)
Transmission: 24-speed semipowershift
Weight: 10,450lb (4,750kg)
Production started: 1997

By the late 1990s there were still just a tiny minority of tractor manufacturers offering any form of suspension system, but they were attracting increased interest as farmers and contractors understood the importance of providing a smoother, more comfortable ride for the driver. By 1997 most of the leading tractor manufacturers were developing suspension systems for the front axle or the cab; however, it was the John Deere company that sparked renewed interest in front-axle suspension.

Suspension System
TLS uses a combination of hydraulic cylinders and gas-filled accumulators to absorb some of the bounce and vibration from the front

wheels. As well as giving the driver a smoother ride, this produces more stability and better steering control when traveling at speed, and it is also said to improve contact between the front wheels and the ground to produce better traction when working with four-wheel drive.

The first 6010 series tractors covered the big-selling 75- to 135-hp (55.9- to 100-kw) sector of the tractor market and were the most popular models in the John Deere range. The John Deere 6910 model was the most powerful model in the series, with 135hp (100kw) available from a six-cylinder engine, although more powerful models were introduced later when the 6010 models were upgraded to become the 6020 series.

Above, left: *The German-built 6010 series tractors from John Deere covered the medium-power sector of the market and were the company's top-selling models.*

BUHLER
⚒ 2000 Winnipeg, Manitoba, Canada

BUHLER VERSATILE 2425

Below: The Buhler Versatile 2425 is built at the same plant in Winnipeg, Manitoba, that had previously built Versatile and New Holland tractors.

When the New Holland group was forced to sell some of its factories in the late 1990s, one of the disposals was the tractor plant in Canada, and the buyer was the Buhler company.

Specifications

Manufacturer: Buhler Industries

Location: Winnipeg, Manitoba, Canada

Model: Buhler Versatile 2425

Type: Pulling tractor

Power unit: Six-cylinder Cummins engine

Power output: 425hp (314kw)

Transmission: 12-speed gearbox

Weight: N/A

Production started: 2000

The Winnipeg factory was originally owned by Versatile, a leading manufacturer of high-horsepower tractors, and Ford bought Versatile to secure its supply of big tractors. New Holland was forced to sell the factory, plus several of its European factories, in order to gain approval under antitrust legislation for merging its tractor and farm machinery business with those of Case I.H. to form CNH.

Versatile Range

Under New Holland ownership the product range built in the Winnipeg factory had included the high-horsepower models with articulated steering, the bi-directional tractor with a reversible driving position, and New Holland's Genesis tractor range. Under the terms of the sale agreement the new owners were able to continue building these models.

The biggest of the red-painted Buhler Versatile tractors is the high-horsepower 2425, featuring four-wheel drive and usually equipped with dual wheels and tires. The power unit is a six-cylinder Cummins engine with a turbocharger and intercooler, and equipped with full electronic management, and the rated output is 425hp (314kw) from 849.8 cubic inches (14 liters) of capacity. A 12-speed QuadShift transmission provides four synchro gears in each of three forward ranges.

CASE IH

2000 **Racine, Wisconsin**

CASE I.H. STEIGER STX440

Taking over the Steiger range in 1986 assured Case I.H. of a strong position in the high-horsepower end of the tractor market, and it also provided the expertise to develop new models for the future.

Specifications

Manufacturer: Case I.H.
Location: Racine, Wisconsin
Model: Steiger STX440
Type: Pulling tractor
Power unit: 904.4-ci (14.9-liter) Cummins engine
Power output: 440hp (326kw)
Transmission: 16-speed powershift
Weight: N/A
Production started: 2000

Above: *Buying the Steiger company, based in Fargo, North Dakota, provided Case I.H. with its own range of high-horsepower tractors, including the rubber-tracked STX440 model.*

Some of the new models arrived in 2000 when the first of the new Case I.H. STX series Steiger tractors were introduced. They featured articulated steering, Case and Cummins engines in the 275- to 440-hp (205 - to 326-kw) range and, on some models, the choice of four-wheel drive or the Quadtrac versions running on four rubber tracks.

Powerful Engine

The STX440 was, for a while, the most powerful tractor in the range, equipped with a 904.4-cubic-inch (14.9-liter) Cummins engine with a 43 percent torque backup. The engine develops its rated power at only 2,000rpm, which is claimed to improve fuel economy and reduce noise and vibration levels. The power is delivered to the wheels or tracks through a 16-speed powershift transmission with electronic speed shifting, and nine of the forward speeds are in the important range of 2.9 to 7.4mph (4.8 to 12km/h), used for field work.

Another facility offered on the STX transmission is Autoskip, a setting that allows the gearbox control to miss every other gear while accelerating from a standing start. This takes much less time than going through every gear to reach the required travel speed on the road.

McCORMICK

2000 Doncaster, Yorkshire, England

McCORMICK MC115

Below: *When the ARGO group bought the former Case I.H. factory in Yorkshire, it chose the McCormick name for its new tractor range.*

Another of the factory disposals resulting from the Case I.H. and New Holland merger negotiations was the recently modernized tractor plant in Doncaster, in England, and it is once more building tractors under the McCormick name.

Specifications

Manufacturer: McCormick Tractors International
Location: Doncaster, Yorkshire, England
Model: MC115
Type: General purpose
Power unit: Perkins four-cylinder engine
Power output: 115hp (85kw)
Transmission: 16-speed gearbox
Weight: 12,089lb (5,495kg)
Production started: 2000

The Doncaster factory was originally owned by International Harvester, and it started building tractors in 1949 under the McCormick brand name that was then owned by I.H. A takeover bid in 1985 brought International Harvester and its Doncaster factory under the same ownership as Case, and Case became the prominent brand name.

Revised Range

When the "For Sale" sign went up at the Doncaster factory in 1999, the buyer was the Italian-owned ARGO group, and as well as the factory the group was also able to buy the exclusive right to use the McCormick brand name on its Doncaster-built tractors. McCormick is one of the most respected brand names from American tractor history, and it has been a valuable asset in establishing the new range in the North American market.

Production of the born-again McCormick range started in 2000 with models inherited from Case, and these included the MC series powered by 242.8-cubic inch (4-liter) Perkins engines from 84hp (62.6kw) upward. The top model in the series is the McCormick MC115 with a 115-hp (85-kw) engine output, and the tractor's specification includes a transmission with 16 forward speeds or 32 speeds with the optional creeper gearbox added.

JOHN DEERE

2001 Waterloo, Iowa

JOHN DEERE 9520T

The letter "T" at the end of the model number of this tractor stands for "tracks," showing that this is a rubber-tracked version of one of the John Deere medium- to high-horsepower tractors.

John Deere's new range of tracklayers announced in 2001 cover seven models in the 8020 and 9020 series with maximum power outputs from 256 to 507hp (190.8 to 373kw). The 9520T is the top model, equipped with John Deere's 6125H series six-cylinder engine with a turbocharger and intercooler. The engine also features a full electronic management system designed to improve the combustion efficiency in order to reduce the fuel consumption and clean up the exhaust emissions.

Transmission

The transmission also features extensive electronic management. There are 18 forward speeds, of which 10 are in the speed range normally used for field work, and there is a combination of powershifting plus automatic changing controlled by the load and the engine speed. The electronic system also provides the facility for a cruise-control setting with the management system automatically maintaining the selected travel speed.

Power is delivered to the tracks through the large-diameter rear sprockets; the steering system is controlled by a steering wheel and operates by varying the track speed independently on both sides of the tractor. Customers for the smaller 8020T series can choose from nine different track options in three different widths, but 9020T models are available with just two widths—30 or 36in (76 or 90cm).

Above: *The 9020T series tracklayers can be fitted with Parallel Tracking, which automatically ensures straight-line steering and correct positioning.*

Specifications

Manufacturer: Deere & Co.
Location: Waterloo, Iowa
Model: 9520T
Type: Tracklayer
Power unit: Six-cylinder engine
Power output: 507hp (373kw) (maximum)
Transmission: 18-speed powershift
Weight: 49,940lb (22,700kg) (fully ballasted)
Production started: 2001

CHALLENGER

⚒ 2002 Duluth, Georgia

CHALLENGER MT865

Having introduced the Challenger 65 crawler tractor with its revolutionary rubber tracks, Caterpillar pulled out of the agricultural market and sold its tractor business to AGCO.

Above: *When Caterpillar pulled out of the agricultural-equipment market its Challenger tractor business was bought by the American-based AGCO group.*

Specifications

Manufacturer: AGCO	
Location: Duluth, Georgia	
Model: MT865	
Type: Tracklayer	
Power unit: Caterpillar 959-ci (15.8-liter) diesel engine	
Power output: 500hp (433kw)	
Transmission: 16-speed powershift	
Weight: N/A	
Production started: 2002	

Instead of merging the tracklayers with one of its other tractor brands, such as Massey-Ferguson or Fendt, AGCO decided to establish Challenger as a new specialized range. It started with the MT700 series models powered by 534.1-cubic-inch (8.8-liter) Caterpillar C-9 engines with power outputs from 235 to 306hp (175.2 to 228.1kw), and in 2002 the company extended the range with four new MT800 series Challengers.

The new arrivals cover the 340- to 500-hp (235.5- to 433-kw) sector, using 728.4- cubic-inch (12-liter) C-12 series Cat engines for the 340- and 380-hp (232.5- and 283.3-kw) models, an 886.2-cubic-inch (14.6-liter) engine for the 450-hp (335.5-kw) model. AGCO finished the range with a 959-cubic-inch (15.8-liter) engine for the 500-hp (433-kw) MT865. All three engines have full electronic management linked to the electronic controls for the transmission.

GPS Navigation

Another advanced feature of the big Challengers is the optional Auto-Guide navigation system using signals from the Global Positioning Satellite (GPS) navigation system. GPS is widely used for identifying the position of ships, aircraft, and vehicles, and on the new Challengers it eases the driver's job by steering the tractor to match the precise width of the implement it is pulling.

The 800 series transmission is a 16-speed powershift, with eight of the speeds in the range of 4 to 9.3mph (6.5 to 15km/h), which is used for most field types of field work. Top speed on the road is 24.8mph (40km/h).

ROC

2003 **Rimini, Italy**

ROC 350

A combination of futuristic styling and, by European standards, a high-horsepower engine made the new ROC tractor from Italy one of the biggest attractions at the SIMA machinery show in Paris in 2003.

Specifications

Manufacturer: ROC

Location: Rimini, Italy

Model: 350

Type: Designed for power-takeoff operation

Power unit: Six-cylinder engine

Power output: 350hp (260kw)

Transmission: Hydrostatic

Weight: 14,635lb (6,630kg)

Production started: 2003

Above: *The futuristic styling of the ROC tractor from Italy was one of the big attractions when it was launched at the 2003 Paris Show.*

According to the manufacturer, the ROC tractor was designed mainly for operating high capacity power-takeoff driven equipment such as powered cultivators and silage machinery, rather than heavy draft work such as plowing, and this explains the high horsepower and the relatively low weight of the tractor. Because the weight is only 6.4 tons (6.6 tonnes) the ROC tractor can be equipped with extra-wide flotation tires designed to operate at a low inflation pressure to minimize soil compaction.

The ROC can be equipped with both front and rear equipment mounting points and power takeoff and, like the Claas Xerion, the complete cab turns hydraulically through 180° to face the front or the rear.

Drive Arrangement

Unlike most systems tractors the four-wheel drive arrangement on the ROC 350 is through unequal-size front and rear wheels, with smaller diameter wheels at the front, and one of the benefits of this format is good maneuverability, giving an outside turning radius of 225in (5.7m).

As well as the 350-hp (260-kw) model exhibited at the Paris Show, ROC also planned a 261-hp (194.6-kw) version, although at that stage the engine make had not been specified.

CLAAS

2003 Le Mans, France

CLAAS CELTIS 446

With its big engine and high-tech features the Claas Xerion was not designed to sell in large numbers, and in order to break into the mass market Claas made a successful bid to buy the French-based Renault tractor business.

Above: *Following the 2003 takeover of Renault by Claas, new Renault tractors are appearing under the Claas name and colors.*

Specifications

Manufacturer: Claas

Location: Le Mans, France

Model: Celtis 446

Type: General purpose

Power unit: Four-cylinder diesel engine

Power output: 92hp (68kw)

Transmission: Shuttle with 10 speeds forwards and in reverse

Weight: 9,702lb (4,410kg)

Production started: 2003

The deal was announced in 2003, and by 2004 the former Renault tractor range was being sold in most European countries under the Claas name and colors. Apart from the Xerion, updated and with a power boost to 335hp (249.8kw) during 2004, the Claas tractor range for 2004 covered the Atles, Ares, Celtis, and Pales ranges, plus the Dionis and Fructus models for vineyards, orchards, and other special situations.

Celtis Range

The small to medium Celtis series tractors were the last new models to be introduced in the Renault range. The tractors were developed by Renault and were launched on the Renault stand at the 2003 SIMA machinery event in Paris, but this was also the occasion when the Claas takeover was announced, which means most of the Celtis tractors have been sold under Claas ownership.

Celtis tractors cover the 70- to 100-hp (52.1- to 74.5-kw) sector of the market, a popular power range on small acreages and particularly on livestock farms. There are four models, all powered by Deere Power Systems (DPS) four-cylinder engines. Special design features include cab doors that open through 180° and can be locked in the fully open position. In addition, the cab roof can be opened to allow the driver to see the front-end loader and its attachment in the fully raised position.

CASE IH

⚒ **2003   Basildon, Essex, England**

CASE I.H. JX1100U MAXXIMA

Case I.H. has introduced a new range of tractors in the 70- to 100-hp (52.1- to 74.5-kw) market sector and equipped them with a new four-cylinder engine developed jointly by three leading engine manufacturers.

Specifications

Manufacturer: Case I.H.

Location: Basildon, Essex, England

Model: JX1100U Maxxima

Type: General purpose

Power unit: Four-cylinder engine

Power output: 100hp (74.5kw)

Transmission: 24-speed powershift with power shuttle

Weight: N/A

Production started: 2003

Behind the new engine is a research and development program financed jointly by Case I.H., Cummins, and Fiat's Iveco engine subsidiary. They operated from a special research center in the United Kingdom, and the 273.1-cubic-inch (4.5-liter) power unit for the new Case tractors was one of the results of what was known as the European Engine Alliance.

Engines

All four of the new JXI-U Maxxima tractors are equipped with basically the same engine, which is naturally aspirated for the 72- and 82-hp (53.6- and 61.1-kw) models and equipped with different levels of turbocharging for the 91- and 100-hp (67.8- and 74.5-kw) versions. Advantages claimed for the new engines include reduced wear rates to minimize oil consumption, fuel consumption has improved by 5 percent compared to the previous engines, and measures to reduce engine-noise levels have achieved a 1.5db(A) reduction.

All models are available in two- or four-wheel drive versions, and there is a choice of three different transmission options. The top-priced option is a 24-speed powershift with a power shuttle. The power shuttle, operated by a control mounted on the steering column, allows the driver to change between forward and reverse without using the clutch pedal.

Above: The four-cylinder engine powering the four-model JXU Maxxima models from Case I.H. is a new design developed jointly by Case, Cummins, and the Fiat group's Iveco engine operation.

NEW HOLLAND
✗ 2004 Basildon, Essex, England

NEW HOLLAND TVT 190

It was no surprise when New Holland joined the rapidly growing list of manufacturers offering a tractor with a continuously variable transmission or CVT. It happened in 2004 when New Holland launched the new TVT series.

Right: *One of the recent converts to constantly variable transmission (CVT) drive systems is New Holland, with its TVT series tractors announced in 2004.*

Specifications

Manufacturer: New Holland
Location: Basildon, Essex, England
Model: TVT190
Type: General purpose
Power unit: Iveco six-cylinder turbo engine
Power output: 192hp (142kw)
Transmission: Constantly variable
Weight: N/A
Production started: 2004

There are five TVT models with power outputs ranging from 137 to 192hp (102.1 to 142kw), and they are powered by high-specification Iveco engines with six cylinders and 400.6 cubic inches (6.6 liters) of capacity. The engines are turbocharged and intercooled, and all feature electronic injection management.

Engine Options

The options list for the engines includes a cooling fan with a variable blade angle that is automatically adjusted by a thermostatic control system. An increase in the temperature of the engine adjusts the blade angle to move a greater volume of air and increase the cooling action. The blade angle is kept to a minimum while the engine is running at less than the optimum temperature after a cold start, as this reduces the time taken for the warming-up process when the engine is running at less than its peak efficiency.

Like other CVTs, New Holland's transmission on the TVT tractors consists of both mechanical and hydrostatic drive systems operating in three speed ranges. The ranges cover creeper speeds, a middle range for field work, and a faster transportation range for road travel. There is also a power shuttle for push-button changing between forward and reverse without using the clutch pedal, and the computerized control system can be set to adjust the engine speed and transmission automatically in order to maintain a constant forward speed when working with equipment operated using power-takeoff.

Bibliography

Ashby, J. E. *British Tractors & Power Cultivators*. Eastbourne, UK: Pentagon Publications, 1949.

Bell, Brian. *Fifty Years of Farm Tractors*. Ipswich, UK: Farming Press, 1999.

Directory of Wheel & Track-Type Tractors. Rome: UN Food & Agricultural Organization, 1955.

Fraser, Colin. *Harry Ferguson Inventor and Pioneer*. London: John Murray, 1972.

Gibbard, Stuart. *Ford Tractor Conversions*. Ipswich, UK: Farming Press, 1995.

Gibbard, Stuart. *The Ferguson Tractor Story*. Ipswich, UK: Old Pond Publishing, 2000.

Gibbard, Stuart. *The Ford Tractor Story 1917–1964*. Ipswich, UK: Old Pond Publishing & Japonica Press, 1998.

Gibbard, Stuart. *The Ford Tractor Story 1964–1999*. Ipswich, UK: Old Pond Publishing & Japonica Press, 1999.

Hafner, Kurt. *Lanz von 1928 bis 1942*. Stuttgart: Franckh Historische Tecnik, 1989.

Hafner, Kurt. *Lanz von 1942 bis 1955*. Stuttgart: Franckh-Kosmos, 1990.

Macmillan, Don. *John Deere Tractors and Equipment Volume I*. St. Joseph, Michigan: American Society of Agricultural Engineers, 1988.

Two Cylinder Collector Series Volume II. Grundy Center, Iowa: Two Cylinder Club, 1993.

Wendell, C. H. *American Farm Tractors*. Saratosa, Florida: Crestline Publishing, 1979.

Wendell, C. H. *International Harvester*. Saratosa, Florida: Crestline Publishing, 1993.

Wendell, C. H. *Nebraska Tractor Tests Since 1920*. Saratosa, Florida: Crestline Publishing, 1985.

Wik, Reynold M. *Henry Ford & Grassroots America*. Ann Arbor, Michigan: University of Michigan Press, 1972.

Williams, Michael. *Great Tractors*. Poole, Dorset: Blandford Press, 1982.

Williams, Michael. *Classic Farm Tractors*. Poole, Dorset: Blandford Press, 1984.

Williams, Michael. *Ford & Fordson Tractors*. Poole, Dorset: Blandford Press, 1985.

Williams, Michael. *Massey-Ferguson Tractors*. Poole, Dorset: Blandford Press, 1987.

Williams, Michael. *John Deere Two-Cylinder Tractors*. Suffolk, UK: Farming Press, 1993.

Williams, Michael. *Farm Tractors*. Guilford, Connecticut: The Lyons Press, 2002

Index